Reading Contemporary French Literature

Warren Motte

Zea Books
Lincoln, Nebraska
2022

Copyright © 2022 Warren Motte.

ISBN 978-1-60962-252-7 paperback
ISBN 978-1-60962-253-4 ebook
doi: 10.32873/unl.dc.zea.1327

Cover design by Nicholas W. H. Motte.

Zea Books are published by the
University of Nebraska-Lincoln Libraries.

Composed in Sitka and Merriweather types,
with Hoefler Text ornaments.

Electronic (pdf) edition available online at
https://digitalcommons.unl.edu/zeabook/

Print edition available from Lulu.com at
http://www.lulu.com/spotlight/unllib

University of Nebraska-Lincoln does not discriminate
based upon any protected status. Please go to
http://www.unl.edu/equity/notice-nondiscrimination

For Marie, once more

Contents

Acknowledgments 6
Introduction 7
Raymond Queneau's Constraint 9
Edmond Jabès's Margins 30
Georges Perec's Work 46
Marcel Bénabou's Rhetoric 62
Jacques Jouet's Exhaustion 80
Marie NDiaye's Narrative 99
Marie Cosnay's Characters 112
Bernard Noël's Trips 124
Jean Rolin's Mourning 134
Jacques Serena's Fever 150
Julia Deck's Geometries 166
Christine Montalbetti's Mission 181
Notes 200
Bibliography 215

Acknowledgments

SOME of the essays in this book have appeared in earlier form in professional journals. I thank the editors for permission to use that material here. I would like to thank Paul Royster for his keen editorial eye, his helpful suggestions, and his unfailing generosity. I am forever indebted to Gerald Prince, from whom I have learned a great deal, and whose friendship I value deeply. Frequent conversations with Philippe Brand, Lydie Moudileno, and Andrew Sobanet have cheered me and enlightened me. I have been lucky to spend a lot of time in the company of Nicholas, Kaitlyn, and Ayla Motte, Nathaniel Motte, and Liz Trinnear, and I am very grateful to them.

Introduction

READING contemporary French literature is an excellent way to spend one's waking hours—and some of the other hours, too, insofar as fiction necessarily brims over into dream. It is certain to keep you on your readerly toes, because French literature in our time is consistently fascinating, provocative, and invigorating. It is moreover unexpected, or very largely so. By that, I mean that it takes us by surprise; and I'm thinking both of the broad corpus of literary production and of the work of individual writers. For if it is true that some writers rewrite the same book over the course of their careers, the best of them address each successive book as a new undertaking, a new experiment in literary possibility.

That is abundantly true of the authors about whom I have chosen to speak in this book. Their work is extremely various, each one of them pursuing a different path. They belong to different generations—roughly three of them from, say, Raymond Queneau to Christine Montalbetti. Their conceptions of literature and their approaches thereto are both distinct and distinctive. Yet all of them write in a *critical* way. That is, they work in full cognizance of literary history and of the tradition that they inherit; they recognize key literary gestures as such; they put those gestures to the question as they deploy them, reshape them to their own purposes, and make them new; they invite their readers to take a critical stance and to participate actively in the construction of literary meaning. Insofar as we readers are concerned, such a writerly posture redounds very much to our benefit, because these people do not take us for fools. And it is consequently all the more incumbent upon us to read this kind of work in a thoughtful manner, in order to justify the confidence that these writers have invested in us.

Raymond Queneau exemplifies the kind of author I have been trying to describe. In any discussion of him, the term "writer's writer" inevitably comes to mind, for he had an enormous influence on the people in his sphere, and on those who came after him. Georges Perec, Marcel Bénabou, and Jacques Jouet can all be thought of as Quenellians, for example, each of them taking that man and his work as their lodestone, in a sense, as they navigate the literary landscape. All three of them would furthermore become members of the group that Queneau cofounded with François Le Lionnais in 1960, the Ouvroir de Littérature Potentielle, or Oulipo. The affiliations of many of the other writers here are less apparent. Edmond Jabès, for instance, seems to surge up out of nowhere—and that idea of "nowhere," emblematized by the desert in his native Egypt, is a crucial one in his work. Marie Cosnay has spent her career at a remove from the principal sources of literary power (by that, I mean the major Parisian publishing houses and the dominant media outlets), pursuing a refreshingly original, strikingly idiosyncratic writerly program. In that very perspective, it is legitimate to suggest that all of the figures addressed here are "strong" writers, in other words, artists whose work is marked by very distinct and notable particularities.

They all display a certain restlessness of spirit, I would add. Georges Perec, for one, expressed the desire to traverse the whole horizon of literary possibility, remarking, "mon ambition d'écrivain serait de parcourir toute la littérature de mon temps sans jamais avoir le sentiment de revenir sur mes pas ou de remarcher dans mes propres traces, et d'écrire tout ce qui est possible à un homme aujourd'hui d'écrire: des livres gros et des livres courts, des romans et des poèmes, des drames, des livrets d'opéra, des romans policiers, des romans d'aventures, des romans de science-fiction, des feuilletons, des livres pour enfants . . ." (*Penser/Classer* 11). He was well on his way to accomplishing that project when he died, at the age of forty-five, in 1982. A similar desire animates the work of the other writers in this volume, though typically they express it in less explicit terms. Reading across their careers, one quickly perceives an inclination toward mobility in each of them, complemented by a commitment to the principle of innovation. In fact, one of the many satisfactions that reading their work provides is the pleasure of discovering where they choose to go in each successive book.

INTRODUCTION

In that sense, it is important to think about our activity as readers, and about the role that work of this sort scripts for us. I have argued that these writers are not indifferent to us. They do not forget us; they do not take us for granted; nor do they order us to sit down and shut up while they tell us a story (though I do not wish to deny that that sort of readerly posture, once in a while, has its own comforts). To the contrary, they demand our involvement. Philippe Lejeune has noted that quality of Perec's work, remarking, "Il y a dans tous ses textes une place pour moi, pour que je fasse quelque chose" (*La Mémoire et l'oblique* 41). The notion of *doing something* may seem self-evident, bound up in the simple act of reading; but I believe that Lejeune is thinking of a more ample kind of participation, and of a textual contract offering us a broader franchise. Like Perec, each of the writers I have chosen is committed to experimentation, and each of them solicits our engagement—not merely our attendance, but our cooperation. They call upon us to understand the specific traditions that subtend their literary practice; they ask us to observe the various strategies that they put into service; they invite us to take part in a significantly articulative dynamic. In short, they offer us a partnership in the ventures that they undertake. It would be churlish of us to decline such an offer, it seems to me, and it consequently behooves us to bring the best of ourselves to the task: our close attention, certainly, our sense of cultural relativity, our intellectual integrity, our agility, our empathy, our boldness—but also (and perhaps principally) our spirit of play. For as earnest as we may be in our desire to occupy ourselves fully and productively in these texts, it is important to remain attuned to the ludic dimension of this pursuit, to the unforeseen pleasures, indeed the joys, of reading contemporary French literature.

Raymond Queneau's Constraint

CONSTRAINT comes in many kinds, many shapes, many nuances. It confines, it restricts, it coerces; it can be cumbersome, forced, and repressive. Yet it is to some degree inherent in any human activity, and becomes particularly apparent in the aesthetic act, where, savantly and cannily exploited, constraint can (paradoxically enough) have a liberating effect, providing a structured locus for creativity and play. Among the writers of our time, Raymond Queneau interrogated that notion with particular insistence; his work, spanning five decades, may be read as a sustained meditation on the uses and abuses of constraint. The import of Queneau's experiments went far beyond the local area of his novels and poetry, moreover: for a wide diversity of writers from the mid-century to the present, his influence was both direct and determinative. Indeed, Quenellian theory of constraint resonates demonstrably in such apparently dissimilar works as Italo Calvino's *If on a winter's night a traveler* and *The Castle of Crossed Destinies*; Harry Mathews's *Cigarettes*; Georges Perec's *La Disparition*, *Les Revenentes*, *La Vie mode d'emploi*, *"53 Jours"*; and Jacques Roubaud's *Quelque chose noir*, *La Belle Hortense*, and its sequel, *L'Enlèvement d'Hortense*. In view of the amplitude of this phenomenon, and of its significance for contemporary writing, I should like to examine Queneau's grapplings with the notion of constraint in some detail, and briefly examine four key texts wherein that notion plays a crucial role: *Le Voyage en Grèce*, a collection of essays, most of which were originally published in the 1930s; *Le Chiendent*, his first novel, published in 1933; *Cent Mille Milliards de poèmes* (1961), an example of exploding textuality; and the last book he published during his lifetime, *Morale élémentaire* (1975).

The first steps in this nascent itinerary of speculation arise out of Queneau's experiences with surrealism. He associated fairly closely with the surrealist group in the late 1920s, but he broke from it and, along with ten others, signed *Un Cadavre*, an astonishingly virulent attack upon André Breton, in 1930.[1] During the next few years (and in fact, to a lesser extent, throughout his career) Queneau reflected steadily upon what he felt to be surrealism's excesses. As he describes these, both in his early essays and in a roman-à-clef, *Odile*, many of them were bound up in what can now be seen (with the wisdom of hindsight) as the dark side of constraint.

Queneau focuses his reflection upon three interrelated constructs, which he casts more or less explicitly as surrealist shibboleths. The first of these is the notion of artistic inspiration. In an article written in 1938, he attacks surrealist theory and practice (as exemplified in automatic writing) quite openly:

> Dans le dernier numéro de *Volontés*, j'ai déjà dit l'intérêt que présentait le récent livre de Rolland de Renéville, *L'Expérience poétique*. On y trouve en effet exposés dans toute leur nudité, dans toute leur crudité, les plus détestables préjugés relatifs à la poésie. Le premier groupe de ces idées reçues concerne la valeur de l'inspiration: 1° l'inspiration viendrait du subconscient (tous ceux qui prétendent actuellement relever le prestige de la poésie acceptent sans discussion, sans réflexion même, cette affirmation qui, si elle était vraie, exprimerait en réalité la dégradation de la poésie); 2° l'écriture automatique serait la forme la plus pure de l'inspiration (impudent sophisme qui résout l'histoire même de ce procédé dont la pratique, tant dans les cercles spirites que dans les clubs littéraires, n'a jamais produit soit que des élucubrations d'une répugnante banalité, soit que des "textes" affligés dès leur naissance des tics du milieu qui les pondit). (*Voyage* 112)

For Queneau, the problem is precisely one of *constraint*: the notion of inspiration, when it is abused so egregiously, stifles the creative impulse. Furthermore, it clears the way for other sorts of abuse, most notably for tyranny. For if inspiration is to be amorphous, haphazard, and ill-defined, there will be a need for an arbiter of inspiration, for someone to declare when inspiration actually and truly visits the artist. As Queneau makes abundantly clear in *Odile*, Breton appropriated this role, constructing the idea of inspiration as a mechanism of control. During this period, Queneau also saw that the absolute opposition of inspiration and structure was radically unproductive:

> Une autre bien fausse idée qui a également cours actuellement, c'est l'équivalence que l'on établit entre l'inspiration, exploration du subconscient et libération, entre hasard, automatisme et liberté. Or, *cette* inspiration qui consiste à obéir aveuglément à toute impulsion est en réalité un esclavage. Le classique qui écrit sa tragédie en observant un certain nombre de règles qu'il connaît est plus libre que le poète qui écrit ce qui lui passe par la tête et qui est l'esclave d'autres règles qu'il ignore. (*Voyage* 94)

Queneau will choose to subvert the notion of inspiration by displacing it, denying its centrality and relegating it to the margins of creativity. In the model he proposes, inspiration is no longer the thurifer of artistic freedom, and the artist is no longer the passive vessel, patiently waiting to be infused from above. Whereas the creative act used to devolve upon a momentary, fleeting visitation, it now finds its motor elsewhere. In short, Queneau locates the creative impulse *within* the artist, rather than without, and subjects it to the latter's will. It is this, to his way of thinking, that will in fact liberate the artist:

> Le poète n'est jamais inspiré parce que maître de ce qui apparaît aux autres comme inspiration. Il n'attend pas que l'inspiration lui tombe du ciel comme des ortolans tout rôtis. Il *sait chasser* et pratique l'incontestable proverbe "aide-toi, le ciel t'aidera". Il n'est jamais inspiré parce qu'il l'est sans cesse, parce que les puissances de la poésie sont toujours à sa disposition, sujettes à sa volonté, soumises à son activité propre. (*Voyage* 126)

When fully articulated, the new praxis that Queneau advocates will include a strong technical component, which stands in stark opposition to the notion of inspiration inherited from the Romantics. Believing that structure is salubrious, and that one cannot, in any case, escape from form, Queneau prescribes that the artist should embrace form willingly and bend it to the purposes of creation. As he attempts to clear away an idealist vision in favor of one that is more frankly materialist, Queneau locates the concrete, the *thing* that will guarantee the efficacy of his formula, in technique: "Le véritable inspiré n'est jamais inspiré: il l'est toujours; il ne cherche pas l'inspiration et ne s'irrite contre aucune technique" (*Odile* 159).

Queneau is aware that an attention to technique imposes constraints of its own. But these constraints, as he surveys them, are of a very different order from the ones imposed by the notion of inspiration. For one thing, the artist is aware of them, and can recognize and define them. For another, they are predictable and significantly more stable than those of the surrealist regime. Most importantly, the artist assumes them freely, and is free to cast them off at any time if a given technique, pursued diligently, fails to be productive. The beauty of Queneau's gesture lies in its canniness and its economy: in effect, he destroys and rehabilitates the notion of constraint with a minimum of wasted effort. Where constraint constricted, it now affords vital space; where it repressed, it now liberates. As Marcel Bénabou has suggested, Queneau's prescription of writing under constraint can be deployed most efficiently in an attack on inspiration, because it subverts and reformulates the very underpinnings of the latter: "C'est donc le paradoxe de l'écriture sous contrainte que de posséder ainsi une double vertu de libération, qui permettra un jour d'évincer la notion même de l'inspiration" (104).

The second surrealist icon that Queneau attempts to shatter is the notion of genius, and, here, his attack follows tactics very similar to the ones I have just described. He takes pains, moreover, to associate genius and inspiration directly and unequivocally, suggesting that the cultural consequences of these ideological constructs gone amok are unredeemably baneful: "Un 'génie' n'est pas seulement un méconnu; c'est aussi un 'inspiré', si l'on en croit cette idéologie, ou plutôt un 'passif' qui attend l'inspiration" (*Voyage* 164). Queneau says that Romanticism arbitrarily dictated that genius must be unrecognized, and points out the logical absurdities of such a position; he argues further that the notion is bound up in a tissue of mysticism from which it cannot be disentangled. He concludes that genius, thus described, is an illegitimate conception that must be firmly and irrevocably renounced (*Voyage* 168).

Elsewhere, however, Queneau points out that the legacy of the Romantic notion of genius was not uniformly negative, that it eventually gave rise to a heightened attention to form; and form, for Queneau, constitutes the ground upon which the battle for literature must be waged:

> En face des scientifisants, les postromantiques, poussés à bout, inventèrent l'art pour l'art qui, isolant définitivement la littérature, la réduisit à des jeux d'oisifs et aux amertumes des génies méconnus (cette singulière invention des temps modernes). Cependant là, la forme survécut, bien que parfois privée de tout contenu; l'estime pour le métier subsista et le goût pour la véritable littérature, mais le tout à la fois un peu fade et un peu faisandé. (*Voyage* 90)

Finally, Queneau attacks the notion of chance. The surrealist veneration of the aleatory, the casual, the random, he suggests, is unhealthy and counterproductive. Once again, his argument devolves upon the consideration that the artist is disenfranchised by such a notion; just as in the case of inspiration, dependence upon chance places the artist in a false position, a slave to forces over which he or she has absolutely no control. The fact that such an idea should be offered as a vision of creative freedom irks Queneau particularly. More importantly, perhaps, he would seem to believe that the notion is simply incorrect; that, objectively considered, chance plays no role in artistic creation. Here, Queneau is perhaps motivated by his idea of the omnipresence of structure, by his conviction that even the most apparently amorphous text is governed by a set of formal rules, whether the artist is cognizant of that fact or not. He will invoke this very cognizance in his attack on the aleatory, suggesting that true and actual creative freedom can be achieved through a lucid exploitation of form. In 1938, he expresses his admiration of *Ulysses* and *Work in Progress* (shortly to be published as *Finnegans Wake*) in precisely those terms: "Rien, dans ces oeuvres, n'est laissé au hasard. Sa part seule lui est abandonnée et tout jaillit librement; car la liberté ne se compose pas de hasards. Tout est déterminé, l'ensemble comme les épisodes, et rien ne manifeste une contrainte" (*Voyage* 133).

In effect, if Queneau devotes such attention to what he describes as the excesses of surrealism, it is because he will use those constructs in elaborating his own theory of literature. But they will undergo a significant process of transformation; in a sense, they will be symmetrically inverted. Thus, the surrealist insistence on inspiration becomes in Quenellian poetics a valorization of practice; the idea of genius gives way to an advocacy of craftsmanship; chance is transmogrified into determination.

Upon these new constructs, Queneau will place others, building an edifice of imposing dimensions. The keystone therein is the notion of form. Clearly, for Queneau, the importance of form is primordial; it serves as the guarantor of aesthetic efficacy and the very locus of artistic value: "Il n'y a plus de règles depuis qu'elles ont survécu à la valeur. Mais les formes subsistent éternellement" (*Bâtons* 33).

His admiration for poetic fixed forms is apparent when, in a text from 1964, he lovingly passes in review the triolet, the virelay, the rondel, the villanelle, the sonnet, the sestina, and the Malay pantoum (*Bâtons* 326-34). Queneau evidences a certain nostalgia as he deplores the fact that fixed forms have fallen into disuse, and argues that the rigor that characterized them should be recuperated and redeployed in other sorts of writing: "Si la ballade et le rondeau sont péris, il me paraît qu'en opposition à ce désastre une rigueur accrue doit se manifester dans l'exercice de la prose" (*Bâtons* 28).

For Queneau also deplores the lack of attention to form in prose, and, most particularly, in the novel:

> Alors que la poésie a été la terre bénie des rhétoriqueurs et des faiseurs de règles, le roman, depuis qu'il existe, a échappé à toute loi. N'importe qui peut pousser devant lui comme un troupeau d'oies un nombre indéterminé de personnages apparemment réels à travers une lande longue d'un nombre indéterminé de pages ou de chapitres. Le résultat, quel qu'il en soit, sera toujours un roman. (*Bâtons* 27)

Where André Gide celebrated the "lawless" character of the novel, that very lawlessness constitutes, for Queneau, another sort of "disaster." And in a bold move, he will propose to repair that disaster. In a conversation with Georges Ribemont-Dessaignes, Queneau avers that he has never seen any essential difference between poetry and the novel—the sort of novel, that is, that *he* wishes to write (*Bâtons* 43). Queneau's astonishing leap of faith reposes on the notion that form can save the novel, and indeed the language in which he casts his new theory has all the resonance of holy writ:

> Il y a des formes du roman qui imposent à la matière proposée toutes les vertus du Nombre et, naissant de l'expression même et des divers aspects du récit, connaturelle à l'idée directrice, fille et mère de tous les éléments qu'elle polarise, se développe une structure qui transmet aux oeuvres les derniers reflets de la Lumière Universelle et les derniers échos de l'Harmonie des Mondes. (*Bâtons* 33)

Queneau's theorizing and his experiments will lean heavily on the concepts of consciousness, will, and determination. He argues for a *conscious* novelistic technique (*Bâtons* 28), and, elsewhere, suggests that the writer's activity can be compared to that of a cruciverbist or a maker of logogriphs (*Bords* 79). The model he proposes is that of a text studiously constructed according to a pre-elaborated plan, a highly structured artifact possessing the virtues of symmetry, rigor, and harmony. The fact that the text should be so strongly determined is of capital importance: the writer, argues Queneau, must be in full *control* of the text, from beginning to end. This explains, perhaps, Queneau's admiration for the exercises in textual generation described by Raymond Roussel in *Comment j'ai écrit certains de mes livres*, where the first sentence of a given work leads through ineluctable teleology to the final sentence, the spooneristic double of the first (*Bords* 79).

It is, I think, this very ineluctability that intrigues Queneau. His wish is for a literary text that is wholly motivated. And that motivation, that determination, must be consciously, lucidly, and painstakingly constructed by the writer, if it is to have any real value. It is here that he locates his version of artistic freedom, a freedom actually deriving from constraint or, as he puts it, "liberté dans la nécessité" (*Voyage* 133).

This, of course, clears away any temptation toward inspiration and the seduction of chance. The text, on the contrary, must result from the writer's conscious intellectual effort. It is on these grounds that Queneau praises Poe, and distinguishes him from his contemporaries: "le poème n'est pas une oeuvre d'inspiration, mais une oeuvre de raison" (*Bords* 79). In postulating a literature of determination, Queneau arrogates extraordinary status for it. He will go so far as to claim the term "classic," casting by implication all other writings into the limbo of unconsciousness: "toute littérature *fondée* doit être dite classique, ou bien encore: toute littérature digne de ce nom se refuse au relâchement: automatisme scribale, laisser-aller inconstructif, etc." (*Voyage* 11). Jacques Roubaud quite correctly sees in this position yet another reaction against the aleatory, and a tactic through which the notion of creative freedom can be reclaimed from the it: "Le caractère intentionnel, volontaire, de la contrainte sur lequel il revient à maintes reprises, avec insistance, est indissolublement lié pour lui à ce vif refus du hasard et encore plus de l'équation souvent faite entre hasard et liberté" ("Mathématique" 56).

Through all of this process, Queneau is able to formulate a notion that will effectively encapsulate his poetics, that of "voluntary literature," a literature of consciousness and high intentionality, of structure and economy, of will and technique. Once again, he postulates the primacy of his model in frank polemic, as he enunciates his credo: "Il n'y a de littérature que volontaire" (Lescure, "Histoire" 32).

When Queneau goes about demonstrating his poetics on the written page, he will turn, curiously enough, toward mathematics. This is perhaps attributable, in part, to the fact that he had excellent early training in that discipline, and indeed came to be a respected amateur mathematician.[2] But I think that on a more profound level Queneau recognized essential affinities and channels of reciprocity between mathematics and literature, or at least between mathematics and the sort of literature that he wished to read and write. Thus, he argues that the determination he finds in Poe's writing devolves upon "une nécessité quasi mathématique" (*Bords* 79).

It is perhaps that mathematics represents for Queneau a world of architectonic harmony, a world where the equivocation and the unstable meaning of natural language hold no sway. Or maybe he sees other virtues in numbers that are not immediately apparent in words. In any case, it is quite clear that it is, for Queneau, precisely a question of a "world," a world that defines itself in opposition to the one we think we know:

> Il n'existe pas qu'un seul monde, lui dis-je, celui que vous voyez ou que vous croyez voir ou que vous vous imaginez voir ou que vous voulez bien voir, ce monde que touchent les

> aveugles, qu'entendent les amputés et que reniflent les sourds, ce monde de choses et de forces, de solidités ou d'illusions, ce monde de vie et de mort, de naissances et de destructions, ce monde où nous buvons, au milieu duquel nous avons coutume de nous endormir. Il en existe au moins un autre à ma connaissance: celui des nombres et des figures, des identités et des fonctions, des opérations et des groupes, des ensembles et des espaces. (*Odile* 26-27)

For Queneau, numbers are more obviously and irrevocably bound up in form than words. They are more material, more concrete, more real: "Réaliste vous voulez dire: les nombres sont des réalités. Ils existent, les nombres! Ils existent autant que cette table, plus que cette table, plus que cette table sempiternel exemple des philosophes, infiniment plus que cette table bang!" (*Odile* 33).

Given this attitude, it is curious to note that Queneau suggests that the artifice behind his first novel, *Le Chiendent* (1933), was primarily linguistic in character. Four years after that novel's publication, Queneau said that *Le Chiendent* resulted from an attempt to translate *Le Discours de la méthode* into contemporary French (*Bâtons* 16-17). Later, he will tell Ribemont-Dessaignes the same thing (*Bâtons* 42). It is not until 1969, in a note published in the *Nouvelle Revue Française*, that Queneau recants (*Voyage* 219-22). In fact, the structure of *Le Chiendent*, as Claude Simonnet demonstrated so elegantly in *Queneau déchiffré*, is based on a series of mathematical constraints. Queneau himself alluded to some of these, notably the division of the novel into 91 sections, 91 being the product of 13 (a beneficent number for Queneau) and 7 (the number of letters in his family name and his two given names) (*Bâtons* 29). And in his conversations with Georges Charbonnier, recorded for French radio in 1962, Queneau returns to the mathematical structure of *Le Chiendent*, suggesting some of the logic behind it:

> J'ai toujours pensé qu'une oeuvre littéraire devait avoir une structure et une forme, et dans le premier roman que j'ai écrit, je me suis appliqué à ce que cette structure soit extrêmement stricte, et de plus qu'elle soit multiple, qu'il n'y ait pas une seule structure, mais plusieurs. Comme à ce moment-là j'étais, disons, un peu arithmomane, j'ai bâti cette

construction sur des combinaisons de chiffres, les uns plus ou moins arbitraires, les autres parce qu'ils m'étaient inspirés par des goûts personnels. Et toute cette construction, en principe, ne doit pas être apparente. C'était pour moi une sorte de guide, et non pas une chose qui devait être manifeste pour le lecteur. D'ailleurs personne à l'époque ne s'en est aperçu. (*Entretiens* 47-48)

Several things should be noted here. First, Queneau, insists upon the arbitrary nature of the constraints involved: they result from whim and strictly personal considerations. That is to say, they are not for public consumption, or, rather, not explicitly so: they are intended to afford structure and form to the work, but are not *themselves* pertinent integers in that work. Second, they are intended, in Queneau's words, as a "guide": they function to stimulate and channel the writer's creativity. In short, were "inspiration" an acceptable word in Queneau's lexicon, one might say that constraint serves to inspire the writer. Finally, in spite of their modesty, the constraints must be rigorous—in a word, *constraining*—if they are to serve the purpose efficiently.

As Queneau elaborates and refines his poetics, these notions will become ever more insistent, along with others that he grafts on to his model. In terms of its practical demonstration, the latter is perhaps nowhere more clear, immediate, and indeed urgently apparent than in Queneau's *Cent Mille Milliards de poèmes* (1961). That text presents itself as a collection of ten sonnets. But each sonnet has been constructed such that any of its fourteen verses may be exchanged with the corresponding verse in any of the nine other sonnets. Thus, to each of the ten first verses, the reader may add any of ten second verses: there are 10^2, or one hundred possiblities for the first two verses. Any of ten third verses may then be chosen, offering 10^3 possibilities, and so forth into starkly vertiginous numerical regions: in fact, there are 10^{14}, or one hundred trillion possible sonnets in the collection. In his preface to *Cent Mille Milliards de poèmes*, Queneau notes one of the thorniest problems the text presents: according to his calculations, if one read a sonnet per minute, eight hours a day, two hundred days a year, it would take more than a million centuries to finish the text.[3] François Le Lionnais, in the postface, casts the problem in a somewhat different light: "Grâce à cette surpériorité technique l'ouvrage que vous tenez entre vos mains représente à lui tout seul une quantité de texte nettement plus grande que tout ce que les hommes ont écrit depuis l'invention de l'écriture, en y comprenant les romans populaires, la correspondance commerciale, diplomatique et privée, les brouillons jetés au panier et les graffiti."

Clearly, *Cent Mille Milliards de poèmes* is a text different from most. And it proclaims its difference boldly. Yet for all of that it encapsulates and puts into practice all of the Quenellian theory I have reviewed thus far: the ten "master" sonnets are obviously highly constructed; that is, there would seem to be very little room for the aleatory in them. Whatever else one wishes to say about them, they are deliberate and polished. Moreover, they are highly determined, as are the "derived" sonnets (quite apart from the problem of apprehending the latter). The work is animated by a powerful attention to form, and the nature of that form is rooted in mathematics. Finally and most pertinently, the text testifies eloquently to an unwavering creative purpose on the part of the poet: in short, *Cent Mille Milliards de poèmes* is a privileged example of *voluntary literature*.

Other, complementary aspects of Quenellian poetics quickly become apparent in this text. The sonnets are executed with a fine attention to detail, and in a manner which implicitly valorizes the process, as well as the product; in a word, they are craftsmanlike. This reflects Queneau's deeply-held belief that the artist must approach his or her work as an artisan: "Le littérateur est l'artiste et l'artiste est artisan. Tous ceux qui ont cherché à faire dévier l'art ou à le limiter ont été de mauvais artisans" (*Voyage* 95).[4] There is also an element of pyrotechnics in *Cent Mille Milliards de poèmes*. Patently, the exercise was a difficult one, a feat that was hard to bring off. Queneau himself subscribes to the doctrine of *difficulté vaincue*, the notion that increasing the difficulty of the problem posed necessarily increases the merit—the value—of its eventual solution. François Le Lionnais, a close friend of Queneau's, formulates this idea quite unequivocally, in a richly dogmatic formalist polemic:

> L'efficacité d'une structure—c'est-à-dire l'aide plus ou moins grande qu'elle peut apporter à un écrivain—dépend d'abord de la plus ou moins grande difficulté d'écrire des textes en respectant des règles plus ou moins contraignantes.

> La majorité des écrivains et des lisants estime (ou affecte d'estimer), que des structures extrêmement contraignantes, comme l'acrostiche, la contrepeterie, le lipogramme, le palindrome ou holorime (pour ne citer que cinq d'entre elles qui ont reçu des noms), ne ressortissent que de l'acrobatie et ne méritent qu'une moue amusée car elles n'auraient aucune chance de contribuer à engendrer des oeuvres valables. Aucune chance? Voire. C'est un peu trop vite faire fi de la valeur exemplaire de toute acrobatie. Le seul fait de battre un record dans l'une de ces structures excessives peut suffire à justifier une oeuvre, l'émotion qui se dégage du sens de son contenu constituant un mérite qui n'est certes pas à dédaigner mais qui reste secondaire. ("Second Manifeste" 24-25)

Queneau himself affirms the value of *difficulté vaincue* in a discussion of the lipogram, a form in which a given letter (or letters) of the alphabet does not appear. There, he points out that the degree of difficulty of a lipogram can be calculated, in function of the frequency with which the letter normally occurs in written language. Thus, the frequency of the letter W being 0.02 in English, writing 100 words without a W would produce a text of difficulty 2; the frequency of E being 0.13, a 100-word lipogram in E would be of difficulty 13, and consequently—according to Queneau—of superior value (*Bâtons* 325).[5]

Finally, there is a clear (and most refreshing) ludic impulse at work in *Cent Mille Milliards de poèmes*. It is proposed as a game (which is not to say it lacks sober import as well[6]), and a wry one at that. For the playfulness that animates the process of production is intended to find its double in the process of reception. This ludic reciprocity is related to Queneau's notion of the poet as cruciverbist or maker of logogriphs. And, for him, it is quite obviously a question of a game solidly based in form:

> Mes premiers livres étaient conditionnés par des soucis d'ordre, je ne dirai pas mathématisant, mais arithmomaniaque, et aussi par un souci de structure ... il y a un côté jeu; c'est un jeu dont on invente les règles et auquel on obéit.
> Ensuite, je pense que je me suis dégagé de cette arithmomanie tout en conservant ce souci de structure, et,

maintenant, de nouveau je m'intéresse énormément à toutes les questions, je ne dirai pas de mathématique du langage, mais enfin du langage en tant que jeu avec des règles, disons un jeu de raisonnement, ou un jeu de hasard avec un maximum de raisonnement. (*Entretiens* 56)

The game in *Cent Mille Milliards de poèmes* is clearly combinatorial in character. And, to return to Queneau's terms, combinatorics defines a point of intersection for mathematics and literature, insofar as both are combinatorial systems. Indeed, for Italo Calvino (who was himself strongly influenced by Quenellian theory), literature itself can be defined in terms of combinatorics and ludics: "Literature is a combinatorial game that plays upon the possibilities intrinsic to its own material, independently of the personality of the author" ("Myth" 79). Jacques Jouet, a French author and self-avowed epigone of Queneau, sees creative (not to say inspirational) virtues in combinatorics: "La combinatoire est une abstraction nécessaire à l'imaginaire d'un écrivain. Elle est séduisante, vertigineuse et source de modestie créatrice" (*Raymond Queneau* 41).

There is yet another dimension of *Cent Mille Milliards de poèmes* that deserves mention. It is the seminal text of the Ouvroir de Littérature Potentielle (Oulipo), a group Queneau cofounded with François Le Lionnais in 1960. Originally numbering ten, the Oulipo now counts forty-one members, living and deceased, among them Georges Perec, Italo Calvino, Marcel Duchamp, Jacques Roubaud, and Harry Mathews. Its collective production has been significant,[7] as have the individual works of its members, largely influenced by the group's literary research. In 1964, Queneau described the Oulipo's work in terms of a formalist quest: "Quel est le but de nos travaux? Proposer aux écrivains de nouvelles 'structures', de nature mathématique ou bien encore inventer de nouveaux procédés artificiels ou mécaniques, contribuant à l'activité littéraire: Des soutiens de l'inspiration, pour ainsi dire, ou bien encore, en quelque sorte, une aide à la créativité" (*Bâtons* 321). What Queneau is talking about is, precisely, structures of formal constraint, structures that the group elaborates, but does not necessarily illustrate in finished works. Often, the Oulipo proposes them freely to other writers who are, one imagines, beached, blocked, brutalized by the false prophets of genius and inspiration. This is what led François

Le Lionnais to speak (only half-jokingly, I think) of the Institute for Literary Prosthesis ("Second Manifeste" 26).

Cent Mille Milliards de poèmes is intimately associated with the Oulipian aesthetic, and with the group's history. Queneau was working on that text in 1960, and the founding of the Oulipo was what motivated him, as he describes it, to finish it:

> J'avais écrit cinq ou six des sonnets des *Cent mille milliards de poèmes*, et j'hésitais un peu à continuer, enfin je n'avais pas beaucoup le courage de continuer, plus cela allait, plus c'était difficile à faire naturellement, quand j'ai rencontré François Le Lionnais, qui est un ami, et il m'a proposé de faire une sorte de groupe de recherches de littérature expérimentale. Cela m'a encouragé à continuer mes sonnets; ce recueil de poèmes est, en quelque sorte, la première manifestation concrète de ce Groupe de recherches. (*Entretiens* 116)

Most importantly for the Oulipo, *Cent Mille Milliards de poèmes* serves as a material demonstration of the notion of *potential literature*, the notion that constitutes the essential principle of the group's research, the privileged object of its interrogations. For, in that text, the vast majority of the sonnets must by necessity remain in *potential* state, rather than assume shape upon a page. The work is a smoothly-functional machine for the production and dissemination of literature; and, its mechanisms are such that this very process calls attention to itself. It is an exemplary text, in the fullest sense of that word.

Many others among the Oulipo's founding principles flow just as naturally out of Quenellian theory. In fact, just as the latter takes its source in a reaction against surrealism, so the Oulipo can be conceived as a sort of anti-surrealism. François Le Lionnais's account of the group's inception leaves no room for doubt on this issue. As he describes it, Queneau wished from the outset to safeguard the Oulipo from authoritarianism, cult of personality, and polemic for polemic's sake, all of which he associated with surrealist excess:

> Au cours d'un déjeuner dans un petit bistrot où on pouvait parler tranquillement, je me décidai à proposer à Raymond de créer un atelier ou un séminaire de littérature expérimentale abordant de manière scientifique ce que n'avaient fait

que pressentir les troubadours, les rhétoriqueurs, Raymond
Roussel, les formalistes russes et quelques autres. Ce projet n'aurait eu aucune chance de lui convenir si nous n'avions été viscéralement d'accord pour écarter de manière radicale toute activité de groupe pouvant engendrer fulminations,
excommunications, et toute forme de terreur. ("Raymond
Queneau" 39)

Jacques Bens, a founding member of the group, formulates the Oulipo's uncompromising position on the surrealist notion of chance, a position that closely echoes Queneau's own: "les membres de l'Oulipo n'ont jamais caché leur horreur de l'aléatoire, des cartomanciennes de salon et du ptit-bonheur-la-chance de bastringue: 'L'OuLiPo, c'est l'anti-hasard', affirma un jour sans rire l'OuLiPien Claude Berge, ce qui ne laisse subsister aucun doute sur l'aversion qu'on a pour le cornet à dés" ("Queneau oulipien" 24).

Much of the Oulipo's production represents, in a very real sense, a conscious playing-out of Quenellian theory. This process is located in a terrain defined by formal constraint, a fact acknowledged, not without humor, in a lapidary self-definition: "Oulipiens: rats qui ont à construire le labyrinthe dont ils se proposent de sortir" (Lescure, "Histoire" 36). Jacques Jouet, for several years the youngest member of the group, insists upon the formal quest, openly wondering where it will lead: "Jusqu'où peut-on aller dans la détermination du texte par la procédure qui l'engendre? Tout le travail oulipien repose sur cette interrogation dont l'examen théorique s'accompagne le plus souvent d'une vérification sur le métier" (*Raymond Queneau* 49).

It has already led to some astonishing works of literature. Italo Calvino's *The Castle of Crossed Destinies* owes part of its conception to the group, and *If on a winter's night a traveler*, as Calvino himself stressed (*Comment*), is distinctly Oulipian in character. Harry Mathews's *Cigarettes* reposes on a combinatoric structure elaborated within the Oulipo, entitled "Mathews's Algorithm" ("Algorithme"). Jacques Roubaud's *Quelque chose noir*, a collection of poems, relies on a textual figuration of the number nine; and his novels, *La Belle Hortense* and *L'Enlèvement d'Hortense*, incorporate certain of the formal principles of the sestina. Georges Perec's *La Disparition* is a 312-page lipogram in E, while, in *Les Revenentes*, E is the only vowel to appear; *La Vie mode d'emploi* is built upon arcane, multiply imbricated systems of constraint that critics are still patiently teasing out; his posthumous *"53 Jours,"* in one of its versions at least, was to have incorporated a different constraint in each chapter *("53 Jours"* 318).

It is Perec who, in an essay on the history of the lipogram, articulates the Oulipo's attitude toward formal mannerism most forcefully:

> Uniquement préoccupée de ses grandes majuscules (l'Œuvre, le Style, l'Inspiration, la Vision du Monde, les Options fondamentales, le Génie, la Création, etc.), l'histoire littéraire semble délibérément ignorer l'écriture comme pratique, comme travail, comme jeu. Les artifices systématiques, les maniérismes formels (ce qui, en dernière analyse, constitue Rabelais, Sterne, Roussel...) sont relégués dans ces registres d'asiles de fous littéraires que sont les "Curiosités": "Bibliothèque amusante...," "Trésor des Singularités...," "Amusements philologiques...," "Frivolités littéraires...," compilations d'une érudition maniaque où les "exploits" rhétoriques sont décrits avec une complaisance suspecte, une surenchère inutile et une ignorance crétine. Les contraintes y sont traitées comme des aberrations, des monstruosités pathologiques du langage et de l'écriture; les oeuvres qu'elles suscitent n'ont pas droit au statut d'oeuvre: enfermées, une fois pour toutes et sans appel, et souvent par leurs auteurs eux-mêmes, dans leur prouesses et leur habileté, elles demeurent des monstres para-littéraires justiciables seulement d'une symptomologie dont l'énumération et le classement ordonnent un dictionnaire de la folie littéraire. ("Histoire" 79)

Perec pursues his brief with considerable eloquence. Clearly, for him, constraining structures are *functionally* liberating, just as Queneau suggested. Speaking of the lipogram, Perec insists upon this point, as counterintuitive as it may seem to his reader: "En ce sens, la suppression de la lettre, du signe typographique, du support élémentaire, est une opération plus neutre, plus nette, plus décisive, quelque chose comme le degré zéro de la contrainte, à partir duquel tout devient possible" ("Histoire" 92).

Marcel Bénabou, another member of the Oulipo, recognizes that such a position is a difficult one to uphold, in that radical formalism is often associated with literary madness and a refusal of humanistic values as they are traditionally expressed in literature: "La contrainte, on le sait, a souvent mauvaise presse. Tous ceux pour qui la valeur suprême en littérature s'appelle sincérité, émotion, réalisme ou authenticité, s'en défient comme d'une dangereuse et étrange lubie" ("La Règle" 101). Yet, in spite of this, he too proclaims the liberating potential of formal constraint, in terms that largely echo Queneau's own: "Cet effet paradoxal de la contrainte, qui au lieu de bloquer l'imagination sert au contraire à l'éveiller, s'explique à vrai dire fort aisément. C'est que le choix d'une contrainte linguistique permet de contourner, ou d'ignorer, toutes ces autres contraintes qui ne relèvent pas, elles, du langage et qui se dérobent plus facilement à notre emprise" ("La Règle" 103).

Just as certain of the foregoing remarks may be seen as the most radical formulations of Quenellian theory, so *Cent Mille Milliards de poèmes* may serve as its most radical demonstration. If the poetics that subtend Queneau's last book, *Morale élémentaire* (1975), are substantially the same, the performance thereof is nonetheless rather different. The book itself is tripartite: the first section contains 51 fixed form poems; the second, 16 prose poems; the third, 64 prose poems. I should like to focus on the fixed form poems, on their *form*, precisely, a form which has by convention (and for lack of any other ready taxonomic tag) come to be called "morale élémentaire."

When Queneau published 19 of these poems in the *Nouvelle Revue Française* prior to their appearance in book form, he offered the following comments upon them:

> Le lecteur aura remarqué qu'il s'agit de poèmes à forme fixe. D'abord, trois fois trois plus un groupe substantif plus adjectif (ou participe) avec quelques répétitions, rimes, allitérations, échos *ad libitum*; puis une sorte d'interlude de sept vers de une à cinq syllables; enfin une conclusion de trois plus un groupe substantif plus adjectif (ou participe) reprenant plus ou moins quelques-uns des vingt-quatre mots utilisés dans la première partie. ("Poèmes" 20)

In presenting them to the Oulipo, he suggested only that they made him think of "une petite musique chinoise, avec des coups de cymbales" (Michèle Métail, "Une petite musique chinoise" 69).

Not surprisingly, the structure of these poems is both studied and rigorous. The groups of nouns and adjectives (or participles) are grouped around the interlude in a pattern that never varies:[8]

NA	NA	NA
	NA	
NA	NA	NA
	NA	
NA	NA	NA
	NA	
	interlude	
	of	
	7	
	verses	
	from	
	1 to 5	
	syllables	
NA	NA	NA
	NA	

Queneau's critics have reacted in various ways to *Morale élémentaire*.[9] Several see mathematical structures at work in the collection as a whole. Michèle Métail, for example, suggests that Queneau included 131 texts in *Morale élémentaire* because 131 is the smallest non-trivial palindromic number, and thus a mathematical figure of harmony ("Une petite musique" 71). She and others, such as Claude Debon, Brunella Eruli, and François Naudin, see the influence of the *I Ching* in the collection. According to Debon, this influence is most pervasive and determinative in the third section ("Sinon comment entrer?" 85); but Métail has argued that the first part of the fixed form poems recalls the structure of a hexagram from the *I Ching* ("Une petite musique" 74). Still other critics, in a more impressionistic manner, are struck by the shape of these poems upon the page; like a Rorschach test, the texts appear to yield up whatever the reader wishes to see in them: an airplane, a human body, a wine glass, a tree, a flower, the sun shining on a house (François Naudin, "Quelques réflexions" 19).

More to the point, I think, is an appreciation of these texts *as form*, rather than as representations of something else. This would seem all the more evident insofar as, unlike *Cent Mille Milliards de poèmes* and *Le Chiendent*, the principles of construction behind these poems seem obscure; that is, if the *what* of their structure cries out from the page, the *why* remains unclear. Queneau himself, in his note on these texts, seems deliberately to discourage his readers from any inquiry in that direction:

> Des "raisons" purement internes ont déterminé cette forme qui n'a été précédée d'aucune recherche mathématique ou rythmique explicitable. Le premier des poèmes ainsi écrit a été proprement "inspiré"; quelques réflexions (l'ourse léchant l'ourson) et une certaine pratique ont provoqué des modifications procurant la forme finalement adoptée. Que le corps du poème (moins l'interlude) comporte trente-deux mots et que l'ensemble présente quinze vers (un de plus que le sonnet) ne résulte d'aucune décision préalable. ("Poèmes" 20)

Queneau's comment is bound up in another aspect of his aesthetic of formal constraint, his characterization of the latter as "scaffolding." When Georges Charbonnier asks him about the role of formal mannerism in his work, and suggests that it often goes unrecognized for a time, Queneau responds in the following manner:

> Ah oui, cela, certainement. À ce moment-là je pensais qu'en effet c'était comme ces constructions, ces . . . comment on appelle ça? ces trucs en fer qui servent aux maçons à ravaler ou à construire une maison, un de ces . . . échafaudages, voilà! Comme ces échafaudages qu'on enlève, c'est exactement ça, qu'on enlève une fois que la construction est terminée.
> Maintenant . . . en jouant sur les mots, on peut dire aussi que la construction reste . . . une fois qu'elle est terminée, l'armature demeure invisible . . . il y a une correspondance entre la nature de l'échafaudage, de l'armature . . . et puis celle de la construction qui reste en place. (*Entretiens* 49-50)

That which remains in these poems is, precisely, *symmetry*; a pure, symmetrical form that is prior to and determinative of the other dimensions of textual function. Jacques Jouet has pointed out that, for all of Queneau's explicit admiration for fixed form poetry, the only fixed forms that he practiced systematically were the sonnet and the "morale élémentaire" (79). Here, too, one may note a certain balance, a certain harmony: Queneau's work on the sonnet inscribes itself within a most venerable formal tradition, while his "morale élémentaire" inaugurates another—a modest and marginal one, certainly, but a tradition nonetheless, as traced by the various other experiments in that form that follow directly upon Queneau's own.[10] This oscillation between tradition and innovation in Queneau's quest for form is indicative of the proportion he attempted to construct throughout his career. For, both in terms of his own work and in terms of his influence upon the literature of his time, the key to Queneau's poetics is *symmetry*, that clash of cymbals which punctuates and gives cadence to his "petite musique chinoise."

Edmond Jabès's Margins

THE SPACE of Edmond Jabès's writing is a vital space, the locus of a lifework that spans six decades and includes some thirty volumes. It remains nonetheless obscure and ill-defined, manifesting the equivocal character and the lack of circumscription of interrogation. For, from the beginning, query is the privileged mode of this body of work. Questioning is by its very nature difficult to locate, and this in itself constitutes, for Jabès, one of its principal virtues: it offers a possibility of discursive openness that stands in radical opposition to the closure of the answer.

As Jabès himself describes it, his interrogative strategy springs from a refusal of affirmation: "If I give a special status to the question, it is because I find something unsatisfactory about the nature of the answer" (Auster 20). This "something" might be articulated in a variety of ways: stasis, determination, convention, unquestioning (and unquestioned) affirmation. For Jabès, all of these notions represent the antithesis of his vision of writing as becoming, as vital process; and he states that distinction with characteristic boldness: "La certitude est région de mort; l'incertitude vallée de vie" (LY 111).[1]

In his conversations with Marcel Cohen, Jabès suggests that the answer is necessarily authoritarian (DL 110-11), in that it seeks to stabilize and guarantee the discourse that surrounds it. Changing terms, one might argue that the status of the answer is central, the point upon which, according to Jacques Derrida, the very notion of fixed structure depends.[2] The status of the question, on the other hand, is *marginal*: it hovers on the edge of structure, continually interrogating and destabilizing the latter. Pierre Missac has noted that the word *marge* occurs with regularity in Edmond Jabès's books (46); it is a key word which may offer ingress to those works. For my part, I should like to postulate the margin as a transcendent figure of Jabès's poetics, and to trace that construct in its various manifestations through his writing, in a manner more interrogative than declarative, attempting to preserve some of the alterity of the question.

Jabès himself is most unequivocal in his appropriation of the margin, not only as scriptoral space, but also as living locus. He tells Paul Auster categorically: "I have always lived in the margins" (9). Early on in the seven-volume *Livre des questions*, he discusses some of the advantages of such a marginal stance:

> J'ai toujours préféré les situations en marge, pour cette position de recul qu'on leur doit et qui nous permet de juger, d'imaginer, d'aimer, de vivre dans l'instant et hors de l'instant, libre mais de cette liberté de l'esclave qui en rêve.
>
> En marge, on devient intouchable au point que l'on a cru que cette position était une position de repli, une retraite en soi, une fuite. (LY 139)

Putting his own writing starkly into question, Jabès insists that he doesn't *belong* to literature, even though he may have wished to belong; that his books refuse this sort of integration; that no qualifying tag is further from his work than the term *oeuvre* (DL 154-55). All of this in spite of the fact that he is steeped in French culture and literary tradition and, most importantly, that he is a creature of the French language: "Si, depuis toujours, je suis rivé à la langue française, la place que j'ai conscience d'occuper dans la littérature de notre pays n'en est pas, à proprement parler, une. Elle est moins la place d'un écrivain que celle d'un livre qui n'entre dans aucune catégorie" (DD 79). Curiously, for one so skeptical of any notion of origin, Jabès states that his process of questioning originated in the spelling errors that he committed as a child (SD 57). These errors, he suggests, are figures of linguistic freedom; freedom, precisely, from the constraints that normative language imposes:

> L'enfant fabrique des mots. Quant à ceux qu'il a volés aux adultes et qui lui sont devenus familiers, il a tendance—lorsqu'il connaît l'alphabet—à les écrire comme il les entend.

> Les mots lui font prendre conscience de son univers. Il ne peut imaginer que le langage, auquel est liée sa liberté, soit plein de contraintes. Le premier mot écrit, par un enfant, est un mot de victoire, le mot de *sa* victoire. Il le défendra le plus longtemps possible et, lorsqu'on le forcera à l'écrire selon les règles, ce sera pour lui une grande déception. (DL 128-29)

In his mature writing as well, Jabès cherishes the distance that separates his idiolect from the body of convention, tradition, and fiat that defines normative language and literature. Here again, simply put, it is a question of the margin, a place that defines itself in stark opposition to the center.

The notion of opposition is a capital one for Jabès. Paradoxically enough, he argues that opposition is in fact the enabling condition for any adherence, in the political sense: "Je pense qu'il n'y a de véritable appartenance politique que critique" (DL 41). For as soon as one speaks of solidarity, he suggests, one necessarily introduces the notion of difference (DL 52). As often as Jabès may reiterate his reluctance to join groups,[3] he has engaged in collective political action upon many occasions: in the 1930s, he belonged to antifascist groups, and he founded the *Ligue des jeunes contre l'antisémitisme* in Cairo; in 1941, again in Cairo, he cofounded the *Groupe antifasciste italien*, and, in 1943, the *Groupement des amitiés françaises*, whose first article proclaimed allegiance to the Free French government (DL 161-62); after moving to Paris in 1957, Jabès loaned his name to a variety of progressive causes, notably the anti-apartheid movement.[4] Clearly, then, Jabès does not exclude solidarity in his own political praxis. But it is important to note that this practice is consistently *oppositional*: the movements that Jabès favors position themselves in opposition to fascism, antisemitism, apartheid. His criticism, in short, emanates from the margin.

Beyond the local level of his writing, and beyond the ample sphere of his practical politics, it would seem that the alterity of the margin enjoys a metaphysical status in Jabès's thought. He speaks of his "répugnance viscérale à tout enracinement" (DL 52), and valorizes the notions of errancy, wandering, and displacement. The principal figure arising out of this discourse is that of the foreigner, a figure who can be defined, most pertinently, only through opposition: "Qu'est-ce qu'un étranger? —Celui qui te fait croire que tu es chez toi" (LD 87). The marginality, the difference that constitutes the foreigner is put into play in a dynamic of *resistance*; and it is precisely that otherness that guarantees the subject's freedom: "L'étranger te permet d'être toi-même, en faisant, de toi, un étranger" (EA 9).

In Jabès's work, this sort of questioning is often bound up in speculation upon the Jewish condition in history, as he erects analogies between marginality and diaspora, the stranger and the Jew, errancy and the sort of exile that was imposed upon him at the time of the Suez Crisis, when he was forced to leave Egypt. These analogies constitute what Jabès calls *resemblances*, and they become apparent as early as the first volume of *Le Livre des questions*. Here, with the eloquence of understatement, Jabès describes the catastrophic reification of marginality:

> Quand l'étoile jaune scintillait au ciel des maudits, il portait le ciel sur sa poitrine. —Le ciel de la jeunesse au dard de guêpe et le ciel au brassard de deuil.
> Il avait dix-sept ans; un âge avec de grandes marges.
> (LQ 171)

Holocaust imposes the literal upon the figural: the abstract distanciation of the margin is rendered concrete in the ghetto and the camp; annihilation translates alienation. Difference is adduced as mortal identity, and institutionalized murder finds its locus in an eccentric, *exterior* space:

> "On l'appelait toujours 'le Juif' et son épouse et sa fille 'la femme et la fille du Juif'." Oui, oui mais encore? [. . .] "Il est mort dans une chambre à gaz hors de France… et son épouse est morte dans une chambre à gaz hors de France . . . et sa fille est revenue en France privée de sa raison. . . ." (LQ 184)

Beyond the immediate context of Holocaust, Jabès suggests that diaspora and errancy result in a heightened attentiveness to the word, to language and history. They become, in a sense, *scripted* in a story that narrates an impossible search for origin:

> Parallèlement à la lecture, antérieure au livre, d'une existence empêtrée entre le geste de Dieu et celui de l'homme, dans cet

espace gratuit où la créature se fond dans la création, les juifs dispersés dans les cinq continents, tandis que leur destin s'aiguille dans les marges, apprennent à concilier les mots de leur vocabulaire avec ceux de leur mémoire originelle. (A 121)

There is a curious phenomenon of convergence at work in this sort of speculation. Postulating the fallen, decentered character of language, Jabès will argue that writing is necessarily a textuality of exile, of nomadism. Or, as Richard Stamelman has suggested, in Jabès, diaspora is the necessary condition of all writing (93). Pushing these *resemblances* still closer, Jabès will sketch the identity of two major terms in his discourse: "Je vous ai parlé de la difficulté d'être Juif, qui se confond avec la difficulté d'écrire; car le judaïsme et l'écriture ne sont qu'une même attente, un même espoir, une même usure" (LQ 132). This short passage has accounted for more critical ink than any other in Jabès's work;[5] for my present purposes, however, I should like to insist upon the notion of convergence, and to note that the point of convergence is, precisely, the margin.

That point, in turn, accedes to whatever materiality it can lay claim to in the book. Here, the latter is not merely a wandering construct; it is, on the contrary, a vital space for both writer and Jew, as Jabès himself makes clear: "In a sense, I am now living out the historical Jewish condition. The book has become my true place . . . practically my only place" (Auster 12; ellipsis in original). For Edmond Jabès writes books about books: in a studied dynamic of infinite regression, the book becomes, under his pen, the world.[6] But that world is a rather strange one, curious and difficult to locate. The Jabesian book is like no other, and has led critics into the most brutal impasses of paradox, denial, and surrender. Gabriel Bounoure, one of Jabès's earliest and most faithful readers, calls *Yaël* an anti-novel (79); Jean-Pierre Téboul speaks of an generic aporia in Jabès (12); and Joseph Guglielmi suggests that Jabès's books offer an unknown sort of discourse (171).

Indeed, the resistance to conventional form would seem to be a deliberate tactic on Jabès's part. In *Yaël*, he addresses this problem directly: "Le livre échappe à toute étiquette. Il n'appartient à aucun clan. Il n'est l'apanage d'aucune classe. Il n'est jamais d'un sillage" (Y 28). The most articulated illustration of such a notion is the seven-volume *Livre des questions*. For there is a book composed of books which vigorously and insistently refuses any easy categorization *as* book within conventional taxonomies. Moreover, this refusal is inscribed with progressively more detail in the *Livre des questions* itself, where it becomes, in fact, a major theme: "j'ai rêvé d'une oeuvre qui n'entrerait dans aucune catégorie, qui n'appartiendrait à aucun genre, mais qui les contiendrait tous, une oeuvre que l'on aurait du mal à définir, mais qui se définirait précisément par cette absence de définition; une oeuvre qui ne répondrait à aucun nom, mais qui les aurait endossés tous" (A 57).

It is not, however, merely a question of generic instablility. Jabès's books trace an itinerary of approach and approximation: "Voici un livre, ou plutôt l'espérance écrite, récrite, de soir en soir, d'un livre" (Y 21); "Voici un livre qui ressemble à un livre—qui n'était pas, luimême, un livre; mais l'image de sa tentative" (LR 11). The book itself, as construct, is always receding from Jabès's pen, refusing to assume material form in the ink upon the page. Practically, this entails a curious phenomenon: the Jabesian book *grows*, as it were, this growth distributed according to figures of imbrication and generation. Thus, the septology was initially conceived as a single-volume work, itself entitled *Le Livre des questions*. With the publication of *Le Livre de Yukel* and *Le Retour au livre*, it became a trilogy. Another trilogy, consisting of *Yaël*, *Elya*, and *Aely*, was added, and assimilated to the first. With the addition of • *(El, ou le dernier livre)*, the septology took shape. But even that shape is far from definitive; Jabès has on occasion alluded to the ten-volume series consisting of *Le Livre des questions* and the *Livre des ressemblances* trilogy.[7] Since then, the *Livre des marges* and the *Livre des limites* have emerged, and continue to evolve, putting anterior works into question, just as they plainly and explicitly arise out of them.

Simply stated, the Jabesian book never *is*; rather, it is always *becoming*. It is a notion that Jabès shares with (among others) Maurice Blanchot, and its status within Jabès's work is pivotal. He speaks of a book whose value resides in its potential, whose textuality points toward an ulterior discourse, whose being is becoming:

> un livre dont il faudrait abolir les mots pour le rendre à sa pluralité blanche; un livre qui serait, à la fois, la part promise et la part refusée du livre; un livre enfin qui se désignerait par

un point dont on ne saurait s'il est blanc, au matin; noir, la nuit, mais que l'on s'habituerait à considérer comme un point à venir, un point en devenir, où rien plus ne subsiste. (EL 24)

Clearly, the locus of such writing is the margin. Doubly and most explicitly so in the case of Le Livre des marges. Composed for the present of Ça suit son cours and Dans la double dépendance du dit (and undoubtedly destined to grow further), this is the work in which Jabès has chosen to group certain of his *textes épars*: lectures, prefaces, homages, occasional pieces, and so forth. He says of them, "Les textes réunis ici sont destinés à demeurer en marge de mes ouvrages. Il faut leur conserver ce caractère marginal, le souligner même, afin que la lecture s'y fasse plus libre" (CS 25). The key notion here, I think, is that of freedom, exemption from constraint and independence from competing orthodoxies. Marginality is, for Jabès, a guarantor of freedom, and the sort of status that he claims for Le Livre des marges with reference to his other work is precisely characteristic of the position he adopts toward the rest of literature in his writerly enterprise as a whole. It is a position of opposition, and indeed of a certain critical vehemence: "La portée du livre est dans sa propre violence, colportée des marges" (EL 47).

Writing, then, will be eccentric: "Écrire le livre, c'est associer sa voix à celle, virtuelle, des marges" (Y 51). It will be a discourse of alterity, erecting itself in opposition to the homogenous, the ortholinear, the totalizing. It will be significantly dynamic, process rather than product, a questioning that plays itself out on each page: "Ma plume, de paragraphe en paragraphe, apprenait à cerner la vérité d'une vocation constamment remise en cause et en doute; acquérait le droit au partage du fruit de la faim, après en avoir payé la dîme; revendiquait le privilège, au nom du resplendissant amour, de se blottir, tel l'amant contre le sein de l'aimée, dans le vocable et dans les marges du livre" (Y 113). Finally, it will be a labor of positive construction, of building, not on traditional scriptoral terrain, which for Jabès is the ground of failure and death, but rather under that ground and (more pertinently) to either side: "Ce long travail souterrain des deux côtés de la mort, un jour, ah ce sera notre voie royale" (E 87).

Once again, it is principally and most emphatically a question of the space of literature. The dilemma, for Jabès, is double. On the one hand, conventional literary space is constraining; the studied closure of the wellmade book stifles and constricts: "Tout est bouché dans l'écriture. L'homme en vain y tente une ouverture pour pouvoir respirer" (RL 62). On the other hand, the space outside of the book is not habitable, it cannot be endured: "Le livre est inséré dans un ailleurs qui nous supprime" (A 148). Thus, Jabès's sometimes-narrator Yukel finds himself outside of the book, where language is deprived of the context that is its condition of possibility, where words are dead things, deprived of any signification (LY 23). This event is a writer's object lesson; clearly, the limits of the book must be tested *within* the book: "Toute sortie hors du livre se fait dans le livre" (Derrida 113).

Jabès proceeds to do just that, in a manner both canny and sure. In an effort to project textuality beyond its normal boundaries, he first inflates the limits of the book, generally through an insistence upon the specular character of the latter: "Derrière le livre, il y a l'arrière-livre; derrière l'arrière-livre, il y a l'espace immense et, enfoui dans cet immense espace, il y a le livre que nous allons écrire dans son énigmatique enchaînement" (E 9). In strict contiguity to that notion, Jabès places another, the idea that one is always hovering at the threshold, that the book is an imposing edifice where ingress itself is problematic. Reader and writer share this ambiguous space at the edge of the book, and the struggle of approach that reading and writing entail: they are located "Au seuil du livre" (LQ 11); in the "Avant l'avant-livre" (A 9); in "L'avant-premier moment de l'avant-livre" (LR 63). That is, more simply stated, the status of both reader and writer with regard to the book is itself marginal, rather than focal.

Within this newly proportioned book, Jabès appropriates new textual space by means of a radical displacement from the center to the margin: "Le lieu du livre est vide emmuré. Chaque page, précaire abri, possède ses quatre murs qui sont ses marges. Les exposer au jour, à la vue, c'est faire basculer les cloisons et le plafond" (EL 28). He carefully stresses, too, the magnitude of that new space:

> —Vous n'avez pas quitté le livre
> Vous ne l'auriez pu.
> Mais, parfois, si larges sont les interlignes, qu'il vous semble fouler un sol nouveau;
> si vastes sont les marges. (LQ 77)

If that space seems vast, it is precisely because the conventional scriptoral act leaves it perfectly vacant. It is "un espace qu'aucune lettre ne désigne" (EL 20), an unused space, and Jabès will recuperate it for his own. The margin's emptiness duplicates that of another privileged construct in Jabès's writing, the desert. Both margin and desert are places of nothingness, of vacuum; as spaces, they are shunned and eschewed. The brilliance of Jabès's tactic lies in a stark, counterintuitive inversion of this commonplace: he, on the contrary, designates that void as the book's proper ground, and has spent a career building upon it: "c'est sur ce rien que j'ai édifié mes livres" (LR 144).

This movement of inversion and displacement is habitual in Jabès's poetics, and it is one that recalls and recapitulates many others. I should like now to propose a figure for that movement and its analogues, that of the Lucretian clinamen. The latter must be understood, I think, as a gesture of revolt and a cipher of freedom, whether in *De rerum natura* or under such disparate pens as those of Alfred Jarry, Harold Bloom, Italo Calvino, and Michel Serres.[8] It is a swerve away from determination, convention, constraint, and authority; it is a startling redirection of process. Like the spelling errors Jabès committed as a child (which he evokes, it will be recalled, as the origin of his questioning), it serves as a guarantor of individuality and creative freedom. For the clinamen *is* an error, precisely: unprogrammatic and consequently unpredictable, it allows for the free play of the system it contributes to elaborate. In order to illustrate this figure, and to account for its capital importance in Jabès's writing, I would like to examine three local instances where he puts it vigorously into play, cases chosen among many others for their amplitude, their pertinence, and for the manner in which they may be seen to play out a certain poetics of marginalism.

The first instance involves words. A significant part of Jabès's project entails a close interrogation of the lexicon: he subjects words to rigorous analysis within the text, deflecting their denotational fields, furnishing them with new and sometimes startling possibilities of connotation. An initial movement here sets words against themselves and each other, in an agonistic dynamic intended to strip them of their false plenitude and reveal them as integers, in their naked materiality. It is a movement that can be figured by that of the clinamen, a swerve away from the given and the predetermined, toward freedom: "Notre liberté résiderait-elle dans la vaine tentative du vocable de se dissocier du vocable?" (Y 34).

Thus, Jabès will set the word against itself, disassembling it, putting its unity and its stability into question, testing its resilience: "Dedans: deux (fois) dans" (P 75). It should be stressed that this sort of process goes far beyond mere punning, or even (construed in a somewhat broader sense) *jeux de mots*. Jabès explicitly castigates those forms as being, in the best case, puerile; in the worst, dangerous (DL 133-34). Rather than give words over into amorphous and arbitrary resonance, Jabès proposes on the contrary to constrain them. And it is clear that he views this as a gesture of freedom: "Plus que de laisser libre cours aux mots, il s'agit donc de les cerner au plus près de leurs possibilités. Notre liberté est là" (DL 132). It is, I think, word play in the fullest sense of the term, animated by a high sobriety of purpose. Jabès puts words into *play* against themselves and each other, a process whose first movement is destructive: "Les vocables ont éventré les vocables" (LY 85). But this initial violence reveals aspects of the word which are normally hidden or obscured; stripped of the mythology of plenitude, the word can be seen as object, as tool ready to hand, as poetic integer:

> Si je prends l'exemple du mot "commentaire" que j'écris "Comment taire?" ce qui me frappe, c'est de voir que toutes mes préoccupations profondes sont déjà étalées là. En effet, commenter c'est faire taire un sens déjà établi, un sens figé. Mais c'est aussi faire taire la perception immédiate que nous avons du texte pour lui laisser une chance de parler par lui-même.
>
> Aussi, s'il m'est arrivé d'écrire Dieu, "D'yeux," c'est pour marquer combien la tentation est grande de chercher Dieu avec les yeux. Car Dieu, n'est-ce pas, c'est l'exigence ultime du regard.
>
> Il va de soi que l'étymologie n'a rien à voir dans tout cela et je comprends très bien qu'un grammarien puisse même s'en divertir. Il va, également, de soi que ma lecture de certains mots est on ne peut plus personnelle et n'a de sens, je le répète, que dans le contexte de ce que je cherche à exprimer. Peut-être, en fin de compte, ne fais-je que revivre l'ivresse

première devant le langage, celle de l'enfant qui, d'instinct,
tire du mot ce qui, pour lui, paraît éternel. (DL 136)

The revelation that Jabès speaks of is initially the author's. But, as it is contextualized within the book, it becomes the reader's. Here, what is additionally revealed is the extreme contingency of signification, for the new sort of signification that Jabès is talking about is built up and sustained only within a skeletal community, that of an author and his public:

> Ce travail sur le mot, il va de soi, réclame la complicité du lecteur. Il témoigne aussi d'une logique qui, à mes yeux au moins, n'est pas du tout gratuite puisqu'elle permet une re-découverte, une relecture du mot. On ouvre un mot comme on ouvre un livre: c'est le même geste. Et cette ouverture est brisure. Nous nous rendons compte à quel point le sens d'un mot, dans la pratique, est affaire de connivence; combien l'acceptation unanime du sens d'un mot est précaire. (DL 134-35)

After this shattering, words are free to signify anew. They are not, perhaps, entirely divorced from their habitual semantic fields; rather, the latter are deflected and (in many cases) augmented. Jabès takes pains to point out affinities and mutual complementarities in his remotivated lexicon, *resemblances*, precisely: "L'attente est patiente marge d'attentat" (EL 21). Yet he makes it clear that these, like the conventional patterns of meaning that they replace or supplement, are, as he puts it, precarious. In a very real sense, for Jabès, words (and indeed language as a whole) testify to the essential and irremediable fragmentation of existence. Whatever structures one may erect to cosmetize or obscure this condition—fields of signification, astonishing verbal reciprocities, poetry—the fact remains that these structures rest upon nothingness. It is a void that words are finally powerless to fill: "Les mots, à jamais, demeurent séparés" (E 33).

In this perspective, the most characteristic word of the Jabesian book is not a word at all. Sarah's cry, the only sound she emits after returning from the camps, stripped of her reason, resonates through *Le Livre des questions*, and well beyond. It is patently averbal, defining a sort of zero degree of language, and it expresses a reality upon which words, finally, have no purchase. It emanates, significantly, from the margins of language, and functions to put language itself harshly into question. In a sense, all of Jabès's words strain toward this cry and toward the margin from which it comes, laboring against easy meaning and the adequacy of mere telling: "Ainsi, l'écriture, d'un ouvrage à l'autre, ne serait que l'effort des vocables pour épuiser le dire—l'instant—pour se réfugier dans l'indicible qui n'est pas ce qui ne peut être dit mais, au contraire, ce qui a été si intimement, si *totalement* dit qu'il ne dit plus que cette intimité, cette totalité indicible" (PL 55-56).

The second swerve I should like to consider involves the notion of the center. In the Jabesian book, writing is subject to a centrifugal movement: it flees the center, constantly spiraling outward. Thus Adolfo Fernandez Zoïla speaks of an infinite transformational process: "C'est ainsi que s'affirme le décentrement, la marginalisation. Les micelles textuelles centrifuges circulent d'un texte à l'autre, toujours apparemment semblables mais toujours différentes. Éparpillement corpusculaire qui sans cesse se féconde, engendrant d'autres vocables, d'autres propos" (12).

I would like to argue that this centrifugal dynamic is accompanied by another movement, by an actual and radical displacement of the center itself, and, further, that this is a deliberate tactic that Jabès deploys. Other readers have noted analogous phenomena. Fernandez Zoïla, for instance, suggests that the centrifugal movement of the Jabesian text results in a plurality of centers (12). For Blanchot, both Judaism and writing originate in a rupture, an event that reveals the center, but at the same time explodes it. The latter becomes "le point excentré qui n'est centre que par l'éclat de la brisure" (879). Gabriel Bounoure, reading *Yaël* and noting the stark dislocation of space, time, voice, and story, is forced to conclude that the center has been decentered (74).

Jabès himself casts the center as an obstacle to be overcome: "Le dernier obstacle, l'ultime borne est, qui sait? le centre" (RL 58). This position makes perfect sense if the center is construed as an oppressive force, and this is precisely how Jabès understands it. Along with Derrida, he recognizes the tyrannical character of the center, and the stifling effect it has upon the structure it purports to organize: "Pourtant le centre ferme aussi le jeu qu'il ouvre et rend possible. En tant que centre, il est le point où la substitution des contenus, des éléments, des termes, n'est plus possible" (Derrida 410). Jabès attacks along two fronts. First, by outright denial. On one occasion, he describes the center as a non-pertinent construct, a vestigial point of reference of an eccentric discourse: "Le centre n'existe pas. Il est le point qui engendre le point autour duquel une parole excentrée s'instaure, une interrogation se développe. Il est le point de non-retour" (DD 79). Secondly, and more effectively still, Jabès displaces the center through questioning it. That is, the progressive interrogation of the center eventually contaminates the latter with precisely the sort of instability and dislocation that is characteristic of the question itself: "Le centre est, peut-être, le déplacement de la question" (RL 57). The crucial result of such efforts is that a marginal discourse can now lay claim to a portion of the authority that was heretofore the exclusive prerogative of the center. It is not that the margin, in turn, becomes central (a trivial and ultimately nonsensical inversion); but rather that power, if necessarily more diffuse, can now be distributed over a broader spectrum of discursive possibility.

Finally, I would like to examine the status of silence and emptiness in Jabès's work. The Jabesian page, instantly recognizable, is like no other. Fragments of language are everywhere; the margins are unstable; the text is dislocated on the page. But the most characteristic aspect of this textuality is, curiously enough, a seeming refusal of textuality: the Jabesian page is recognizable not because of its ink, but rather because of its blankness. It confronts the reader most directly with the primordial question of these writings, a question that Jabès himself is careful to articulate: "Comment lire un récit émaillé de blancs?" (LP 19). How indeed? Moreover, it is not merely a question of reading the *récit*, for the *blancs* themselves demand to be read as well. Jabès suggests to Marcel Cohen that these white spaces figure death, and that a writer must dole them out with circumspection:

> La mort, c'est l'espace blanc séparant les vocables et qui les rend intelligibles, c'est le silence qui rend audible la parole orale.
>
> C'est pourquoi le blanc est si redoutable sur une page. Les écrivains qui, aujourd'hui, emploient abusivement le blanc ne savent pas toujours le tort qu'ils font à leurs propres écrits. Le blanc, en leur donnant trop de résonance, étouffe les phrases.

> En élargissant démesurément l'espace vital dont a besoin le mot, celui-ci s'effrite inexorablement. Peu d'écrivains savent se ramasser dans une parole suffisamment forte pour résister à pareille pression du silence, à pareille étendue. Et cependant, écrire ne peut être qu'affronter ce silence. (DL 146)

Yet, as much as one may recognize the utility of silence and even (more pertinently still) its necessary ubiquity, it is still very troubling, both theoretically and functionally. Derrida, for one, calls silence the inaccessible, and says that the idea of silence is disarming, even as he argues that we must elaborate a language that preserves silence (385). Susan Handelman, reading Jabès, concludes that the latter is dealing in a "shadow side" of language, where emptiness is the only thing preserving narrative coherence: "Yukel and Sarah's story, Yaël and Elya's story, the rabbis' stories, the stories of the Jews in their various wanderings have been woven together, yet the narrative is not smooth. What holds them together are the open spaces of the Book, which can somehow accommodate them all; they are undergirded by Nothing" (68).

There is more at work here than the simple eloquence of the void. The blank page is the locus of writing, that which will become the space of literature: "La page blanche est un silence imposé. C'est sur ce fond de silence que s'écrit le texte" (DL 127); but, paradoxically, the emptiness is also, and simultaneously, *what is written*: "Nous n'écrivons que la blancheur où s'écrit notre destin" (EA 95). Clearly, Jabès views silence as vital, even as he holds it to be a figure of death. Once again, this is strongly characteristic of the inversions he practices, and it can be schematized as a swerve away from plenitude, ink, and speech toward the emptiness, whiteness, and silence of the margin.

In his defense of silence, Jabès is not alone. Maurice Blanchot, in an early essay on *Le Livre des questions*, offers a powerful brief: "L'interruption est nécessaire à toute suite de paroles; l'intermittence rend possible le devenir; la discontinuité assure la continuité de l'entente" (870). Blanchot's thought and that of Jabès follow very similar lines here, and Jabès would seem to agree with Blanchot's thesis, as far as it goes. Indeed, a passage from *Le Retour au livre*, published shortly after Blanchot's essay, may be read as a response to the latter:

"Un espace est nécessaire à la lecture du monde. La lisibilité est dans le recul" (RL 79). I would submit, however, that Jabès goes beyond the position that Blanchot sketches out. He is not interested in silence and emptiness merely as guarantors of understanding. Their status, for him, and the role they play within his work are far more ample.

Jabès is concerned, precisely, with the void itself, with the abyss, the fault, the *faille*. His concern is such that he looks for such phenomena (or indeed *coerces* them) not only where they occur most naturally—between words or sounds, between phrases and locutions, between the two sides of a dialogue—but also within the word itself: "Briser le mot, faire jouer les mots dans les brisures du mot, c'est aller au plus proche par le chemin le plus direct" (CS 72); "Pénétrer dans le mot par le truchement de sa différence" (LD 45). Jabès insists that an analytical process such as this is necessary in writing, and can produce effects that are nothing short of vertiginous: "Un espace un peu plus large—la séparation de deux syllabes, par exemple—dans le mot, une faille inattendue, la cassure d'une lettre ou sa chute dans le vide, provoquent un tel jeu dans ce mot que celui-ci se voit entraîner dans une série de métamorphoses qui l'annule à mesure qu'elle progresse" (EL 21).

This process, carried out on the level of the individual word, is intimately bound up in Jabès's poetics as a whole, of which it may be taken as figural. For the essence of Jabès's writing resides in the fragment: more than the letter, more than the word, more than the phrase, more than the story, more than the book, it is the fragment that is the privileged integer of this body of work. The text it produces appears as shattered; broken and dispersed; damaged and in need of repair. Yet Jabès argues that this very brokenness points insistently toward unity:

> C'est dans la fragmentation que se donne à lire l'immensurable totalité. Aussi est-ce toujours par rapport à une totalité controuvée que nous affrontons le fragment; celui-ci figurant, chaque fois, cette totalité dans sa partie reçue, proclamée et, en même temps, par sa contestation renouvelée de l'origine, devenant, en se substituant à elle, soi-même origine de toute origine possible, décelable.
>
> De cette fertile "déconstruction" qui opère dans les deux sens—de la totalité afin de déboucher sur l'ultime fragment et de l'infime fragment enfin, en s'annulant au fur et à mesure

dans le néant du fragment prépondérant, de reconstituer, à travers son effacement, cette totalité—l'oeil est le guide, le phare. (CS 53)

The space that the fragment affords is the locus of free play in the book, a marginal space where textuality arises and is nourished: "la forme aphoristique est l'expression profonde du livre, car elle permet aux marges de respirer, car elle porte en soi la respiration du livre et exprime l'univers en une fois" (Y 51). Textual fragmentation recapitulates the dislocated character of existence, moreover; it is in this sense that Jabès proposes the book as the world. But it is also—crucially—a tactic that allows Jabès to avoid the proscription of representation, allows him, simply stated, to *write*:

> —Pourquoi—lui demanda-t-il—ton livre n'est-il qu'une succession de fragments?
> —Parce que l'interdit ne frappe pas le livre brisé, répondit-il. (PL 45)

Broken book, shattered writing: yet another swerve away from midpage, toward the margin. Like so many other, analogous acts in Jabès's work, it is a gesture of revolt and an appropriation of freedom. More urgently still, it is a movement of survival, one that is accomplished, finally, in a resounding silence: "Ici, s'éteint le langage" (LR 144).

Georges Perec's Work

SORROW and melancholy color Georges Perec's writings from his first published works onward. In some texts, those attitudes are explicit and insistent, while in others they are more muted. Works such as *Un homme qui dort*, *W ou le souvenir d'enfance*, "La Clôture," and *Récits d'Ellis Island* are clearly composed in a minor key, and present themselves to us in the first instance as lamentations. In others, like *La Disparition* and *La Vie mode d'emploi*, a major key dominates. Yet, in the manner of the best blues tunes, that key and the mood it connotes are continually called into question by plaintive notes and voicings, effects that serve to redirect our reading into avenues that are far darker than the ones first imagined. Undoubtedly, the sadness that Perec expresses in his work has many different objects. There is a commonality that runs through much of it however, a fundamental similarity of approach and tone that recurs with regularity throughout his writings. More organized, more structured, less anecdotal and more profound than other kinds of sorrow that Perec expresses, the phenomenon that interests me is a sustained mourning, and its object is his parents.

For the benefit of those readers who may be unfamiliar with Perec, allow me to provide a few biographical details. I shall be very brief here. Georges Perec was born in Paris in 1936. Both of his parents were Polish Jews who had come to France in the 1920s. His father enlisted in the French army, and was killed on the final day of the *drôle de guerre*, in June 1940. His mother was arrested and interned in Drancy, then deported to Auschwitz in February 1943. She did not survive, though what exactly became of her was never determined.

Many critics have read a story of personal torment in Perec's work. Philippe Lejeune, for instance, sees in Perec "une écriture autobiographique du manque, de la faille, du malaise" (*La Mémoire et l'oblique* 43). It is particularly useful in Perec's case to broaden the field of what we mean by "autobiography," for his work as a whole is uncommonly shaped by the writing of the self, whether it is a question of obviously confessional texts or not. Wherever the self is placed on stage, the effect that Lejeune notes becomes apparent, as if there were something about the self itself that causes the writing to hesitate, to stutter. Let me repeat that there are, without a doubt, many objects of melancholy in Perec's writing. Moreover, I certainly do not wish to propose Perec's grief as either single or static: to the contrary, it is both multiple and constantly mobile. The sadness that Perec feels over the loss of his parents finds expression in his texts in many different ways, taking many different forms and investing many different sites. I am persuaded however that within such variety striking patterns of similarity exist, linking text to text in a kind of oblique narrative discourse.

I would like to begin to account for that phenomenon through a notion that Freud develops in "Mourning and Melancholia." (And I have no qualms about bringing Freud to bear in considering a writer who was analyzed by Françoise Dolto in his preteen years, by Michel de M'Uzan in his early twenties, and by J.-B. Pontalis in his mid-thirties.) In that essay, discussing "the economics of pain," Freud speaks of the "work of mourning," wherein the subject comes to terms with the reality of the loss of a loved one.[1] That process, Freud suggests, is a painful one, but it serves to prolong the psychic existence of the lost object in crucial ways, for if the subject were to accept the loss immediately and in the entirety of its implications, the ego would be overwhelmed. Freud insists that the work of mourning is a very gradual process, "carried out bit by bit, at great expense of time and cathectic energy," a point upon which other students of the phenomenon concur.[2] He argues further that the work of mourning takes place in "piecemeal" fashion, proceeding in fits and starts rather than in a continuous, uninterrupted manner. Finally, he adumbrates an end for the process, and with it a prospect of eventual recovery: "The fact is, however, that when the work of mourning is completed the ego becomes free and uninhibited again."

Freud's construct seems very cogent to me, granted what we know—or think we know—about the way people deal with intense personal loss. It is particularly apt, and useful too, when one considers Georges Perec's writing, because it offers a way of reading the kind of oblique narrative that I mentioned earlier. I would like to insist, for a moment, on both of the terms that compose it. I am convinced that a very great deal of the sorrow, regret, pain, and bewilderment that Perec expresses in his texts can be read systematically as mourning behavior, and that Perec stages such effects in utterly deliberate (if not quite programmatic) fashion. In other words, he is conscious of his mourning *as* mourning. Though I do not wish to belabor the issue of intention unduly, the consideration of consciousness is an important one. Freud distinguished between mourning and melancholia precisely on the grounds of the subject's awareness, arguing that the melancholic may be aware of *whom* he or she has lost, but unaware of *what* has been lost in him or her. "This would suggest," he argues, "that melancholia is in some way related to an object-loss which is withdrawn from consciousness, in contradistinction to mourning, in which there is nothing about the loss that is unconscious" (245). Georges Perec is the most conscious of writers. He knows all too well the places where the trauma has scarred him; and he spends a great deal of his writerly energy in making those scarifications legible to others.

In that sense (and turning now to the other term in Freud's construct), the process of grieving that Perec undertakes is very clearly organized as *work*. That is, whatever form it may take in his writing, it presents itself as effort, as labor, as toil, and as a behavior that is above all purposeful. Perec seeks an active engagement with his grief, recognizing that, unattended and undirected, it is something that would threaten to cripple him. As Julia Kristeva has noted, the alternative that the death of a beloved person poses to the subject is a radical one, and one that persists in very precarious equilibrium: "loss, bereavement, and absence trigger the work of the imagination and nourish it permanently as much as they threaten it and spoil it" (*Black Sun* 9). Under the influence of his mentor Raymond Queneau, Perec came to recognize the work of the imagination *as* work, refusing the idea of artistic inspiration in favor of a vision of the artist as first and foremost an artisan, a worker. He recognized, too, that such work is productive, whether the product be a sonnet, the elaboration of a new and intricate literary constraint, or an itinerary of inquiry and reflection allowing him—however tenuously—to keep despair at bay.

From text to text then, in different guises and according to different terms, Perec pursues the work of mourning. He proceeds in a manner that may seem disjunctive and interrupted at first glance, in fits and starts, a "piecemeal" project as it were. The tone in which it is articulated remains largely consonant throughout however, a meiotic tone in which less is said in order to mean more.[3] I should mention here that I invoke the term "meiosis" in its rhetorical sense, for in the lexicon of medicine it means something quite different and inapposite, defined by the OED as "the state of a disease in which symptoms begin to abate." Whatever else one might think of it, it is important not to be too sanguine about Perec's work of mourning. Clearly, it is an undertaking that remains very much in process in his writing up to the moment of his own death. It presents no recognizable prospect of the kind of full recovery that Freud postulated at its hypothetical endpoint; nor does the "cure" hold the promise of anything other than a provisional and fragile—but nonetheless vital—psychic balance.

Before I turn to specific instances in Perec, I would like to suggest another way to conceive Freud's term, imagining for the moment "work" not as a behavior, but rather as the product of that behavior. In such a perspective, one might usefully think of "the work of mourning" in Perec as the work itself, the oeuvre, the individual work of literature and also the body of writing as a whole. Certain texts—*W ou le souvenir d'enfance*, to name the most obvious one—can be considered productively in such a light, as elaborate and carefully constructed memorials. When for instance Perec states in *W* that "Ma mère n'a pas de tombe" (57), that painfully laconic utterance takes its place in a variety of textual isotopies. Chief among them is a metaliterary discourse which suggests that one of Perec's purposes in *W* is precisely to construct a site of remembrance and mourning for his mother, a grave, a tomb, in his writing. And I am persuaded, too, that it is legitimate to view Perec's oeuvre as a whole in a similar manner. I do not mean that such a reading of Perec's work should exclude others, but only that it constitutes a vitally important and inevitable facet of a body of writing that is as remarkably multidimensional as any of which I am aware.

In what follows I shall try to read the notion of "work" doubly, both as activity and as product, vexing the one against the other in order to find their points of mutual complementarity. Having argued that there are many sites of mourning in Perec's writings, and that the expression of his grief is multiple and various, sometimes obvious and sometimes far more covert, I have chosen to focus upon four sites. Taken first individually and then considered together, they seem to me representative of the different shapes that mourning adopts in Perec, both in terms of the way that work is carried out and in terms of the kind of works in which it results.

The first and most readily apparent field of mourning in Perec I would like to point toward is in *W ou le souvenir d'enfance*. Many of his readers, myself included, have commented upon that text as a discourse of lack wherein Perec grapples with the articulation of concerns that remain, for him, largely unsayable.[4] *W* is a hybrid text in which chapters of fiction alternate with chapters of autobiography, approaching the problem of catastrophe from different angles; and at times one mode of literary expression clearly tries to express what the other just as clearly cannot. As Perec describes it, the fundamental problem devolves upon the problem of memory. His autobiographical narrative begins thus:

> Je n'ai pas de souvenirs d'enfance. Jusqu'à ma douzième année à peu près, mon histoire tient en quelques lignes: j'ai perdu mon père à quatre ans, ma mère à six; j'ai passé la guerre dans diverses pensions de Villard-de-Lans. En 1945, la soeur de mon père et son mari m'adoptèrent.
>
> Cette absence d'histoire m'a longtemps rassuré: sa sécheresse objective, son évidence apparente, son innocence, me protégeaient, mais de quoi me protégeaient-elles, sinon précisément de mon histoire, de mon histoire vécue, de mon histoire réelle, de mon histoire à moi qui, on peut le supposer, n'était ni sèche, ni objective, ni apparemment évidente, ni évidemment innocente?
>
> "Je n'ai pas de souvenirs d'enfance": je posais cette affirmation avec assurance, avec presque une sorte de défi. L'on n'avait pas à m'interroger sur cette question. Elle n'était pas inscrite à mon programme. J'en étais dispensé: une autre histoire, la Grande, l'Histoire avec sa grande hache, avait déjà répondu à ma place: la guerre, les camps. (13)

The first thing that should be noted about this passage is the immediate and unconditional denial of the kind of project which the title of the text implicitly announces. That is, having erected a horizon of readerly expectation based on the notion of memory—and memories—Perec very deliberately devastates that horizon in the first sentence of his autobiographical narrative. He erects in its place the beginning of an amnesic memoir where what is memorialized is precisely the lack of any reliable connection with the past. In the French original, his play on the ideas of "story" and "history" (the French word *histoire* can mean either) is particularly pungent, erecting tensive relations between the two, and suggesting that a story of personal catastrophe is rendered largely moot by the far broader and perhaps more compelling context of historical catastrophe in which it takes shape. The sort of negative narration that Perec launches here will characterize the rest of *W*, if in different ways and in varying degree. It will be characterized too by an extreme recursivity, an effect that Perec deploys with some ostentation in the first sentence of the final paragraph I quoted, where he rereads—and indeed rewrites—the inaugural sentence of his autobiographical narrative. That technique serves many purposes in *W*, but most interestingly it materializes and inscribes upon the page the kinds of gestures that real anamnesis requires, that is, looking back, recalling, and reconsidering.

Whenever Perec does look back, however, he fails to find what most people take as a matter of course and fundamental entitlement: *his* story. "Mon enfance," he states, "fait partie de ces choses dont je sais que je ne sais pas grand-chose" (21). Among all of the memories that an adult might expect to retain from childhood, Perec seeks most urgently for some trace of his parents, some recollection that corresponds to lived experience, something upon which he can now rely. Faced with the absence of such memories, he turns toward invention, imagining emblematic situations, couching them in the conditional and the hypothetical, even suggesting to his reader upon one occasion that they are not "entièrement implausibles" (22). In short, he turns to writing:

> J'écris: j'écris parce que nous avons vécu ensemble, parce que j'ai été un parmi eux, ombre au milieu de leurs ombres, corps près de leurs corps; j'écris parce qu'ils ont laissé en moi leur marque indélébile et que la trace en est l'écriture: leur

souvenir est mort à l'écriture; l'écriture est le souvenir de leur mort et l'affirmation de ma vie. (59)

He is aware—painfully and preternaturally so—that the writing of the thing is not the thing itself, and that the gap of representation cannot be bridged. Perec defines himself as a writer, though: that's what he is, and more importantly still, that's what he does. In other terms, having come squarely up against the interdict that amnesia places on the telling of his "own story," he turns to his *work*. He postulates for that work the kind of organic connection with his parents that his memory cannot provide to him, a "trace" which allows him to say, at the very least, that his parents once were, that they are now no longer, and that they deserve some kind of memorial, however artificial and constructed it might be.

The most eloquent site of such a memorial in *W ou le souvenir d'enfance* is undoubtedly the page in the very middle of the text which separates the first part of *W* from the second. It is framed by empty pages, and it is itself empty, apart from an ellipsis enclosed in parentheses (85). If the alternation of chapters were to be respected, a chapter of the autobiographical narrative should be placed there; and coming after a passage of that narrative where Perec saw his mother for the final time, one might expect that it would provide information about her death. As I mentioned earlier, however, Perec has never been able to find any such information; and what he puts in its place, escaping from language as it does and suspended as it is, clearly points toward something that remains well beyond language—and perhaps beyond thought, too.

Recognizing the importance of that moment, I would like to consider another one to which less critical attention has been paid, and in which Perec's work of mourning may be still more unmistakable. In the tenth chapter of *W*, Perec discusses a photograph of himself and his mother in some detail. Among the remarks he offers is the following one: "J'ai des cheveux blonds avec un très joli cran sur le front (de tous les souvenirs qui me manquent, celui-là est peut-être celui que j'aimerais le plus fortement avoir: ma mère me coiffant, me faisant cette ondulation savante)" (70). Gazing at the photograph, Perec sees material evidence of the way his memory has failed him. For the photo tells him incontrovertibly that he was *there*, with his mother, in precisely the kind of intimate setting he was forced to imagine in other circumstances; yet he recalls nothing of the scene. The possibility that this failure to remember might be a refusal to remember—and thus a betrayal—haunts him. Working though that nexus of problems, quite literally in this instance on the page, he recasts it in another form, admitting that the memory is "missing," and creating for it a privileged status for it within the devastated register of erasure that *W* constructs. This one would be *the* one, Perec tells us. It would be the perfect image of parent-child intimacy. The contact of body to body that one takes for granted in such a relationship is performed here as a fundamental drama. The gesture at its center is capitally important. Perec's mother arranges his curl perfectly, both by virtue of the fact that she was an exemplary mother and also because (as he mentions elsewhere in *W*) she was a hairdresser: that was her other job, her *work*, in life.

His work, right now, is to remember that moment, a moment that must have occurred, even if he is forced to resort to the hypothetical mode in order to give it shape. The fact that Perec places the evocation of this most important missing memory in parentheses is typical of the meiotic strategy upon which he relies throughout *W ou le souvenir d'enfance*, where less always means more. It may be usefully compared to the ellipsis in parentheses in the middle of the book, but here language has not abdicated—or not quite. What is crucially at issue is the parental touch, the act that emblematizes and guarantees everything else that Perec longs to recall in a past with which he is so bleakly out of touch. Metaphorically then, it figures the kind of contact with the past that eludes him, Moreover, it suggests the sort of contact that he seeks in the telling of his story, for stories are always told to an audience, however virtual. Yet as touching as his story may be, it is clear from the way Perec works through it that he deems that last sort of contact to be hypothetical, just like the others.

The second site of mourning that I would like to visit spans several of Perec's works, and first becomes apparent in *Un homme qui dort*. Toward the end of that text, which is surely the most melancholy and introspective of Perec's fictional works, the narrator (a version of Perec himself in deliberately transparent disguise) gazes at his face in the mirror: "Quels secrets cherches-tu dans ton miroir fêlé? Quelle vérité dans ton visage? Cette face ronde, un peu gonflée, presque bouffie déjà, ces sourcils qui se rejoignent, cette minuscule cicatrice au-dessus de la lèvre [. . .]" (168). Among the details that the narrator offers as he reads his own face, it is the scar that interests me the most, for I believe that it is the best example of the sort of legible scarifications that I mentioned earlier. Earlier in the novel, the narrator alludes to Antonello de Messine's *Le Condottiere*, "le portrait incroyablement énergique d'un homme de la Renaissance, avec une toute petite cicatrice au-dessus de la lèvre supérieure, à gauche, c'est-à-dire à gauche pour lui, a droite pour toi" (116-17). The coincidence of the scars, and (more obviously still) the deliberate repetition of the phrase "incroyablement énergique" in the narrator's account of his own face (168) suggest both the importance of the scar in the semiotics of the self and the kind of totemic identification that the narrator invests in the Condottiere. Extratextual evidence confirms that Perec shares his narrator's fascination with the Condottiere, for that figure returns frequently in works such as *Espèces d'espaces*, *W ou le souvenir d'enfance*, and *La Vie mode d'emploi*. Moreover, Perec mentions in *W* that he himself has a scar on his left upper lip. He speaks about it at some length in that text, remarking that he received it in boarding school during the war at the hands of another boy who attacked him with a ski pole. "Pour des raisons mal élucidées," says Perec, "cette cicatrice semble avoir eu pour moi une importance capitale: elle est devenue une marque personnelle, un signe distinctif" (141). He adds that though he wears a beard, he shaves his upper lip so as not to hide his scar. Further, he points out that Jacques Speisser, the lone actor in the film version of *Un homme qui dort*, also has a scar on his upper lip, "presque exactement identique à la mienne: c'était un simple hasard, mais il fut, pour moi, secrètement déterminant" (143).

Reading this ramifying network of signs, it gradually becomes apparent that Perec sees the scar as the material trace of personal catastrophe. He received it shortly after he was orphaned, and the injustice of the incident with the ski pole is the very emblem of the sort of arbitrary, unmerited punishment that he suffered since the death of his parents, a suffering that continues to impede his efforts to come to terms with his life as he writes *Un homme qui dort*. In such a perspective, it is the token of the fact that (as his narrator puts it) "tu ne sais pas vivre, que tu ne sauras jamais" (27).[5] His scar is the material testimony that something is dreadfully wrong with the individual who is marked by it, the trace of what Jonathan Cohen has termed the "basic neurotic reaction," that is, "a psychological reaction that is simultaneously a moral reaction: namely a deep conviction of badness and defect" (4). It is moreover the only unchanging, constantly recognizable trait in a face that dramatically eludes its bearer. When the narrator of *Un homme qui dort* ponders his face more deeply, he often sees nothing more than a bovine parody of a human face: "Parfois, tu ressembles à une vache" (169). Yet even in those moments, the scar remains.

That Perec should choose to display his scar so openly—on his face and in his writings—is extremely eloquent; and it may legitimately be interpreted as an effort to make his work of mourning visible. If the scar does indeed incarnate the kind of "truth" that the protagonist of *Un homme qui dort* looks for in his face, that truth is a very difficult one. It is imbricated in a narrative that is both local and general in its dimensions, interweaving personal and historical holocaust. The implications of that narrative are dire ones for the person who feels bound by it, and those bonds are made stronger still by virtue of the fact that the story itself is a formative one. In other words, while Perec may feel that his scar and the story that it tells describe him in important ways, he may also feel, more tellingly still, that it has determined who he is. Thus Perec may be even more deeply committed to that story than it might at first seem; and that notion may help to explain some of his more pronounced and elaborate mourning behavior. As Cohen puts it, in a tone of understatement that rivals Perec's own, "It appears to be far more difficult than we have realized to give up anything we think we know for certain, especially when it has been learned under early, adverse circumstances" (202).

In *La Disparition* it is the individual, precombinatory letter that serves as the principal locus of mourning. The absence, the *disappearance* of the letter E from the alphabet provides the novel with both theme and structure—and that consideration holds true on the level of anecdote as well as on a far more sober and compelling discursive level. Thus, Perec mentions a hospital ward with twenty-six beds, all of them occupied with the exception of one; a collection twenty-six in-folio volumes where the fifth volume is missing; a horse race with twenty-six entrants, one being scratched; and twenty-six boxes, with the fifth being absent. Thus too, the novel's chapters are numbered from one to twenty-six, but there is no fifth chapter; and its parts are numbered from one to six (like the sequence of vowels and the semi-vowel Y), but there is no second part.

The characters in *La Disparition* turn around this conceit without being able to understand it or—still less—to articulate it, and they are consequently benighted by it. They recognize only that something is lacking, and that this very lack is deeply threatening to them: "Mais il a disparu! Qui? Quoi? Va savoir! Ça a disparu. À mon tour, aujourd'hui, j'irai jusqu'à la mort, jusqu'au grand oubli blanc, jusqu'à l'omission" (55). When characters upon rare occasion do manage to grope their way to the fundamental truth that organizes their world, they are rewarded by death. Ottavio Ottaviani, for instance, recognizes the lipogrammatic character of a manuscript, remarking that it has no letter A; but before he can add that it likewise has no E, he falls to the ground and dies (297). Olga Mavrokhordatos expires with a single, potently lacunary word on her lips: "Maldiction" (213). And the novel itself ends in a generalized death that encompasses both the fictional world that it has constructed and the generative constraint that has allowed it to come to be. Let me quote that ending here, in literal (if alas not lipogrammatic) translation:

> la mort,
> la mort aux doigts d'airain,
> la mort aux doigts gourds,
> la mort où va s'abimant l'inscription,
> la mort qui, à jamais, garantit l'immaculation d'un Album qu'un histrion un jour a cru pouvoir noircir,
> la mort nous a dit la fin du roman. (305)

We might well have suspected such an ending, granted the title of the novel, for the French *disparition* means both "disappearance" and (by euphemism, but nonetheless clearly) "death." Moreover, if the absence of a sign is always the sign of an absence, one might expect the letter E to signify beyond what is immediately apparent on the page. For my part, I am persuaded that the E serves Perec as the *literal* enfiguration of his parents; that its absence is the one essential and inescapable reality of *La Disparition*, just as the absence of his parents is the one essential and inescapable reality for Perec; and that the consequences it dictates in the fictional world of the novel are metaphorically descriptive of his parents' fate—and eventually, too, of the fate Perec foresees for himself. It is possible to read such analogical relations strictly within the boundaries of the evidence the novel offers, but one can also call upon other moments in Perec's work to confirm them. The dedication of *W ou le souvenir d'enfance*, for example, reads "pour E," and the fact that the letter E is phonetically identical in French to the tonic pronoun *eux* suggests that Perec means the "them" who stand—in their absence, of course—at the center of that text. And when Perec refers, in an interview dating from 1979, to "la disparition de mes parents pendant la guerre" ("Entretien" 9), it is not by chance that he quotes the title of the book which, up until that time, had afforded him the most literary notoriety.

In that light, the kind of achievement that writing a three-hundred page novel without the letter E represents deserves to be reconsidered. It is not merely an astonishing feat of literary acrobatics (as some readers greeted and dismissed it shortly after its publication), though the virtuosity it puts on display is undeniable. It can be viewed simultaneously as the result of extremely hard and resourceful work, and as the working through of a variety of exceedingly difficult problems, both technical and existential. How might one write at all without the letter E, the most frequently-used letter in the alphabet, the beginning and the end of *écriture*? Granted the constraint he has imposed upon himself, Perec cannot say "mère," "père," "parents," "famille," "eux." In other terms, those are words that are quite literally impossible in the lexicon he has chosen to use. Nor can he write his own name, in which that letter occurs four times, without doing it a violence which leaves it beyond recognition. One might reflect on the implications of that sort of ablation for the self designated by that name, the same self that proposes to bring this impossible piece of work to fruition.

As daunting as those obstacles are, however, they are less fearsome than the climate of incipient doom that pervades *La Disparition*, and which must be read, too, as part of Perec's work of mourning. When Olga cries "Maldiction," her misspoken utterance speaks in fact directly and precisely to an issue that haunts the novel from beginning to end. Variously referred to as a "damnation," a "law," a "talion," there is a death sentence hanging over each of its characters. It becomes clear moreover that, more than anything else, this is a family matter, a question of inheritance, "la damnation qui *ab ovo* nous poursuit," as one character puts it (289). Freud remarks that people who suffer severely from grief must often grapple with a "delusional expectation of punishment" ("Mourning" 244), and upon first consideration one might suggest that Perec is projecting such an expectation into his novel. But I think that things are far more complex than that. Perec is far more canny than that, and his awareness of what he has undertaken in *La Disparition* is far more trenchant than that. For he has taken that topos and turned it to his own advantage here. He has taken a talion and turned it into his own kind of law. He works through his task, following the dictates of that law to the letter—but it is in fact the *letter* that he has chosen. The significance that he invests in that letter is his own; and he can clearly claim it as such. The same is patently true of the novel to which that absent letter gives form—and the same is true also of his grief.

The fourth and final instance of mourning in Perec that I have chosen deals with words and their fate, in a strange fable of language whose hero is Albert Cinoc. One of the most appealing characters in all of Perec's fiction, Cinoc occupies a small but nevertheless vital space in that most spacious of novels, *La Vie mode d'emploi*. When we come upon him there, he is clearly not expecting visitors: "Cinoc est dans sa cuisine. C'est un vieillard maigre et sec vêtu d'un gilet de flanelle d'un vert pisseux" (359). Cinoc's profession is a very unusual one: "Comme il le disait lui-même, il était 'tueur de mots': il travaillait à la mise à jour des dictionnaires Larousse. Mais alors que d'autres rédacteurs étaient à la recherche de mots et de sens nouveaux, lui devait, pour leur faire de la place, éliminer tous les mots et tous les sens tombés en désuétude" (361). His vocation becomes his avocation, but in reverse as it were. Increasingly fascinated by the words that he "kills," Cinoc begins to read old literary works in order to find words that have fallen out of lexical currency, in order one day to write a dictionary of forgotten words. "En dix ans il en rassembla plus de huit mille, au travers desquels vint s'inscrire une histoire aujourd'hui à peine transmissible" (363).

As Marcel Bénabou has pointed out, Cinoc resembles Perec in several ways. Like Perec, Cinoc is of Polish Jewish origin; other people are uncertain how to pronounce his name, a name whose orthography changed many times during his family's long journey from Cracow to

Paris; lastly, Cinoc is deeply devoted to words (Bénabou 26). Both the name and the word serve Perec as sites of mourning, in ways that are analogous and mutually illuminative. Cinoc's neighbors wonder (singly and in an impromptu neighborhood conciliabule) how to pronounce his name; and Perec offers a catalogue of their efforts, twenty variations ranging from "sinos" to "shinoch" to "chinots." Though Perec's own name was perhaps not as badly misused as Cinoc's, a fundamental similarity remains: both are "foreign" names, not easily reconciled with standard French onomastic practice. As such, they both mark their bearers in important ways. The history of the spelling of Cinoc's name is likewise vexed. From the original "Kleinhof" it went through a variety of permutations as four generations of Cinoc's family migrated through Europe; Cinoc himself is unable to reconstruct that history in any satisfactory way. In *W ou le souvenir d'enfance*, Perec remarks that his own family name underwent a similar transformation, for strictly similar reasons (as did his mother's maiden name, too), and that other people always misspell it as either "Perrec" or "Pérec" (51-52).[6]

We commonly take the name as something profoundly embedded in personal identity; and the history of a name can tell us much about the history of a family. In Cinoc's case, and in Perec's, the name describes an itinerary through place and time and a process of considerable transformation. Through his description of what Bénabou calls Cinoc's "aventures onomastiques" (30), Perec is constructing a parable of his own experience, and that of the family to which he once belonged. Though his tone is reasonably lighthearted on the surface, the tale it tells by implication and analogy is a far more somber one.[7] For the name is not given, once and for all; contrary to what we often assume, it is subject to change due to circumstances that may seem largely arbitrary, circumstances well beyond the control of the individual who bears it. Names, even those with which we are supposedly intimate, may elude us in pernicious ways. Perec remarks in *W ou le souvenir d'enfance*, for example, that he made no less than three errors in transcribing his mother's maiden name before finally getting it right (55). The dismal truth that strikes him there, a truth he returns to in a very different manner through the mediation of Cinoc, is that one can become estranged from one's name—and estranged too from one's family, from one's history, from one's "own story."

In a similar manner, as words fall into desuetude, they take with them small portions of the memory of language. Considered in that perspective, the work to which Cinoc devotes himself, in both its vocational and its avocational dimensions, is strongly suggestive of the kind of work that Perec himself carries out. In both cases, one gesture gives rise to—and enables—another. Cinoc eliminates words from the lexicon, yet that very act, performed over many years, causes him to engage upon his project of lexical archaeology. The former involves systematic and deliberate forgetting, the latter an equally systematic and deliberate remembering. Moreover, as Perec stages his account of Cinoc's work in the pages of *La Vie mode d'emploi*, he recapitulates Cinoc's gestures in significant ways. Perec offers examples of the words Cinoc "kills," in effect recalling them and inscribing that process of recollection in his novel, a process he offers to share with his reader. Similarly, when he turns toward the dictionary of forgotten words that Cinoc is preparing, he provides three pages of such words, accompanied by their definitions, hauling them up out of linguistic amnesia and inviting us to savor them in remotivated form, as fully reinfranchised linguistic signs.

What intrigues Cinoc most about those words is the lost narrative whose trace they contain, or, as Perec puts it in the passage I quoted earlier, "une histoire aujourd'hui à peine transmissible." Perec is likewise devoted to a lost narrative, to a story that is almost impossible to tell. He mourns for that story just as he mourns for the people that inhabited it: his mother, his father, and indeed the self that he imagines to have been his own. Perec works through that mourning in the telling of other stories, stories that may bear the trace of the one which has been lost. He deploys many different strategies of mourning, testing each in turn, hoping to find one that will work, yet recognizing throughout that none of them will work—if by "work" one means something that will ease the pain of separation for good. It is in a sense the writing of mourning, the *work* of the work, which allows meaning to come forth, even—especially, perhaps—when that meaning bears only a fragile resemblance to the incomparable and perfectly abundant meaning that has been lost.

Philippe Lejeune suggests that Perec's writing has a "convivial" character to it, arguing that, "Il y a dans tous ses textes une place pour moi, pour que je fasse quelque chose" (41). His insight is an important one, I believe, since it neatly articulates a feeling that is widespread among Perec's readers. I for one have benefited from Perec's writerly hospitality, in focusing much of my own work upon his over the years. Granted that, I am tempted to invoke one more site of mourning, among the very many that I have not mentioned. Perhaps a part of our experience in reading Perec, now, is bound up in a kind of mourning for him. Not a mourning for the man, I hasten to add, but rather a mourning for the writer, for both the written and the unwritten. Reading Perec elicits that mourning and allows us to come to terms with it. It may quite possibly allow us to come to terms with other kinds of mourning, too. Those terms must remain provisional, however, and they must be renegotiated continually. For in the final analysis, it's really not a question of completion, either in Perec's case or in ours. Freud must have known that, despite what he suggests about mourning's end, because he concludes his essay on this note: "As we already know, the interdependence of the complicated problems of the mind forces us to break off every enquiry before it is completed—till the outcome of some other enquiry can come to its assistance" (258). For my part, I shall suspend my discussion of this last site of mourning right here, proposing it as a prolegomenon to a broader conversation, whose assistance will be most welcome.

Marcel Bénabou's Rhetoric

IT'S DAMN near impossible to write about Marcel Bénabou's books. They present a limpid, armored surface where the kind of handholds one normally looks for in a text are rare and extraordinarily precarious. Every utterance in them is so deeply bound up in irony and doubt that the prospect of saying anything frank and valid about them appears dim at best. Every gesture the critic might be tempted to make seems to have been anticipated by author, and parried in advance as it were, just as if Bénabou had deliberately followed the script for the puzzle-maker that Georges Perec laid out in *La Vie mode d'emploi*.[1] In short, if reading Marcel Bénabou's books is consistently—indeed extravagantly—pleasurable, writing about them is hell on wheels. That bit of whining aside (there will be no more, or not very much more), let me begin. But I would like to say in passing that it is the inalienable right of every academic to whine. Moreover, it is a right we must also accord to Bénabou himself as we try to come to some sort of terms with his books (for he, too, is an academic, and a distinguished one at that). Allow me then to start with something relatively easy in order to work my way, crab-like, toward the impossible.

Marcel Bénabou was born in the Sephardic community of Meknès, Morocco in 1939. At the age of seventeen, he went to Paris to study at the Lycée Louis-le-Grand, matriculating thereafter at the École Normale Supérieure. He earned his doctorate at the Sorbonne, and made his living as a Roman historian at the Université de Paris VII. He joined the Ouvroir de Littérature Potentielle (or "Oulipo") in 1969, and served nobly as that group's Definitively Provisional Secretary. His first book, published in 1976, is a work of historiography entitled *La Résistance africaine à la romanisation*, and I'll say no more about it, because it's his three other books, *Pourquoi je n'ai écrit aucun de mes livres* (1986),

Jette ce livre avant qu'il soit trop tard (1992), and *Jacob, Ménahem et Mimoun: Une épopée familiale* (1995) that interest me here.[2] Each of those books may be read as a sustained meditation on the impossibility of writing; and granted his insistence on that theme, it's a wonder that there are any books signed "Bénabou" to write *about*.

Pourquoi is a deeply duplicitous, deliciously perverse text in which Bénabou attempts to explain why, though he was "born" to literature, he hasn't written any books. It's a book that is always beginning, built on hesitation, erasure, and a hallucinating series of false starts; reading it, one feels as if one were walking in wet cement. More than anything else, it presents itself as a prolegomenon to another book, an ideal, virtual, and clearly impossible one that Bénabou would certainly write, if only he were able. As maddening as they may be, Bénabou's tortured maunderings in *Pourquoi* are also consistently amusing, and indeed the book won the 23rd Xavier Forneret Black Humor Prize. *Jette* is a book about the discontents of writing and reading, and it begins with the following exhortation: "Allons, pose ce livre. Ou plutôt jette-le loin de toi. Tout de suite. Avant qu'il soit trop tard. Pas d'autre issue pour toi, crois-moi, que cette résolution." (9). Layering ironies upon ironies, *Jette* has much to say about the way writers and readers cleave to literature, even when—perhaps especially when—literature is at its most embattled as a cultural commodity. The title that Bénabou chose for his fourth book was *On écrit toujours le même livre*, but his publishers demanded that he change it to *Jacob, Ménahem et Mimoun: Une épopée familiale*. That's a pity in my view, because the original title is a very apposite one, functioning both candidly and with the same kind of canny duplicity one finds in Bénabou's other titles. On the one hand, Jacob is yet another preface to another, impossible book, one which sketches out nonetheless a possibility that animates all of Bénabou's writing since *Pourquoi*: "de parvenir un jour à cette performance: faire du livre inachevé et inachevable non un accident fâcheux dû à mon incompétence, mais un véritable genre littéraire, avec ses normes et ses préceptes propres" (*Jacob* 244). On the other hand, the close and affective focus on Bénabou's family and the community in which they lived is quite different from what one finds in his previous work.

Yet that apparent shift of focus is an inevitable one for Bénabou, since the dilemma of the impossible book is for him, at the outset, deeply intricated in the question of origin. "J'ai longtemps cru que l'on naissait écrivain, qu'il suffisait ensuite de laisser mûrir en soi, un nombre convenable d'années, ce précieux germe, pour qu'apparaisse un jour le premier livre, comme était apparue auparavent, à son heure, la première dent," he states in *Pourquoi* (61). For he has always assumed that writing is his vocation; and if he was born into a community of "chosen" people, he himself was "chosen" for literature (*Pourquoi* 91). His family, after all, had their place in literature: Pierre Loti had described a visit to Bénabou's great-grandfather's home in his travel book, *Au Maroc* (1889). He feels, too, that there must be a place reserved for him in the literary pantheon, by virtue of his vocation; yet he finds himself desperately—and unequally—struggling to find ingress into a domain which he had always assumed was his own, by birthright. The struggle with the vexations of origin assumes another shape in *Jacob*. Having been a precocious child, one who learned languages easily and who wrote those languages with an astonishing fluency, his dream now is "redevenir, comme je l'avais été jadis, non celui qui parle des autres, mais celui dont les autres parlent" (*Jacob* 17). Moreover, Bénabou locates that book's genesis in a sentence he had written more than thirty years prior to the narrative "now" of *Jacob*, in the library of the École Normale Supérieure, a sentence that he found limpid and full of portent. Alas, everything he wrote thereafter seemed bland and hopelessly inadequate in comparison, yet another example of the tyranny of origin.

That tyranny paralyzes Bénabou and renders his desire to achieve literary distinction still more afflicting. And in ineluctable metamorphosis, what begins as desire slowly changes into obsession: "Certes, l'écriture avait été jusque-là pour moi plus qu'un désir, plus qu'un projet, plus qu'un plaisir: une véritable idée fixe" (*Pourquoi* 68). His double conviction, that he in fact *is* a writer, and that nevertheless it is impossible for him to write the kind of books he was born to write, resounds throughout his work in cries of anguish.[3] Both sides of that conviction are articulated in a textuality that resembles profession at certain moments, and confession at others. In the section of *Pourquoi* entitled "Adieu au lecteur," Bénabou describes his will to write as a kind of spiritual illness, one for which he is unlikely to find a cure, asking his reader to think about this book, and to reflect on a question that is clearly rhetorical in nature: "N'est-il pas le récit d'une rencontre sans cesse différée, d'un amour contrarié, semé d'obstacles et de traverses, victime d'illusions et de regrets? D'un amour malheureux, et finalement peut-être impossible, celui de son auteur avec une certaine idée de la littérature" (129). There is wryness and self-parody at work in that question, and those will not be lost on the reader. Yet there is also a nostalgia for a moment when art could provide a cure, for a moment when, "par le biais de l'écriture, l'émergence du passé cesserait d'être le mal pour devenir le remède" (*Jacob* 27).[4]

The past, however, and more perniciously still, his *memory* of the past, are two of the things Bénabou identifies that render writing impossible for him. In the first instance, he feels that his debts to the past are legion, and their liquidation is an axiomatic condition of any serious literary venture he might undertake, "Car j'ai eu très tôt le sentiment d'être chargé d'une grande quantité de dettes, involontairement contractées dès ma naissance, et jamais réglées" (*Jacob* 28). He describes his first debt as the fact that, through a miracle, a piece of luck, or an accident of history, he had escaped the Holocaust. When, after the war, he becomes aware of the annihilation of European Jewry, he feels as if he had overheard a dreadful secret, and he is unable to talk about it, even with his brothers, to whom he normally confided everything. He worries, too, about how he can prove himself "worthy" of having been spared—and sets himself thus a task that is clearly an impossible one. "Telle fut la première de mes 'dettes.' Elle me pesait d'autant plus que je l'avais toujours gardée secrète, ne trouvant personne à qui en parler, ni personne pour me dire auprès de qui je l'avais contractée" (*Jacob* 32-33). His second debt is to his parents. As the last male child in a family of eight children, his parents had wanted him to become a rabbi, but despite regular attendance at rabbinical school during his childhood summers, Bénabou never took to it, and he alludes to the days he spent there as "parmi les moins agréables de mon enfance" (*Jacob* 36). He feels indebted also to the community in which he grew up in Meknès, suggesting that it was a doubly marginalized one, first with regard to mainstream Sephardic culture, second with regard to the Ashkenazic tradition in Europe; and he experiences the need to render some account of that group. That need becomes more urgent as he realizes that his community is threatened by a new diaspora, through the emigration of its members to other countries, chiefly Israel, France, and Canada. "Tout semblait donc avoir conspiré pour me faire aboutir à . . . un livre," he says (*Jacob* 49; ellipsis in original).

By the time Bénabou finally sets out to write the kind of book he knows he has always owed to literature, however, various sorts of distances vex his project. He is well into his maturity,[5] and sees his childhood only at a considerable remove; he too has emigrated from Morocco, and now lives in Paris; his cultural horizon is no longer the one that he inherited from his parents and his community. And the thorniest problem of all is that the vehicle he has chosen for his project, literature, is something that he conceives *now* in a very different fashion, because as a child, "literature" for Bénabou meant "sacred literature." While vestiges of that remain in his mature literary vision, for example his suggestion that reading and praying are linked for him (*Jacob* 55), the discovery of "profane literature" was nevertheless a determinative event in his childhood. Secular writing intrigued him deeply, and profane books allowed him to imagine a world outside of his family circle. Beginning with Greek and Roman literature, he would soon discover French literature and, most tellingly, the French novel. Balzac, Hugo, Dumas, Verne, Zola, and even Amédée Achard, Jean Jalabert, and Pierre Benoît sketched panoramas that Bénabou found infinitely seductive, and worthy, too, of imitation. Initially, though, far from affording him a way to repay his debts, his interest in secular writing served merely to compound them, because he saw it as a sort of betrayal, an impression that will continue to complicate his conception of the literary act.[6]

On the surface of things, his relation with literature and with its medium, language, is that of the prince to the kingdom. Under the tutelage of family members, he had learned a variety of languages (French, Hebrew, Arabic, Latin) as a child, and he was known in his circle as someone who read bulimically, someone who would undoubtedly become a writer one day. He discovers secular literature, however, very largely on his own, and in a fashion that approaches the clandestine. He looks upon it, moreover, like stout Cortez's men, with wild surmise, amazed by its novelty and its vastness. What impresses him most, perhaps, is its otherness, for clearly this is a domain that is radically different from that of the literature he had come to know until that point. Those two considerations account very largely for the equivocal way Bénabou regards literature: one the one hand, his gaze is that of an insider; on the other hand, he sees himself (both by force of circumstance and by avocation) as an outsider.

That equivocal stance is closely analogous to the way Jacques Derrida describes his own relationship with the French language and its literature. The argument Derrida adumbrates in *Le Monolinguisme de l'autre* is an intricate one, and I cannot do it real justice here. Suffice it to say that Derrida, having been born a French-Algerian Jew, and having among other things been stripped of his citizenship by the Vichy government,[7] feels that his relationship with his "mother tongue" is neither simple nor immediate, an issue that he formulates with characteristic pungency: "Oui, je n'ai qu'une langue, or ce n'est pas la mienne" (15). Moreover, Derrida describes his first encounters with French literature as problematic, in a manner that is similar to Bénabou's own: "La découverte de la littérature française, l'accès à ce mode d'écriture si singulier qu'on appelle la 'littérature-française,' ce fut l'expérience d'un monde sans continuité sensible avec celui dans lequel nous vivions, presque sans rien de commun avec nos paysages naturels ou sociaux" (76).

It is, then, a question of distance and disparity that Bénabou faces as he confronts his project, where all along he had assumed that he would find closeness and familiarity. His past looms far behind him; his cultural, social, and intellectual contexts have shifted dramatically in the interim; and his memory of things, when closely examined, proves unreliable. It's not that he lacks for childhood memories; but rather that he finds them too abundant: "Je découvris ce qui me nuisait, c'était la profusion, le foissonnement, l'hypertrophie, de la mémoire. Ou plutôt la tyrannie que cette mémoire, encombrée d'un passé marocain qui se refusait à passer, exerçait sur mon rapport à la réalité" (*Jacob* 21). Having kept reams of notes about his past for many, many years, Bénabou finds when he comes to look them over that they no longer correspond to what he remembers. In other words, he comes abruptly up against a difficult truth that many autobiographers before him have grappled with, in a variety of different ways: memory and the *writing* of memory are not quite the same thing. Memory itself may be more or less reliable, more or less faithful to lived experience; but the representation of memory (in whatever medium) entails a set of operations that necessarily distort and deform their object.

How can he hope to overcome—or at least attenuate—that difficulty in the impossible project to which he has mortgaged his body and soul? The short answer to that question is that Bénabou has chosen to write impossible books.[8] He appeals to two traditions, both sacred and profane, as he elaborates the notion of the impossible book and configures it to suit his purposes. On the one hand, Bénabou invokes the Judaic notion of the book as transcendent signifier of existence, a textuality that encapsulates and preserves the life of the community and that of every individual in it. On the other hand, he alludes to the more contemporary, secular debate on the book as an experimental ideal, a debate that one can trace back to Mallarmé. Bénabou suggests obliquely that those two traditions are conflated in his project, slyly referring to "La stricte orthodoxie mallarméenne de mon cheminement" (*Jacob* 49). The idea that intrigues him most profoundly is that of resistance. A book worthy of its salt will resist being written; and it will only be successful in the degree to which that resistance manifests itself upon the page in a writing that strains toward the book. That resistance in the act of production must make itself felt in the act of reception, too. And indeed each of Bénabou's books resists classification according to the conventional taxonomies we apply to literature. Claude Burgelin, for instance, offered the following description of *Pourquoi*: "Un livre qui est à la fois épopée, roman d'amour, autobiographie, méditation philosophique, poème, essai critique; un livre qui est monologue, dialogue, polylogue; un livre enfin qui parodie et subvertit tous les modes d'expression susnommés par le pastiche, la dérision, le calembour et autres jeux paronomastiques" (2).

In short, since Bénabou's writings reject our attempts at classification, we are left with the "default" term, *book*. It is a term that appears in every one of his titles (if we recall that the original title of *Jacob* was *On écrit toujours le même livre*), and each text interrogates that term in a sustained, rigorous, and at times comical fashion. "Certes, je n'ignorais pas le goût de la plupart des auteurs pour les titres obscurs, ambigus, énigmatiques même, qu'ils croient les plus aptes à réveiller la curiosité (toujours un peu somnolente, il faut bien le dire) du lecteur," says Bénabou in *Jette* (38). In a chapter of *Pourquoi* entitled "Titre" he alludes to his own title as "une provocation" (*Pourquoi* 17), and alludes explicitly to Raymond Roussel, author of

Comment j'ai écrit certains dee mes livres, which is arguably the most duplicitous titles in the modern canon—until one encounters *Pourquoi* itself, that is. Twice in *Pourquoi*, echoing both Diderot and Magritte, Bénabou assures his reader that "*ceci n'est pas un livre*" (20, 121; emphasis in original). Yet we readers are perhaps not wholly convinced. Nor are we meant to be. These texts are highly structured after all, and testify to a deliberation that seems Flaubertian in its focus. One might cite in support of that hypothesis the symphonic structure of *Jette*, with its four "movements"; or the use of the organizational principle of the triad in *Pourquoi*, where each of the three parts includes three chapters with three subchapters each;[9] or the three main discursive modes of *Jacob*, which deal with history, literary form, and personal memory, respectively.

Bénabou quotes Georg Christoph Lichtenberg's reflections on the notion of the book at the threshold of *Jette*, in order to persuade his reader—just in case the title had left any doubt in his or her mind—that books and their discontents will be foregrounded in the volume the reader is about to enter: "C'est à peine s'il existe une marchandise au monde plus étrange que les livres: imprimés par des gens qui ne les comprennent pas; vendus par des gens qui ne les comprennent pas; reliés, censurés et lus par des gens qui ne les comprennent pas; bien mieux, écrits par des gens qui ne les comprennent pas" (7). As Bénabou's narrator in *Jette* casts about in every direction among theories of the book in order to find something that might correspond to his own exalted conception of that ideal, he gradually becomes aware that the ideal book he longs for so desperately is one that, by its very nature, can never be made manifest in mortal form: "Je devrais bien le savoir, pourtant, que la chose (comment l'appeler autrement?) que je cherche n'est ni dans les livres que j'ai lus ni dans ceux que je projette de lire. Elle n'a quelque chance de se trouver que dans ceux dont je n'ai même pas idée, et qui sans doute, quelque effort que je fasse, ne trouveront jamais l'occasion de paraître sous mes yeux" (167).

That lesson is an important one for the narrator of *Jette*, for Bénabou (whose amanuensis the narrator is), and for the reader, as well. As Bénabou conceives of it, the book must remain a virtuality, the object of a discourse whose only valid modes are conditional, hypothetical, and interrogative. Writing each of his books, he speaks primarily about how the book *might* have been written, granted a set of optimal—and impossible—conditions. In the first instance, those conditions devolve upon the writer himself, and the minute gestures that he performs upon the page. If only he were the writer he had always imagined himself to be, before he actually sat down to write; if only his technique were equal to his ambition; if only the image of himself he sees on the page corresponded to the writer's face he imagines he might possess; *then* he might write the book that he envisions. Yet the image of himself that his prose reflects is not a flattering one. The insistent emblazonments of the writing act in Bénabou's books, and the many puns on his own name inscribed therein[10] serve mainly to paint a portrait of the artist as a middleaged neurotic, a benighted scribbler who, watching himself writing, can write about nothing other than that watching. It's not that such apparent narcissism fails to trouble Bénabou; toward the end of *Jacob* he bemoans the fact that, having set out to write a book about his family and their community, he has written a book about himself (227), indulging in an orgy of ego. Yet in a sense, Bénabou's sin is merely a pale imitation of the one the book itself commits, over and over; for the book watches itself, too, and with a keenly critical eye, constantly comparing itself to other books and coming up short. Despite Bénabou's disingenuous assertion in *Pourquoi* that he dreams of "un livre en somme qui ne se donnerait aucune des facilités de la mise en abîme ou des jeux spéculaires" (32), the books he has written play lustily on the notion of textual specularity,[11] as if that topos, which functioned earlier in this century as the very signature of "serious" writing, had in its dotage become ripe for parody.

In those moments when the reflection of the distant ideal of the book becomes more and more imperious in the text, the reader may come to realize what the book may represent for Marcel Bénabou: more than anything else, it's a mirror that is carried along a bookshelf. His own bookshelf, as evidenced by the intertextual references in *Pourquoi*, *Jette*, and *Jacob*, is sumptuously furnished and dangerously overladen; one can almost hear it groan. Allow me to list those references here[12] in order to offer some idea of the dimensions of the allusive network in Bénabou's books (and also, I admit, for the sheer joy of the catalogue). In the 600-odd pages of his three books, he manages to invoke, directly or more obliquely, the following figures: Ecclesiastes, Homer, Aesop, Pythagoras, Sophocles, Euripides,

Socrates, Plato, Aristotle, Demosthenes, Epicurus, Cicero, Virgil, Livy, Seneca, Martial, Tacitus, Tertullian, Apuleius, Plotinus, St. Augustine, Moses Maimonides, Dante, Abraham Abulafia, Annius of Viterbo, Rabelais, Bonaventure des Périers, Scève, Ronsard, Montaigne, Francis Bacon, Shakespeare, François Maynard, Hobbes, Descartes, Corneille, La Rochefoucauld, La Fontaine, Pascal, Spinoza, Boileau, Racine, La Bruyère, Montesquieu, Voltaire, Rousseau, Diderot, Lessing, Chamfort, Georg Christoph Lichtenberg, Sade, Louis-Sébastien Mercier, Goethe, Joseph Joubert, Jean Paul, Chateaubriand, Hölderlin, Walter Scott, Novalis, Schelling, Schopenhauer, Stendhal, Alfred de Vigny, Heinrich Heine, Delacroix (the painter's *Journal*), Balzac, Hugo, Dumas *père*, Gogol, Poe, Michel de Guérin, Musset, Thackeray, Herman Melville, Henri Amiel, Baudelaire, Flaubert, the Goncourt brothers, Jules Verne, Edmond About, Emile Zola, Thomas Hardy, Odilon Redon (his *Journal*), Mallarmé, Henry James, Nietzsche, Verlaine, Lautréamont, Huysmans, Pierre Loti, Isaac Leib Peretz, Rimbaud, Joseph Conrad, Sholem Aleichem, Jules Laforgue, Jules Renard, Miguel de Unamuno, Israel Zangwill, Rudyard Kipling, H. G. Wells, Julien Benda, Gide, Proust, Valéry, Alfred Jarry, Thomas Mann, Rilke, Raymond Roussel, Apollinaire, Amédée Achard, Jean Jalabert, Max du Veuzit, the Tharaud brothers, Edmond Fleg, James Joyce, Franz Kafka, Jean Paulhan, György Lukács, Maurice Sachs, Pierre Benoit, Pierre Jean Jouve, Pierre Reverdy, Franz Werfel, Jean Cocteau, Walter Benjamin, Antonin Artaud, Georges Bataille, Jorge Luis Borges, Henri Michaux, Michel Leiris, Raymond Radiguet, Raymond Queneau, Jean-Paul Sartre, Paul Nizan, Maurice Blanchot, René Char, Simone de Beauvoir, Jean Genet, Malcolm Lowry, Cioran, Lawrence Durrell, Edmond Jabès, Maxence Van der Mersche, Albert Camus, Roland Barthes, Louis Althusser, Josefina Vicens, Italo Calvino, Pierre Bourdieu, Jacques Derrida, and Georges Perec.

    The intertextual play in Bénabou's books ranges far beyond mere reference, and beggars the notion of literary allusion as we commonly understand it. The insistent references to other writers serve undoubtedly to put Bénabou's erudition as a reader of literature on display; they locate his own books in a context of literary tradition; and they suggest the kinds of directions that he intends to pursue. But their principal function rejoins a far more trenchant and ironically focused metaliterary discourse: these are the writers who render Bénabou's *own* writing impossible. In *Jacob*, Bénabou speaks of the "gymnastique intellectuelle" he engaged in when he encountered new sorts of literary language, saying that the imitation of other styles of writing became a sort of game for him; yet it was "à la longue nocive: elle m'a très tôt habitué à modeler ma parole sur celle d'autrui" (117).[13] Imitation may be the sincerest form of compliment, yet serious literature cares not a whit for compliment. For the paradoxical constraint that serious literature imposes on a writer is to carve something utterly new and original out of a venerable linguistic and cultural patrimony.

The horns of this dilemma, tradition and innovation, respectively, pierce Bénabou to the bone as he begins to reflect upon the way he might inaugurate his career as a writer, looking for inspiration in the books he reads: "J'étais donc de longue date préparé—j'allais dire programmé—pour y chercher aussi un modèle pour le livre à écrire. Je passais plusieurs semaines—les premières que je consacrai pour de bon à mon projet d'épopée familiale—à réfléchir à la chose, essayant de transposer, au besoin en l'adaptant, la construction de tel ou tel de mes livres favoris" (*Jacob* 124). Well, he found models—all to many of them. Rather than enabling the project he wishes to undertake, those models paralyze him. What kind of boldness is demanded of a would-be autobiographer when he sees Montaigne's *Essais*, Stendhal's *Vie de Henry Brulard*, and Sartre's *Les Mots* looming on his bookshelf? Imagine the hubris of a writer who would try his hand at the epic, when he is thoroughly steeped—indeed drowned—in Homer, Virgil, and Dante. What can one hope to accomplish in the realm of the bildungsroman after *Wilhelm Meister's Apprenticeship* and *L'Éducation sentimentale*, or in the künstlerroman after *A Portrait of the Artist as a Young Man* and *Doctor Faustus*? How can this "Marcel" pretend to say anything about things past when Proust's "Marcel" has already said it all? Unable to achieve the mimetic virtuosity of Pierre Menard, Bénabou finds himself as lost in the literary world as Emma Bovary.

Among all of the distinguished precursor figures Bénabou invokes, there is one whom he returns to again and again, one who had recently walked the road Bénabou wished to travel, and who left his imprint upon it. Georges Perec, Bénabou's longtime friend and fellow-Oulipian, provides a model that Bénabou finds perhaps the most impossible of all. Yet it nonetheless a model that Bénabou constantly holds before himself as he writes. The chapter of *Pourquoi* entitled "Première page" begins with a lengthy pastiche of Perec's first novel, *Les Choses*; and toward the end of that book Bénabou alludes to "un com*père* ex*quis*—un com*père* ex*pert* et qui n'allait pas tarder à devenir un maître" (123; my emphasis), encoding Perec's name homophonically in his own text, and acknowledging his role as a literary mentor. In the chapter of *Jacob* entitled "Modèles," Bénabou regrets that he was unable to complete certain texts that he had conceived in collaboration with "un compagnon trop tôt disparu," mentioning the titles of projects that he and Perec had worked on together (111). Thinking about the difficulties that his family epic presents, he muses, "Et j'en venais presque à envier cet ami qui, à mon déferlement de mémoire, avait un jour pu opposer, sur le ton du défi, un cinglant: 'Je n'ai pas de souvenirs d'enfance!'" (*Jacob* 225), quoting Perec's own bold assertion in the opening pages of his *W ou le souvenir d'enfance*. When Bénabou frets about projecting too much of himself into the description of his ancestors, and the risk that "en fin de compte ce seraient eux qui paraîtraient faits de moi, beaucoup plus que moi d'eux" (*Jacob* 238), he is alluding to Vigny's celebrated phrase: "Si j'écris leur histoire, ils descendront de moi"; but it is also that phrase which Perec had chosen as the epigraph for a book about his family that he intended to write one day.[14] Briefly stated, the model that Perec presents for Bénabou is a heroic one, a model that consequently does not brook facile imitation; and though Perec is not the only heroic writer in Bénabou's overcrowded hall of fame, he is undoubtedly the preeminent one.

Not all of Bénabou's heroes are writers of literature; several of them are characters in literature. In a chapter of *Pourquoi* entitled "Heroes," he mentions some of the characters from fiction and mythology whom he holds most dear, figures like Ulysses, Jonas, Gulliver, Hercules, Samson, Job, Don Quixote, Sisyphus, Penelope, Tantalus, and the Danaïds. It's a curious group that he cites, and upon reflection it may occur to the reader that these characters are heroic precisely by virtue of the fact that they struggle against overwhelming odds, and often in vain; they are beset, they wait, they yearn, and they bear their torment nobly. Such a vision of the heroic appeals immensely to Bénabou, and suggests to him that he himself might aspire to a small degree of heroism, for isn't the task he has set himself both Sisyphean and Quixotic in nature, doesn't he endure its torments with the patience of Job, doesn't he write, erase, and rewrite the text he's working on, like Penelope at her loom? Or perhaps an antiheroic status would be enough to ask for, since real heroes are so few and far between in our corrupted age. He sees himself upon occasion as an irresolute hero, a "Hamlet de bibliothèque à la démarche flottante" (*Pourquoi* 33). At other times, he wonders if a writer who knows the end of his life will coincide with the end of one of his books, and who has thus decided never to finish any of them, might inspire our admiration (*Pourquoi* 28). But there's the rub: Marcel Bénabou is not content to be merely a hero; he must be a hero of a book. And not just any book, but his own book, the very one he finds impossible to write. In other words, he longs to be both the hero who writes and the hero who is written *about*. Everyone can distinguish a writer from his hero, he remarks offhandedly and with shameless duplicity in *Pourquoi* (20). As Bénabou harangues his reader with this theme over and over again, he or she may be prompted to wonder if reading Bénabou's books is not, in itself, a modestly heroic activity....

But no: that way lies madness. It is writing—and only writing—that is heroic, according to Bénabou. The toughest thing about it is choosing one's moment, a process that demands an almost superhuman circumspection. One would certainly not wish to write before becoming fully mature: who wishes to read the egregious scribblings of yet another beardless, jejune tyro? But literary maturity is hard to come by if one does not write; in that perspective, it's always too early for Bénabou. And it's always too late as well, for other people—Balzac! Melville! Flaubert! Proust! Kafka! Queneau! Perec!—have already written, and have produced works that render the very idea of further writing laughably otiose. For Bénabou, in other words, writing is always suspended between precipitance and belatedness.[15] Perhaps it would be enough to live the literary life in faithful devotion, without actually writing. Faced with the classic alternative of writing or living, however, Bénabou finds himself incapable of either, and resigns himself to a kind of tormented literary quietism.

Paper itself seems to mock any ink Bénabou might be inclined to inscribe upon it. In *Pourquoi*, he speaks about his curious relations with paper, telling the reader how he was always buying it in his earlier years, hoarding it, saving it for the day when he would finally write. He worships the whiteness, the freshness, the untainted potential and promise of paper, and looks upon it with a fetishistic, jealous gaze. "Le papier blanc, lui, m'impressionne, et je fais tout pour lui conserver sa pureté," he says in *Pourquoi* (96); he protects it, however, all too well. During his vacations from school, far from the madding crowd, he would lay the paper he had lovingly collected out before him, along with all the other tools of the writer's trade, persuading himself that finally the moment had come—yet no inspiration was ever visited upon him, and in none of those estival Edens did he actually succeed in writing. For writing is something that can be approached only through epiphany; yet he or she who waits for epiphany may wait a long, long time.[16]

In a section of *Pourquoi* entitled "Au lecteur," Bénabou anticipates his reader's objections to the kinds of claims he intends to stake for himself:

> Sans doute pensez-vous que, si considérable que puisse être le nombre des livres (toutes catégories confondues, du libelle de quelques feuillets aux plus vastes encyclopédies) qui ont été produits depuis plus de sept mille ans (une évaluation au moins approximative doit certainement figurer dans quelque ouvrage spécialisé), il est pour le moins déraisonnable de prétendre fonder sa singularité sur le simple fait que l'on n'a pris aucune part personnelle à cette toujours renaissante production; en un mot, n'avoir écrit aucun livre ne devrait pas à vos yeux suffire à définir un homme, ni même à l'accabler. Nul, je crois, n'en disconviendra. (12)

His rhetoric here is a particularly contrary one, arguing as it does the very premise that he wishes to invalidate. It is moreover emblematic of a broader gesture toward literature and its traditions that is calculated to imbricate Bénabou's own book—this "non-livre" as he calls it (*Pourquoi* 121)—solidly therein. For Bénabou is writing literature from beneath as it were, elaborating a subversive prose, trying to tunnel up into literature before literature and the watchers at its gates become aware of the threat. Or rather, in a ploy worthy of the wily Ulysses, he places before those gates a gift that, with any sort of luck at all, will enable him to take possession of the city.

Bénabou's repeated apostrophes to the reader serve two main purposes. On the one hand, they function to orient our reading of his books—or more precisely to *constrain* our reading, because, appearances notwithstanding, these are the most tyrannical of texts. On the other hand, they adumbrate a theory of reading as an activity that necessarily conditions writing in all of its manifestations. In *Pourquoi*, he speaks of the irrepressible desire to read that has animated him since he was a child, suggesting however that his impulse was rooted in a luminous contingency: if he did read so vastly, it was always in order one day to write (51). Yet far from enabling writing, reading is what makes writing impossible for him. Speculations on the reciprocal vexations of reading and writing echo throughout his books. At times he postulates reading as being prior to writing, arguing that he is first and foremost a reader; at other times he insinuates that, born to write, he has always read through a writer's eye. His remarks are intended not only to tell us about himself, but also to tell us about ourselves, to make us reflect recursively on our own reading practices, on the way we approach literature, on the various strategies we deploy in our efforts to find meaning in texts.

That sort of topos finds its most sustained manifestation in *Jette*. The narrator is a reader, one who is laboring—mainly in vain—to come to terms with a text of uncertain origin and authorship whose opening lines exhort him simply to throw the book away before it's too late. More than anything else, *Jette* is a discourse on reading and the impossible demands it places on us, and I would like to examine that discourse in some detail. Like Bénabou's own books, the volume the narrator of *Jette* is holding in his hands is full of advice to the reader; yet most of the time that advice is not particularly reassuring: "Ce livre où tu viens ainsi d'entrer sans précaution ni prudence, tu ne sais pas encore que tu cours, comme moi, le risque de t'y perdre" (11). The narrator struggles long and nobly to make sense of the text, yet all his efforts serve only to render that text still more obscure. Two activities are at issue in *Jette*: reading, very simply conceived (that is, the identification of words on the page), and interpretation. In the first instance, it is reading that proves impossible for the narrator: "Mais ici, il s'agissait de tout autre chose: j'étais incapable de déchiffrer un titre, qui s'étalait pourtant sous mes yeux. Mieux, incapable d'identifier l'origine des caractères qui avaient servi à le composer!

Exactement comme si j'étais devenu analphabète!" (38-39). It's the fault of the letters, after all—it's the alphabet itself that is illegible. That is a vision of radical catastrophe that will pursue the narrator of *Jette* even into his dreams; and later in the book he recounts an especially harrowing one:

> Les lettres, légères, se confondaient, puis s'étalaient en larges coulées sombres qui dégringolaient en silence. Les mots, quand j'arrivais quand même à en saisir deux ou trois au passage, étaient vides: comme des coquillages sur la plage. Alors, moi-même lettre parmi les lettres, je finissais par m'agglutiner à ce magma. Et par m'y perdre. Aucune place pour moi, dans aucun des ensembles qui s'esquissaient (118)

For many of us, books may be the stuff of dreams; but for the narrator they are quite simply nightmarish. Frustrated in his readerly efforts, he puts the book down, intending to come back to it afresh; yet when he does, he finds that the text has changed (76). Nonetheless, he will return to it again and again, laboring to read it, with a single-minded constancy that resembles nothing so much as love. His love affair with the book, however, will culminate only in enervation, exhaustion, and incompletion: "Si lire—comme écrire, comme parler—est un acte d'amour, j'en étais arrivé, avec ce livre, à ce point blême de la nuit où les amants, épuisés et pourtant inassouvis, hésitent à se livrer un nouvel assaut, et rêvent seulement d'une gorgée d'eau fraîche" (145).

The narrator's problems with simple reading being what they are, it is less than surprising to find that his hermeneutic efforts are also foredoomed. He reflects on the great medieval tradition of exegesis, and upon the distinguished commentators and glossarists who animated it, how they could read *through* the various arcana—rebuses, anagrams, chronograms, cryptograms—of the texts they dealt with. But he, of course, is not one of them: "Leur esprit était rompu de longue date à ce genre de labeur. Le mien ne l'était pas assez" (90). He will try a variety of heuristics on for size, discarding them one after the other as each proves to be of no avail. On one occasion, he is tempted to abandon the path of logic and intellectual rigor that once seemed to offer such promise, in order to test interpretive modes grounded in quite another set of norms:

> Il me parut clair que je devais changer de stratégie. Me rabattre séance tenante sur une recherche plus à ma portée. Plus conforme aussi aux habitudes des marchands d'oracles. Or, sur quoi reposent, depuis des siècles, tout le crédit, toute la fortune des sibylles, nécromants, prophètes, pythonisses, oniromanciens et diseuses de bonne aventure, sinon sur l'usage quasi exclusif de mots à double sens, de formules ambiguës? (93-94)

Yet his efforts there, too, will result in failure, and he will declare himself "Bloqué, captif, défait, écrasé, foulé aux pieds, en un mot vaincu" (144).

As the narrator confesses his defeat, one of the games that Bénabou is playing becomes apparent. It's a game that might be called "loser wins," and, as Michel Beaujour has pointed out, it is a game that is particularly dear to the avant-garde.[17] One can of course play a game according to the rules; but that possibility does not interest Bénabou, for he finds the rules impossible ones to follow, and in any case they have given rise to an imposing corpus of texts that he cannot pretend to rival. One can, however turn one's back on the rules—or pretend to do so—and declare oneself out of the game, a move that offers a set of quite different possibilities. In effect, what this entails is a reconfiguration of the game according to new protocols, ones which, upon examination, depend closely and symmetrically upon the old ones. For the eschewal of rhetoric is itself a rhetorical gesture; and when Bénabou's narrator declares himself defeated, we must take his words in a rhetorical manner. By analogy, Bénabou intends that we should read *through* his narrator's lamentations. When the narrator castigates, for instance, "ces injonctions, ces interjections, ces interrogations! Et cet amalgame d'ironie, de pathos et de rhétorique" that he sees upon the page of the book he's trying to read (125-26), we are prompted to reflect upon the page of the book that we are reading, and upon the ironical, duplicitous, and ludic relations that yoke those two pages. When toward the end of *Jette* the narrator says, "Mon entreprise était donc en train d'échouer" (243), we are encouraged to reflect on Bénabou's own project, one that is likewise drawing to an end, but which may just eventuate in something other than outright failure.

In short, we, too, are invited to participate in the game. As players, our role demands the kind of brazen ruse, the sort of cheerful bad faith, that Bénabou displays throughout his work, as he turns the categories of possibility and impossibility, success and failure, on their heads and exploits them to his advantage. We must play what is said against what is meant, what we're told against what is whispered in our ear, and what we read against what we understand. Like any game, this one involves an element of risk; and Bénabou is quick to recognize and articulate the risk that he runs: "je redoutais de devoir un jour tomber entre les mains de certains de ces habiles qui, munis de scalpels mal effilés et de grilles rouillées, se jugent en mesure de déceler sous un silence un cri, derrière telle absence un signe, et dans la dénégation méme les traces d'un aveu" (*Pourquoi* 110-111). Bénabou longs nonetheless for a perfect reader, one who would be equal to the kind of impossible book he would most certainly write, if only he were able. Or perhaps one who, reading through the imperfections of the books Bénabou has written, would see, shimmering on a distant horizon, the outlines of an impossible book: "Le vrai lecteur n'est-il pas celui qui est capable de construire le lieu où la dispersion prend sens?" he asks toward the end of *Jette* (224).

Clearly, that's a tall order. And I don't mean to suggest that he has found that sort of reader in yours truly, for he most emphatically has not. In fact, Marcel Bénabou is as likely to find the perfect reader as he is to write the perfect book. In the meanwhile though, we imperfect readers may be persuaded to accept an imperfect writer's invitation, and ponder a series of impossible questions, just possibly finding some consolation there, wondering aloud why he has not written any of his books, why we must throw this book away before it's too late, and why it is that one always writes the same book.

Jacques Jouet's Exhaustion

IN THE COURSE of his career, Jacques Jouet has patiently constructed one of the most astonishing bodies of work in contemporary French literature. During that time, he has published more than a hundred volumes in a variety of literary genres. By turn a poet, a novelist, a playwright, a short story writer, an essayist, a lexicographer, and a member of the Ouvroir de Littérature Potentielle (Oulipo), Jouet never seems to rewrite himself—and such a consideration alone would serve to distinguish him from many of his peers. As diverse as they otherwise may be, one finds in each of Jouet's books a vast literary curiosity, a deep impulse toward innovation, and a will to test the possibilities of literature through the elaboration of what may appear in retrospect to be an evolving catalogue of the various forms available to a writer today. In short, Jacques Jouet is an experimentalist in the noblest sense of that word, a writer whose work comes to us fresh, each book a "new" book, all of them clearly the product of a literary imagination animated by a keen, ludic intelligence. Having followed his work closely for many years, I also believe it is legitimate to suggest that Jouet is a man of letters (as antiquated as that term may sound to our postmodern ear). He belongs thus to a species that is gravely endangered in our time and latitude; and consequently it is in an ecological spirit, conservationist but not conservative, that I shall present this account of his work.

In an influential essay first written in 1967 and much-anthologized since, John Barth offered some remarks on what he called "the literature of exhausted possibility," or "the literature of exhaustion" (64). Taking as his principal touchstones Samuel Beckett and Jorge Luis Borges, Barth examined the hypothesis, current at that time—and in ours, too, *plus ça change*—that the novel is coming to the end of its possibilities as a literary form:

> Suppose you're a writer by vocation—a "print-oriented bastard," as the McLuhanites call us—and you feel, for example, that the novel, if not narrative literature generally, if not the printed word altogether, has by this hour of the world just about shot its bolt, as Leslie Fiedler and others maintain. I'm inclined to agree, with reservations and hedges. Literary forms certainly have histories and historical contingencies, and it may well be that the novel's time as a major art form is up, as the "times" of classical tragedy, Italian and German grand opera, or the sonnet-sequence came to be. No necessary cause for alarm in this at all, except perhaps to certain novelists, and one way to handle such a feeling might be to write a novel about it. (71-72)

Barth describes his own works, such as *The Sot-Weed Factor* and *Giles Goat-Boy*, as "novels which imitate the form of the Novel, by an author who imitates the role of Author" (72), arguing that in a period of exhaustion the novel turns back upon itself, imitates and parodies itself, offering a funhouse-mirror image of what we imagined that literary form to be.

In Jacques Jouet's work, genre reflects upon itself in ways that are fundamentally similar to the ones Barth describes, for in each of the expressive modes that Jouet adopts, he plays boldly with generic protocol and convention, subtly but firmly putting literary tradition into question. Yet the sort of "exhaustion" that one notes in his writing is perhaps more closely akin to an idea expressed by one of Jouet's fellow Oulipians, Georges Perec. In a piece written for *Le Figaro* in 1978 entitled "Notes sur ce que je cherche," Perec spoke about another kind of literary exhaustion: "Si je tente de définir ce que j'ai cherché à faire depuis que j'ai commencé à écrire, la première idée qui me vient à l'esprit est que je n'ai jamais écrit deux livres semblables, que je n'ai jamais eu envie de répéter dans un livre une formule, un système ou une manière élaborés dans un livre précédent" (*Penser/Classer* 9). Further along, Perec adds: "mon ambition d'écrivain serait de parcourir toute la littérature de mon temps sans jamais avoir le sentiment de revenir sur mes pas ou de remarcher dans mes propres traces, et d'écrire tout ce qui est possible à un homme d'aujourd'hui d'écrire: des livres gros et des livres courts, des romans et des poèmes, des drames, des livrets d'opéra, des romans policiers, des romans d'aventures, des romans de science-fiction, des feuilletons, des livres pour enfants . . ." (11; ellipsis in original). The principle of exhaustion that subtends Perec's remarks—and the one that helps to structure many of his major texts in fact—is loosely derived from mathematics, and more specifically from combinatorics. Just as a given series of permutations may be said to "exhaust" the possibilities of a combinatory system, so too it may be claimed that a given set of texts (a collection of poems, a series of novels, even an oeuvre) labors *toward* the exhaustion of literary possibility. Especially if, like yet another Oulipian, Italo Calvino (and others theorists, too, such as Vladimir Propp, Gérard Genette, A. J. Greimas, Umberto Eco, and Tzvetan Todorov), one feels that literature is essentially combinatory in character.[1]

Such a vision of literature, it seems to me, is the one upon which Jacques Jouet has founded his poetics, and it is in that perspective that his work may be termed "exhaustive." Like Perec, Jouet's work testifies to his urge to experiment in a broad variety of genres and forms, putting each to the question as he works his way strategically across the horizon of literary possibility. In the domain of poetry, for instance, he has written lyric poetry, narrative poetry, dramatic poetry, occasional poetry of various kinds, and even a modest census report (*107 Âmes*, about which I will have more to say later). Venerable fixed forms such as the triolet, the sestina, and the sonnet interest him intensely, as do more recent fixed forms such as the "morale élémentaire," invented by Raymond Queneau, and the "poème de métro," a form that he himself invented. He has edited a volume devoted to Western experiments in the Malaysian "pantoum" form, and he has for decades written a daily "poème adressé du jour," a text addressed to one specific reader and sent out to him or her by mail once it is completed.

Trying to keep up with Jouet can be exhausting, granted the heady pace he sets (if I may kvetch just a bit); and accounting for his work in an exhaustive manner, in view of its dimensions and its heterogeneity, seems to me well nigh impossible. In what follows I should like to take a few soundings in his oeuvre, looking over his shoulder as he strives toward the exhaustion of literature. I will not mention all of his texts; among those I do mention I shall dwell on some more than others; and I will most surely *not* pretend to exhaust the interpretive possibilities of any of them. I would like to proceed from the outside in, as it were, narrowing my focus progressively upon those works that I feel to be most central to his literary project as a whole, and ending with poetry because I believe that Jouet is in the final analysis a poet, and that every piece of writing he undertakes is characterized by a strong and uncompromising poetic impulse.

I would like to begin with a brief discussion of two of Jouet's works that do not—upon first consideration at least—seem to belong to the "creative" dimension of his writing, *Les Mots du corps dans les expressions de la langue française* and *Raymond Queneau*. The former intrigues me in that it offers a privileged view of Jouet's relations with language, and his fascination with language in and *for* itself; while in the latter, as Jouet writes about the work one of his mentor figures, he brings his own nascent vision of poetics closely into focus.

In *Les Mots du corps*, Jouet proposes a defense and illustration of the way the French language invokes the body in fixed expressions. He deals with a corpus of 433 expressions, and devotes extended entries to 176 of them, ranging from the familiar ("rendre tripes et boyaux"), to the more exquisite ("pâle comme une merde de laitier"), to the literary ("faire catleya," which Jouet torturously grafts onto the body through etymology, claiming that "orchid" derives from the Greek *orkhidion*, "testicles"), to the hopelessly vexed ("con comme une bite"). In his preface Jouet mentions that the entries in *Les Mots du corps* are composed of three kinds of material. First, lexicographical and linguistic data, compiled from sources as disparate as Wartburg's *Französisches Etymologisches Wörterbuch* (the mere mention of which makes many former graduate students in French literature quail with unremedied trauma, including yours truly), Furetière's 1690 *Dictionnaire universel*, and Jacques Cellard and Alain Rey's inexhaustible *Dictionnaire du français non-conventionnel*. Second, a citational apparatus where Jouet situates the expressions in a literary-historical context, drawing on writers from Rutebeuf to Michel Leiris and from Rabelais to Alphonse Allais. Finally, a "fictional" dimension, in which he himself elaborates stories intended to illustrate the expressions he has chosen to work upon. Clearly, one of the things Jouet is attempting to do in *Les Mots du corps* is to harmonize tradition and innovation, old and new, taking language at its most fixed and static (most of the time, we use clichés such as these offhandedly and uncritically) and reinvigorating it, mobilizing it, making it speak anew through a voice that is patently and explicitly literary. What guides him throughout is his intuition that these expressions are deeply attached to our experience of language: "Il m'est vite apparu que le corps est un bon microcosme de la langue. Il est certainement l'un de ses lieux métaphoriques les plus féconds. Je devrais dire lieu d'échange métaphorique, une des plaques tournantes de la langue. Tous les chemins y mènent, tous les chemins en partent" (8). That kind of "intersectivity" is deeply imbricated in *Les Mots du corps*, and it is moreover one of the features that Ross Chambers noted in dilatory or (as he puts it) "loiterly" literature (*Loiterature* 9). It is Jouet's pleasure to digress in this book, following the meanders of the various intersections he comes upon, in a kind of "constructively dilatory" itinerary of just the sort that one notes throughout his career as a writer. Briefly stated, then, Jouet's principal concerns and techniques in *Les Mots du corps*—exhaustiveness, reinvigoration of tradition, intersectivity, productive digression—seem to me to be closely similar to those which color his work as a whole.

Written for La Manufacture's "Qui êtes-vous?" series, *Raymond Queneau* bears only a distant resemblance to the formulaic, dry survey that one may associate with monographs of that type. The writing here is bold and elegant; the analyses that Jouet offers are intellectually rigorous and provocative, devolving upon moments in Queneau's work that address problems encountered by many contemporary writers, both in the avant-garde and the mainstream; Jouet's project, finally, is characterized by a playful perspective that is wholly consistent with his subject and most refreshing for his reader. The main body of the book is devoted to an essay entitled "Raymond Queneau, la règle de plaire et la règle de penser." Jouet evokes the notion of literary madness as he examines Queneau's early flirtation with surrealism, and his subsequent inquiry into *fous littéraires*, or (as Queneau himself preferred to call them) "hétéroclites." While Queneau suggested that his study had cost him three years and resulted in nothing other than a 700-page manuscript, the *Encyclopédie des sciences inexactes*, rejected by both Gallimard and Denoël in 1934, Jouet argues that this "descente aux enfers de l'intelligence" (21) would nourish all of Queneau's later work. The discussion of Queneau's aesthetic of literary determination is informed by Jouet's own experience as a writer and as a member of the Oulipo, founded by Queneau and François Le Lionnais in 1960. Jouet pays homage to the seminal text of the Oulipo, Queneau's *Cent Mille Milliards de poèmes*, as he offers readings of some of the hundred trillion sonnets which that work engenders. From that potentially exhausting exercise, he turns to a consideration of the curious reciprocity of novel and poem in Queneau's work, and to the encyclopedic impulse that insistently animates the latter. Finally, he addresses the question of autobiography, and its role in the fictional regime: Jouet's wariness here resembles Queneau's own. Along the way, Jouet faces up to one of the thorniest formal problems encountered by Queneau scholars, that of the eponymous adjective. Radically rejecting base sectarianism in favor of a good-natured (if patently wry) pluralism, Jouet uses "quenellien" (15), "quenéen" (21), "quenalien" (21), "quenien" (39), "quenéifien" (50), and "quenouillard" (124). Readers of Queneau often find that his work presents difficulties precisely because his writing seems to anticipate most of the critical strategies that are brought to bear on it; for his part, Jouet chooses to play squarely upon that notion, reading Queneau through Queneau with admirable deftness and subtlety. Many Oulipians have written critical studies of Queneau,[2] and one interesting by-product of such exercises is that it often allows them to hone their own literary ethos more sharply; such is the case of Jouet's *Queneau*. Undoubtedly the principal precursor figure (along with Perec) in Jouet's literary lineage, Queneau's way of seeing literature in the first instance as form and patient construction inspires Jouet's own writing abundantly from its beginnings to the present. One can also trace Queneau's influence in the ludic impulse that subtends Jouet's work; in his urge to experiment with literary potential; in his recognition of the reciprocal affinities of even the most apparently disparate literary genres, and the way he exploits those affinities even as he avails himself of the specific possibilities of a given genre; and finally in his will to expend himself utterly within literature, both as a reader and as a writer.

Throughout his career, Jouet has practiced the short story. Several of these, such as *Histoire de Paul Gauguin et de son divan*, *L'Évasion de Rochefort*, *Muséification de Notre Dame*, *La République romaine*, *La Scène usurpée*, and *Ce que rapporte l'Envoyé*, were published in small volumes, while many others appeared in collections organized around a given theme. *Le Bestiaire inconstant* is a collection of twenty-three stories about animals, from dogs and cats to hermit crabs, moths, and cockroaches. Taking his place in the venerable tradition of the bestiary, Jouet gives free rein to the human-all-too-human tendency to anthropomorphize, and the various beasts who figure in these pages are invested with some of the drollest characteristics of homo sapiens. There are very few gods here (Yahweh does make a cameo appearance on pages 53-54), but the Devil plays a significant role in the collection, popping up in nearly all of the stories and offering an enticing array of temptations. Romillat, the hero of the eleven stories in *Romillats*, is a man whose very *ordinariness* beggars the imagination—both the readerly imagination and the writerly one. Like Bartleby, like Peter Schlemihl, like Schweik, like Oskar Matzerath, like Hans Schneir, he is an idiot in the highest sense, a nullity of a man who is hopelessly benighted by the puny vicissitudes of his existence, but one who remains entirely—if impossibly—himself. Romillat's profile is curiously indistinct. He is married or divorced, cuckolded or not, and has two or three children; he may have taught in a high school; and from time to time he disappears. As undefined as this man may be, he provides us nonetheless with a lens through which our own most banal, quotidian behaviors appear extravagantly bizarre. *Actes de la machine ronde* also contains eleven stories. Despite the apparent dissimilarity of these texts ("L'Escalier du soleil" is written in alexandrine verse, for instance, rather than in prose), there are a variety of mutual reciprocities that circulate among them, echo effects devolving upon structural, thematic, and stylistic considerations. First things and the notion of origin interest Jouet here, as he turns his imagination to the invention of pottery ("Le Tour du pot"), the conundrum of the chicken and the egg ("La Première Poule"), and the fundamental question of human voice ("La Voix"). There are many aspects of *Actes de la machine ronde* that project outside the collection, too, pointing toward other moments in Jouet's work. Such is the case, for example, of "Un Soir à Thèbes," which takes as its background the encounter of Oedipus and the Sphinx, a mythico-literary topos that recurs with insistency in Jouet's writings. Clearly, that scene is a crucial one for Jouet, and he returns to it often, in his prose, theater, and poetry, trying to imagine how it could be told otherwise, what other answers

Oedipus might have imagined, what new narrative twists might be injected into it—in short, how a writer today might reappropriate that ancient cultural moment, painstakingly and exhaustively, and make it signify in new ways.

As Jouet reflects upon literary genre, the principal tactic he deploys is the metaphorization of genre itself. That is amply true of his theater, as the title of his first collection of plays, *La Scène est sur la scène*, suggests. Moreover, the utterance "la scène est sur scène" occurs as the first stage direction in nine of the fourteen texts included here, and in six of the thirteen plays in his second volume of collected theater, *Morceaux de théâtre*. Clearly, one of Jouet's intentions is to offer some comment on theater itself as a cultural practice, through an examination of its fundamental protocols and its conditions of possibility. In carrying out that program, Jouet will return to some of the most important touchstone figures in the dramatic tradition, from Aeschylus (*Les Vaincus*, *Scène* 37-59) to Shakespeare (*Hamlet, une parallèle*, *Scène* 15-35), reconsidering their gestures, walking in their footsteps yet proposing new itineraries for the drama they imagined. Sophocles and his Theban Sphinx loom large here, too, in *Question* (*Scène* 237-40) and *Autre question* (*Morceaux* 227-34); and the moment of truth in those encounters hinges on a young girl's poetic agility in both cases, much to the Sphinx's chagrin. Other morsels into which Jouet sinks his theatrical teeth are borrowed from novels, from writers as diverse as Mary Shelley (*Monsieur Frankenstein*, *Scène* 191-236) and Jules Verne (*Tour de la scène en 80 minutes*, *Morceaux* 71-120). Some of the characters Jouet places upon his stage are fairly well known, like Jesus Christ (*Jésus enseigne les Goliath*, *Morceaux* 31-69); while others, such as his very own Romillat (*Le Jour où Romillat changea de compagnie*, *Scène* 241-83) are distinctly less so. Jouet's plays have been produced in Paris and Ouagadougou, in Pernand-Vergelesses and Saint-Genis-Pouilly. Several of his texts[3] were performed at the annual Rencontres Jacques Copeau, from 1991 through 1997, and many were elaborated in close collaboration with directors and actors—even with apprentice actors, as in the case of *La Sortie au peuple* (*Morceaux* 263-70). The collaborative dynamic that is essential to theater in its productive dimension interests Jouet deeply. In the summers of 1997 and 1998, for instance, he spent time in Burkina Faso working with a variety of other playwrights, directors, and acting ensembles; one of the texts resulting from that work, *Trois fois trois phrases*, appears in *Morceaux de théêtre* (271-87).

That same sort of collaborative spirit has animated a fair share of Jouet's literary activity, from his early days in writers workshops and his affiliation with the Oulipo (he became a member of that group in 1983) to the present. At least one other such project deserves mention here. In 1996, along with Claudine Capdeville, Georges Kolebka, and Pierre Laurent, Jouet founded a collection at the Éditions Plurielle. From then until 1998 they published a series of very short, happily playful texts (none of them longer than fifteen pages) in their collection, aptly—and paronomastically—entitled "Les Guère Épais." Recruiting a variety of authors, including several Oulipians,[4] they printed these texts in editions limited to 150 copies, and sold them by subscription, in batches of three. Twenty-three of these volumes had been produced when, in April 1998, the Éditions Plurielle declared an end to the "Guère Épais," to the cruel dismay of their limited (but doggedly faithful) readership.[5] Several things about this project interest me. First, the establishment of a patently anti-establishment publishing venture, a parody of mainstream publishing in a sense, an operation whose literary aspirations are very modest indeed and denuded of literary imperialism. Further, I am intrigued by the stance taken by the "Guère Épais" collective with regard to the marketplace, the decision to sell books by subscription to a well-defined (though very small) public, apparently without the intention to profit, and by the way they maintained close, dialogical relations with their readership through the amusing circulars that accompanied each set of texts they sent out. Finally, I have been impressed by the quality of the texts that have appeared in the "Guère Épais," where less—in this case at least—has proved to be more; and I have found the ludic spirit that colors them most refreshing indeed.

Turning away from small literary forms and collaborative effort for the moment, I would like to discuss Jacques Jouet's novels. Just as in his theater, Jouet plays genre against itself when, almost two decades into his career, he tries his hand at the novel form. In *Le Directeur du Musée des Cadeaux des Chefs d'État de l'Étranger*, the notion of the catalogue plays a central role. For the Director's task is to bring together all of the gifts offered to the French Republic over the years by foreign dignitaries, classify them, and display them in a museum.

This man is the ultimate collector: with admirable method and deliberation, he will identify, count, describe, and list these gifts prior to placing them, *thing* upon *thing*, in his museum, in a process of accretion and apposition whose very nature is inscribed in the novel's title—and in its structure, too. His joys and his struggles are those of any collector: the rapture of enumeration, the challenge of coercing coherence from an inchoate mass of data, the elaboration of a logical, rigorous, systematic world. Each gift has a story, of course, and these stories, taken together, offer a droll, idiosyncratic vision of history. Highly ironic relations pertain between the givers and receivers of the gifts, and indeed between the gifts themselves. As the gifts multiply, so do the narrative possibilities of Jouet's novel. Shadowy creatures lurking in these pages propel those possibilities along: the nefariously subtle caretaker of the museum; a young woman recently appointed Minister of Ceremonies, Rites, Pomp, Etiquette, and National Memory; and a depraved political hatchetman known only as "Le Capitaine." Each has an intrigue to play in the museum, and as those intrigues collide they engender surprising effects. Not the least interesting of the latter is the way in which the continual imbrication of plot inflects the generic character of Jouet's text. At times, it reads like an historical novel; at others, like a detective novel, a love story, a political potboiler, a sentimental education, and so forth. What we have here, in short, is a novel of the novel, a fiction of fictions. Like his Director, Jacques Jouet is a collector. He assembles in this text an impressive display of narrative possibility. Inevitably, one concludes that the novel of the museum *is* the museum: strolling through its halls, one is continually astonished at the protean vitality of a literary form which, not so long ago, seemed to be foundering. The moral of this tale, I think, lies in the fact that the novel is an infinitely generous genre; for, if each gift in this museum is a story, each story is also—and perhaps more importantly—a gift.

In *La Montagne R*, Jouet changes terms, but his fundamental tactic of the metaphorization of genre remains the same. Here, rather than as a museum, the novel is cast as a mountain. The conceit of the story is simple enough, yet engagingly droll: the leaders of a fictional republic decide to build a 1500-meter mountain near the capital, both to provide jobs through a massive public works project and as a monument to national prestige. The project will go awry (as indeed it inevitably must), but not in the way we might expect. The novel is divided into three parts. The first is devoted to the speech of the President of the Republican Council, as he outlines that project to the legislature. It's a canny parody of contemporary political discourse, particularly amusing for those readers who recognize that "politspeak" is a language which scoffs at national and cultural boundaries, and who are assailed by its egregious brayings on a daily basis. The second part takes place after the project has come to a halt. A young woman interviews her father, a minor contractor who had worked on the mountain for many years. She asks him about his daily life during those years, about the status of the workers on the mountain, particularly that of the many foreign workers, about the reasons for the accidents that happened on the site and which eventually brought work to a standstill. Here, Jouet deals with other political issues, such as race and class; yet he also sketches the very local and conflictive politics that may animate family relations. Finally, the people responsible for the mountain are put on trial, and the third part of the novel stages the testimony of a writer named "Stéphane" who had been commissioned to write a fictional account of the project. He is a shadowy, elusive figure: he may have ghostwritten the President's speech, he may have sent the young woman to interview her father, and so forth. Yet he realizes, as we do, that certain affinities link the mountain and his own writerly task, and flaw them, too, in similar ways: "Écrire un roman, c'est avoir une montagne, comme ça, à fabriquer de toutes pièces sur un terrain mitoyen du vôtre" (94). National monuments, like novels, dig their foundations deep into the human imagination; yet in politics, as in literature, things are very rarely what we first imagine them to be. Throughout *La Montagne R*, language is put on trial. Testing language in several different discursive contexts, in each of which language is strained to the breaking point, Jouet asks his reader to think about its limits as a heuristic tool and to question its potential as a vehicle of truth, whether it is deployed in the flatulent discourse of a corrupt public official, the veiled whisperings of a conflicted family, or the deliberately—and professionally—prevaricative testimony of a novelist. It is the latter figure who intrigues me the most in *La Montagne R*, for the role Stéphane plays therein is strictly figural of the one Jouet himself plays. And clearly, the game that Jouet proposes to the readers of his novel is one which hinges upon the notion of textual specularity. At the simplest level, Stéphane's Montagne R novel is emblazoned within Jouet's own, each mirroring the other. When Stéphane describes the travails and writerly struggles he endures as he labors to write his virtual text, we readers are encouraged to reflect on the kind of work that resulted in the real text which we are holding before us. Yet the relations between these two texts are not perfectly reciprocal, and multiple ironies animate those relations, the most obvious among them being the fact that Stéphane, unlike Jouet, cannot finish his novel. In other words, the doubling effects that Jouet elaborates in *La Montagne R* are asymmetrical, carefully skewed to his own advantage. And the way he exploits his character is double in the same fashion, for Stéphane serves as both example and counterexample. At certain moments, Stéphane's account of his project may be read as a faithful description of the kinds of concerns that any successful novelist must face; at other times, his woeful maunderings are intended to suggest the worst nightmares of a failed novelist. I would like to argue, moreover, that it is legitimate to read in this passage a theory of the novel which Jouet claims as his own. From a writer's perspective, a novel in progress looms up like the Montagne R does on the landscape of the République. It is artifice, but it imitates the real. Its dimensions are impossible ones, and its conception beggars its execution. What it chiefly demands is a labor of artisanry rather than art, work rather than inspiration. Most importantly, a novel is a *chantier*, a building site. Literature is constructivist in all of its phases, Jouet argues, in its production and its reception, in both writing and reading alike. For if his novel offers a mirror to the writer, it also offers a mirror to the reader, and indeed Jouet confronts us throughout *La Montagne R* with our own reading act, inviting us to reflect upon it as a constructive activity, to watch ourselves as we test different interpretive strategies, attempting to build coherence and meaning. When Stéphane becomes, in the end, the unfortunate object of his society's scorn, it is principally because, unlike Jacques Jouet, he has failed to negotiate the Montagne R's terrain. That terrain features a steep upside, and its downside is a vertiginous, precipitous one. But that's the way it is with mountains—and with this novel, too.

In Jouet's third novel, *Fins*, he plays on the principle of narrative closure. *Fins* tells the stories of two Parisian couples and their marital adventures, which are by turn loony and poignant. It is composed of

216 paragraphs (or passages), each containing a brief narrative that takes its place in the broader narrative economy of the novel, each of them "closed" in some fashion. In his postface to the novel, Jouet speculates on this structure: "Comment faire pour que le roman finisse à chacun de ses pas? Est-ilm possible d'écrire un roman qui se termine à tout moment, dont chaque unité—ici le paragraphe—le mène à son terme, à un terme possible? J'ai cherché ça, sans avoir peur, aussi, de l'oublier parfois" (122). The second constraint that Jouet sets for himself in *Fins* is based on a fixed poetic form that reached its apogee under the pen of poets like Arnaut Daniel, Dante, Petrarch, and Tasso, the sestina.[6] That form involves the distribution of rhymes in a poem of six stanzas composed of six lines each, according to a rigorously permutational pattern. In *Fins*, the permutational integers are the number of sentences in each paragraph. The first paragraph contains one sentence, the second two, and so forth. In the seventh paragraph, another permutation begins, in which the order is shifted: 6, 1, 5, 2, 4, 3. The second permutation beings in the thirteenth paragraph, with a shift that is symmetrical to that in the second set: 3, 6, 4, 1, 2, 5. Jouet follows pattern in Fins until all of the combinatoric possibilities of his algorithm ($6 \times 6 \times 6 = 216$) have been, precisely, *exhausted*. In his postface, he explains that the formal constraints he has adopted in *Fins* are meant to respond to Raymond Queneau's call for more structural rigor in the novel, which Queneau enunciated in an essay entitled "Technique du roman," first published in 1937: "Alors que la poésie a été la terre bénie des rhétoriqueurs et des faiseurs de règles, le roman, depuis qu'il existe, a échappé à toute loi. N'importe qui peut pousser devant lui comme un toupeau d'oies un nombre indéterminé de personnages apparemment réels à travers une lande longue d'un nombre indéterminé de pages ou de chapitres. Le résultat, quel qu'il soit, sera toujours un roman" (*Bâtons* 27). Yet by Oulipian standards, Jouet's constraints in this novel are relatively supple, and quite deliberately so; he confesses in his postface that formal rigor is not the first principle of his novelistic practice as a whole, making explicit allusion to the passage from Queneau that I quoted: "Ce qui ne veut pas dire que, pour ma part, j'aie fait ou que j'aie l'intention de faire tous mes romans de cette façon. Je m'intéresse aussi beaucoup aux romans 'troupeau d'oies'" (121). What does seem to me to be worthy of our readerly attention in *Fins* is Jouet's will to totalize within a carefully

circumscribed field of action; his recognition that storytelling, both in its production and its reception, is fundamentally combinatoric in character; and his desire to go to the very *end* of the literary task he has postulated for himself, invoking the very notion of the end as one of his subjects and playing lustily upon it.

Jacques Jouet began his literary career as a poet, and a poet he remains. In what remains to me, I would like to discuss three of his collections of verse, *107 Âmes*, *Navet, linge, oeil-de-vieux*, and *Frise du métro parisien*.

107 Âmes contains 107 poems, each sketching the portrait of a different, real person. In his preface, Jouet describes the work's conceit:

> Au moment de rédiger chacun des poèmes qui composent *107 Âmes*, je ne connaissais de la personne en cause—bien réelle—que ses réponses écrites à un questionnaire confectionné par mes soins. Un rabatteur, que j'avais requis, s'était chargé de convaincre une personne de son choix d'accepter le contrat. Il lui avait transmis le questionnaire, puis me l'avait retourné rempli. Une fois le poème écrit, j'en livrais deux exemplaires au rabatteur, qui donnait l'un d'eux au sujet. (9)

His questionnaire contained ten questions, nine of which devolve upon basic, objective demographic data: name, age, profession, place of birth, family situation, housing, income, and so forth. The tenth question is a departure from the coldly administrative tone of the pollster; in it, Jouet asks his subject to describe a determinative event in his or her life. The poems in *107 Âmes* share a common form: three stanzas of six verses each. The verses are relatively short, and are mostly composed of seven syllables (a few poems are composed in octosyllables, and one poem [75] in verses of nine syllables). In what Jouet refers to as the most Oulipian of his major texts, he has used (in addition to the three-sestet structure of the poems) two systems of constraint. First, the exhaustion of the data furnished in his subjects' responses to the questionnaires: "Ma règle était d'utiliser les informations fournies par le questionnaire rempli, toutes ces informations, rien que ces informations" (11). Second, as Jouet remarks in his preface, each poem incorporates a rhyme scheme that Harry Mathews unearthed in the first of John Berryman's dream songs. The rhyme is distributed over three verses. In the first, Jouet posits a stressed consonant (or consonants), in the second, a tonic vowel; the third verse conflates them. As unusual as it may be, the effect achieved by this technique is nonetheless that of rhyme: "En quelque sort, donc, le troisième vers est en consonance avec le premier, en assonance avec le deuxième. Il rime avec la somme des deux" (12). Such a device points to Jouet's deep interest in rhyme as a general literary principle, an interest that colors in one way or another many of his major works, whether the "rhyming" function hinges on sounds, on themes, or on structures. Among those 107 souls, then, there are 58 females and 47 males (two don't report their gender). Among the 102 reporting their age, the youngest is 8 and the eldest is 89. Their average age is 36. Among the subjects 18 years of age or over, 27 are single, 37 are married, 8 live in concubinage, 1 is separated, 6 are divorced, and 9 are widowed. Apart from those of French nationality, there are 9 Germans, 4 Americans, 2 English, 2 Belgians, a Romanian, a Greek, a Scot, a Senegalese, an Argentine, an Italian, an Irishman, a Turk, a *Québécois*, a Portuguese, an Australian, and a Japanese. 27% of the subjects are "foreigners." 39 subjects reside in Paris or the Parisian Region, 50 in the French provinces, and 17 in other countries. 8 subjects live in studio apartments, 41 in larger apartments, 5 in public housing projects, 37 in single-family dwellings, and 1 is without fixed domicile. There are among them bookkeepers, a disc jockey, a librarian, architects, secretaries, students galore, gardeners, artists, teachers, farmers, social workers, mechanics, housewives, psychologists, unemployed people, engineers, a doctor, a nurse, masons, a trade union official, a carpenter, an interior decorator, factory workers, retired people, a florist, an archivist, a cook, and a political organizer who was once a hunger striker in a Belfast prison. Their average income is 7,579 francs per month. The lowest reported income (apart from the homeless person, whose income is presumably nil) is 1,500 francs per month; the highest is 25,000 francs per month. Though such a reading may be starkly lacking in soul, it does point to a fundamental concern in *107 Âmes*. For if Jouet does not pretend to rival the État Civil, his project is nonetheless animated by a registrar's care for exactitude and exhaustiveness. As much as *107 Âmes* is "about" the subjects who responded to Jouet's questionnaires, it is about the society in which they live. And in this, Jouet's intentions are at least *modestly* Balzacian. The notion of modesty is, I believe, a key principle in

107 Âmes. Jouet has remarked of these texts, with characteristic understatement, "Ce ne sont pas des épopées." One would have to agree with him: the formal concision of the collection is anything but epic; there are few heroes, few heroic labors; the focus seems to be on the ordinary, rather than the extraordinary. Clearly, Jouet is proposing a different kind of poetry. For what he has elaborated here is a soulful formalist poetics, one which is quietly, modestly, resolutely humanist, and consistently informed by the firm intuition that "les gens valent plus que leurs drames" (36).

We hear from every quarter that poetry is a dying art, confined to an ever-more constricted circle of quirky amateurs, doomed by cynical publishers who regard poetry manuscripts with the kind of loathing one normally reserves for terminal disease. Yet all of a sudden, out of the blue, comes *Navet, linge, oeil-de-vieux*, a three-volume collection of verse of 938 pages. *Navet, linge, oeil-de-vieux* is many things; but principally, perhaps, it is a resounding affirmation of the vitality of poetry as a cultural practice. From April 1, 1992 to the present, Jouet has set himself the task of composing a poem a day, and this collection records the first four years of his experiment. There are lots of different kinds of poems here. Some are short, a few comprising only one word. Some are long, including a poem Jouet returns to periodically over the four-year period, written in alexandrines and terza rima (using the same Berryman-inspired scheme of internal rhyme found in *107 Âmes*) which includes—thus far—4002 lines. There are poems on the still-life that lends its title to the collection, and which Jouet kept on his desk during those years, composed of a turnip, a linen napkin, and an "oeil-de-vieux" (a clear, square, biconcave lens used by landscape painters). There are occasional poems, free-verse poems, and fixed-form poems (such as Queneau's "morale élémentaire"). There are "poèmes de métro," composed according to a constraint which dictates that each verse must be composed between the various stations of a trip on the Parisian subway. There are examples of a form Jouet calls the "poème adressé," that is, a poem written with a certain person in mind, playing in some manner upon that person's name, and sent out by mail to that person as soon as it has been composed. Jouet explains the impulse that animates his "addressed poems" in a publicity flyer that accompanies *Navet, linge, oeil-de-vieux*:

> Le poème adressé, pour moi, est un genre de poésie.
> Il est titré du nom de la personne à qui il d'adresse, daté et localisé. Il puise un peu de sa substance dans le nom de la personne à qui il s'adresse.
> Afin de tempérer le rêve déraisonnable d'un grand nombre de lecteurs pour un petit nombre de poèmes, j'aime a contrario m'imposer d'écrire un grand nombre de poèmes, chaque poème n'étant lu, dans un premier temps, que par un lecteur.
> La poésie peut être faite pour pas grand monde, comme ne disait pas Isidore Ducasse.[7]

There are many poems on painting here, and indeed the collection is dedicated to painters; one is left with the impression that Jouet is proposing poetry as a lens, a way of seeing and framing the experience of everyday life. That concern for the quotidian colors each text here, if in very different ways. For *Navet, linge, oeil-de-vieux* may also be read as a journal, as a poet's diary. Unlike most diaries, however, the tone of this work is not intimist in character; rather, it is broadly public. To the hoary (and paralyzing) Romantic notion of poetry as inspiration, Jouet opposes a vision of poetry as work and as practice, in short, a conception of poetry as an integral rule of daily life. His muse is a simple one here; and, if one is willing to provide the hard labor that poetry demands, "inspiration" comes fairly easily. From time to time, one buys a new turnip to replace the old one, and that seems to turn the trick: "Allons chez le primeur / puis chez l'imprimeur" (471). Speaking of that latter figure, it should be remarked that P.O.L's publication of this vast collection is a bold, truly stunning gesture that renders a remarkable service to French poetry and to all those who read it, just when we were beginning to believe that nobody cared.

Frise du métro parisien, finally, is the apotheosis of the "métro poem." It is also, I feel, a sustained meditation on a certain idea of poetry—and of literature in general. In his preface to *Frise du métro parisien*, Pierre Rosenstiehl quotes an early métro poem of Jouet's, one that offers a useful definition of the genre itself:

> Un poème de métro est un poème composé dans le métro, pendant le temps d'un voyage.
> Un poème de métro compte autant de vers que votre voyage compte de stations moins un.

> Le premier vers est composé dans votre tête entre les deux premières stations de votre voyage (en comptant la station de départ).
> Il est transcrit sur le papier quand la rame s'arrête à la station deux.
> Le deuxième vers est composé dans votre tête entre les stations deux et trois de votre voyage.
> Il est transcrit sur le papier quand la rame s'arrête à la station trois. Et ainsi de suite.
> Il ne faut pas transcrire quand la rame est en marche.
> Il ne faut pas composer quand la rame est arrêtée.
> Le dernier vers du poème est transcrit sur le quai de votre dernière station.
> Si votre voyage impose un ou plusieurs changements de ligne, le poème comporte deux strophes ou davantage. (5)

In order to test the *potential* of the poetic genre he had invented, Jouet imagined a trip on the métro wherein he would pass through every single station on the Parisian subway system at least once, with a minimum of reduplication. He called upon Rosenstiehl, a fellow-Oulipian and a professor of mathematics specializing in theory of labyrinths and graphs, in order to help him map out the most efficient itinerary. Jouet took his trip on April 18, 1996, beginning at 5:30 AM and finishing at 9:00 PM. What resulted was *Frise du métro parisien*, a poem of 490 lines, distributed in 49 stanzas. I would like to consider just a few aspects of the text, in order to give some idea of its tone and of how it may been seen to put into play some of the more fundamental considerations of Jacques Jouet's poetics. First, I hope that I am on safe ground in suggesting that the "métro poem" is an urban genre; nonetheless, Jouet evinces therein a pleasure that is nothing short of pastoral: "Je ne suis pas moins heureux que si je marchais, ce matin, dans la campagne" (15). In similar manner, throughout his text, poetry turns back upon itself in the kind of reflexive gesture Barth spoke about, examining its own traditions and conditions of possibility. Moreover, Jouet casts the poetic act here as a *vital* activity taking place in the real world, bound by real-world constraints: this a poet with a train to catch. He reflects, too, upon the notions of rhythm and time, and the way in which this poem written on the subway necessarily conflates those important poetic notions beyond any possibility of disintrication. For the compositional rhythm that he has imposed upon himself leaves him no time for anything but his composition: "Il ne m'est laissé le temps de rêver à autre chose qu'au poème" (17); and the small integers of time in his trip from station to station impose a subterranean rhythm upon his poem. He writes to pass the time, surely—but also to feel time passing. And he writes in that most quotidian space of the cityscape, the place where one's time usually does not seem to signify, in an attempt to persuade us that even the most banal, everyday experience may be lived poetically. The long day he spent there must have been an exceptionally exhausting one for Jouet, following his sleek combinatoric to the exhaustion of the métro system. Striving, too, to exhaust the poetic form he had imagined, he finds that the very idea of exhaustion, when closely examined and put to the test, suggests recursively—and perversely—a plenitude:

> Impossible d'avoir sérieusement le sentiment
> de simplement commencer d'épuiser un lieu parisien, comme disait un autre,
> puisque parcours et perception ne se livrent à aucune espèce de réduction,
> mais décuplent, centuplent et tentaculent
> les noyaux du réel encore germables après qu'on a bouffé le premier bon du fruit.
> Tout lieu est un riche lieu. (17)

In its rich specularity, *Frise du métro parisien* enacts just that sort of commentary upon itself, within itself. Read as the projection of a certain theory of literature, it may also be seen to enfigure Jacques Jouet's oeuvre as a whole as he moves from station to station, genre to genre, book to book, along an itinerary that is consciously circular. One of the remarks he offers as he goes around and around in the métro reveals what he is actually about in his poem; and it may be taken also as a singularly apposite formulation of his literary enterprise from its beginnings to the present: "Je veux seulement faire oeuvre ronde" (25).

Marie NDiaye's Narrative

CRITICS generally agree that a closely cultivated strangeness of mood constitutes one of the hallmarks of Marie NDiaye's fiction, though they frame that effect in different ways. Dominique Rabaté remarks, for instance, "Le lecteur qui entre dans l'oeuvre de Marie NDiaye est immédiatement saisi par un sentiment d'étrangeté. Le monde où il pénètre est soumis à des règles dont les lois lui échappent, mais dont la logique s'avère implacable."[1] Ambroise Teko-Agbo suggests that NDiaye "valorizes [. . .] the problem of the strange and invites us to reflect on the place of the strange and the stranger in our societies."[2] Nora Cottille-Foley argues that, "Dès son premier roman, *Quant au riche avenir*, Marie NDiaye donne à entrevoir l'expérience de cette étrangeté propre au processus de la perception."[3] Shirley Jordan takes a broader view still when she invokes "la panoplie ndiayïenne de générateurs d'instabilité,"[4] seeking a manner of understanding the phenomenon of strangeness in NDiaye's work that allows for more multiplicity and more diversity of conception and execution. For my part, I would like to draw the focus a bit closer, in order to concentrate on one technique among the several that Marie NDiaye typically deploys in an effort to persuade us that things are not quite what we might have imagined them to be.

In each of NDiaye's fictions, there are moments that leave us nonplussed, that flaunt the norms of narrative logic or causality which the rest of the text puts in place, unexplained and apparently unexplainable things that distinguish themselves dramatically from the narrative landscape upon which they are staged. Those moments are relatively easy to identify, since NDiaye offers them to us with playful obviousness,[5] but they are difficult to theorize in a satisfactory fashion. Many of them fall somewhere between what Gerald Prince has called the *unnarratable* and the *unnarrated*,[6] verging more or less toward one of those categories, depending upon the case, yet never wholly reducible thereto. Some of them cannot be described in those terms however, since they are not "events," properly speaking. Rather, they can be conceived as textual lacunas: moments when explanation lacks, for instance, or moments which seem to be predicated upon something else which has not been furnished to us. For lack of a better way to designate them, I would like to think of those phenomena as instances of "negative narrative," imagining them as negative images of telling, ones wherein what is left *unsaid* is promoted to a crucial role in the process of literary signification. In what follows, I would like to examine a few such instances in Marie NDiaye's work, quite briefly and in a very pragmatic manner, regarding each of them as exemplary of a broader strategy of subversion of narrative convention.

In the early pages of *Un temps de saison*, it quickly becomes apparent that something is very wrong indeed. That situation, in itself, is not a rare one in NDiaye's fictions; to the contrary, the worlds she constructs are each a bit off-kilter.[7] In *Un temps de saison*, however, we are never told what occasions that strangeness, and we must fall back upon a precarious process of narrative inferencing. As we engage in that process, we look to Herman, the novel's protagonist, because the way that he finds himself benighted in the provincial village where the action is set is closely analogous to our readerly situation, and his groping attempts to understand his dilemma closely figure our own. Herman recognizes that his position in the village is a marginal one, and despite the fact that he has spent many summer vacations there, he remains very much a stranger. That otherness is suddenly amplified when for the first time he stays in the village after the notional end of the vacation period. "Peut-être n'aimait-on pas ici," Herman speculates, "que les étrangers fissent connaissance de l'automne, qui en quelque sorte ne les regardait pas, et considérait-on comme indiscrète cette immixtion dans la mystérieuse existence de l'arrière saison?" (17). Has he overstayed his welcome? It is in any case the first time a Parisian vacationer has remained in the village after the end of August, and that exceptional event is duly noted by the villagers. "Herman était le premier Parisien qu'il voyait sous la pluie d'automne," remarks one young man, "et dans ce froid mordant qui ne manquait jamais de tomber ici dès le premier septembre, pour ne s'en aller qu'aux environs du quinze juin" (22-23). Moreover, that event seems to be imbricated somehow in the disappearance of Herman's wife and son—though why it might be so is a matter of conjecture.

Both events, that is, the decision to stay a while longer in the village and the disappearance of Herman's family, are starkly anomalous ones, and perhaps their affiliation resides in their anomaly. When Herman consults the police in his efforts to find his wife and son, the transgressive character of his situation is brought home to him:

> Aucun villageois n'avait jamais disparu, avait affirmé le gendarme, ce que croyait Herman avec conviction. Mais il était tout autant persuadé qu'une mésaventure de ce genre n'avait jamais frappé un étranger au cœur de l'été, et, comme ils semblaient être, Rose et lui, les premiers à pénétrer dans l'automne, ils faisaient aussi, les premiers, les frais d'une expérience unique. (25)

That unique experience is largely comparable, I think, to our own readerly experience in *Un temps de saison*, for we too are obliged to cast about for meaning in a world whose laws very largely escape us, a world that Marie NDiaye has elaborated with a view toward ensuring that we should be starkly ill-equipped for our task. It is not the first time we have encountered such a world. One thinks of Kafka, of course, and also of Beckett, and perhaps even of Robbe-Grillet. The deliberation with which NDiaye plots Herman's dilemma, and ours, is most striking indeed, however.

More than anything else, her strategy devolves upon a refusal to *tell*. If it becomes clear that Herman has decided to stay in the village during "la mauvaise saison" (94), the reasons for that abrupt and uncanny change in the weather are never provided. That's just *how it is*, as Beckett might put it. That curious state of things in *Un temps de saison* is constructed in the negative mode, upon the shaky narrative ground of the unsaid. We are never told, for example, why Herman's wife and son have disappeared, nor where they have gone. Though we know that his wife is named "Rose," we never learn his son's name, for he is always referred to obliquely, by epithet: "notre fils," "l'enfant," "le petit," "le garçonnet," and so forth (10, 11, 13). When a woman whom

Herman has encountered offers an explanation for the disappearance of Herman's family, the notion that she advances is one that leaves Herman more bewildered still, for that notion is so utterly bald and unexplained that he cannot come to terms with it: "Pourtant Métilde, une seule et unique fois, lâcha un mot qu'Herman tourna et retourna dans son esprit sans parvenir à le lier clairement dans son esprit à son affaire mais qu'elle avait bien prononcé au sujet ce celle-ci. Elle parla de la fréquence des avatars dans cette région humide" (89).

Among all of those instances of the unexplained, one seems to trouble Herman more than the rest. When he goes to ask a neighbor if she has seen his wife and son, she receives him with a prodigious courtesy: "elle ne cessait de lui sourire et de pencher délicatement son front vers lui dès qu'il prenait la parole, dans un mouvement d'exquise urbanité qui déconcertait le professeur" (13). Her manners are "si curieusement raffinées" that Herman is disarmed (14). He encounters the same weird effect when he asks a policeman for help, when he takes his case to the town hall, and when he tells his story to a group of local people at the Hôtel Relais (20, 30, 58). "Ce peuple est si courtois," he muses, "qu'il me tient prisonnier plus sûrement que par des ordres et des interdictions" (31). Clearly enough, that courtesy is something which distinguishes the people of this provincial town from the Parisians to whom Herman is largely accustomed. Yet the politeness that the townspeople display is so exaggerated, so ill-adjusted to circumstance, so singular and insistent, that Herman cannot account for it. Moreover, it seems to have very little to do with the actual inclination of the natives, for they are not especially hospitable folk, nor are they particularly eager to help Herman find his family. As the head of the local Syndicat d'Initiative puts it, "Je connais cette région, on y est d'une politesse extrême mais on n'y rend service que de la manière la plus superficielle aux étrangers" (38-39). In short, Herman finds himself in a world that he cannot fathom, despite his best efforts.[8] That, more than anything else, is what drives *Un temps de saison* along, providing a narrative interest founded upon a failure to understand. Throughout the novel, we readers certainly share Herman's inability to come to grips with that world—unless we are willing to imagine the latter in different terms, putting our usual interpretive categories and strategies of reading into abeyance for a moment, and reading a bit *otherwise*.

In each of her fictions, Marie NDiaye attempts to coax her reader toward that other kind of reading, placing obstacles in her texts that make conventional manners of reading either impractical or outright impossible. Often, those obstacles devolve upon the unsaid, in unexplained and aporetic moments wherein logic breaks down. Such moments are abundant in *La Sorcière*, and many of them cluster around the theme of sorcery itself. Lucie, the novel's protagonist, is by her own account a poor excuse for a witch. She is very much at a loss when it comes to understanding her own powers. And in any case she feels that they are paltry ones when compared to those of her mother. That she has inherited them is something that she never doubts; and she accepts, too, that she must somehow pass them along to her twin daughters, Maud and Lise. NDiaye frames sorcery, then, as something that is matrilineal in character. Yet it is not always transmitted smoothly, for in a curious effect of alternation of generations, the powers that Lucie's mother wields and those which her daughters will eventually exercise are significantly more developed than Lucie's own. Or is it in fact Lucie's own failure—or refusal—to understand her sorcery the very thing that diminishes it? Her mother seems to have no troubles of that sort, in any case, and her daughters are eager to understand, displaying even in the early stages of their apprenticeship "un touchant désir de venir à bout de l'énigme" (10) that astonishes Lucie. Granted that she is the narrator of this tale, however, her own bewilderment with regard to sorcery serves to cast that topos as something well beyond our ken, something that we readers are not equipped to understand, for reasons that are never made explicit.

The fact that witchery should be a closely-guarded secret in *La Sorcière* clearly lends force to that effect. In particular, men must never know what accounts for it, nor how it is transmitted. Indeed when Lucie decides to initiate Maud and Lise, she chooses a site far removed from any fatherly gaze: "Nous nous installions à l'abri des regards de leur père, au sous-sol. Dans cette grande pièce froide et basse, aux murs de parpaings, fierté de mon mari pour son inutilité même (vieux pots de peinture dans un coin, c'était tout), je tâchais de leur transmettre l'indispensable mais imparfaite puissance de ma lignée" (10). It is perhaps not surprising that sorcery should be wrapped in secrecy; the occult, after all, is something *occulted*. Yet Lucie experiences her sorcery as a shameful secret, as something that afflicts her family, rather than as a gift. Lydie Moudileno has argued persuasively that anathema plays a key role in Marie NDiaye's fiction, suggesting that a hereditary stigma is the source of Fanny's difference in *En famille*, and the reason for her exclusion from broader social groups.[9] A similar phenomenon is at work in *La Sorcière*, I think, and one that is just as perplexing in terms of its origins.

The manifestations of sorcery in the novel are likewise baffling, for they are staged nakedly, and with no explanation. Taking a trip on a train with her daughters, for example, Lucie awakes to find that they have left the compartment. Looking out the window and seeing two crows flying alongside the train, she assumes that they are Maud and Lise—and so must we, granted the signs that the text provides (111). Yet the "why" of that incident, and the "how," and the "whereby," are all elided in the narrative, leaving that incident to stand alone, as it were, unbuttressed by conventional logic or causality. Things play out in the same manner when, a bit later, returning on foot to the train station with her daughters, Lucie reaches out to grasp their hands, and encounters feathered wings instead (136). In both cases, the way those events confound Lucie sets the terms for our own reception of them, and announces beyond doubt that the fictional world which NDiaye puts on offer here is fundamentally and crucially different from our own.

One could point out many other instances of that effect in *La Sorcière*. There is the moment when Lucie, during a visit to her mother, discovers a little box with a snail inside it, and realizes that the snail is in fact her father, upon whom her mother has cast a spell (173). One thinks, too, of the way that Lucie's former neighbor Isabelle reappears in the narrative, largely transformed, and now presiding over her own "university" (153). Or of the way that Lise quite naturally "sees" that it will rain tomorrow (50). In every case, those moments come to us nakedly, with no explanation, and we must cope with them as best we can.

Perhaps the most troubling moment among all of the unexplained incidents in *La Sorcière* is the one where an unknown woman greets Lucie as if she knew her—or indeed as if they were somehow related. Furthermore, it is nicely emblematic of the sort of negative narrative that animates the stories NDiaye tells. Lucie encounters that woman, merely in passing and apparently by chance, as she is walking through town, and the entire incident is cast in a patently uncanny mode:

> Je coupai par le parking d'un grand magasin de meubles, traversai un quartier de vieilles maisons aux murs pelés, abandonnées quelques années auparavant, habitées de nouveau, depuis peu, par des familles émigrées de contrées que le Garden-Club proposait souvent à des clients pour leur semaine de rêve.
> —Bonjour, ma soeur, dit gravement, en me croisant, une femme au long vêtement jaune.
> Elle se glissa dans une maison dont le crépi tombé par plaques montrait les pans de bois pourri d'humidité. Notre pavillon du lotissement, là-bas, loin derrière les hangars et les grandes surfaces de bric-à-brac, me parut alors proscrit, confiné ridiculement dans une retraite confortable et funèbre dont Isabelle elle-même, ma véritable soeur, ne sortait pas, tournant et retournant le long de murs invisibles dans sa luxueuse voiture faite pour engloutir des routes sans fin, ou l'arpentant dans ses chaussures de course rebondissantes qui lui donnaient l'air, bien qu'elle fût lourde, de s'apprêter à l'envol.
> —Bonjour, ma soeur, répondis-je, troublée.
> Le vêtement jaune repassa fugitivement derrière la vitre brisée d'une petite fenêtre, au premier étage. J'entendis une voix vive et gaie, puis un grand rire de fillette. Plus haut, du linge mis à sécher dégouttait négligemment sur la façade noircie de fumée et de crasse.
> J'attendis un instant devant la porte, frissonnant dans mon imperméable, espérant vaguement je ne savais quoi—que la femme ressorte, qu'elle m'apostrophe encore de cette manière si agréable, sûre d'elle et désintéressée? Pouvait-elle être, cette étrangère, ma soeur d'une façon ou d'une autre, et comment le savait-elle? (62-63)

Clearly, this event puts Lucie to the test in crucial ways, because it raises a series of questions to which she can find no ready answers. By the same token, it also puts us to the test, because it challenges our interpretive skills, too, and resists our efforts to come to terms with it. Who is this woman who greets Lucie so familiarly? Upon what is the sorority that she invokes founded? Why does Lucie fail utterly to recognize her, whereas she herself seems to recognize Lucie so easily? Several other things may strike us as curious here. The fact that Lucie should respond to the woman's greeting in kind, for instance, and in perfect symmetry, despite the fact that she doesn't recognize her. Lucie's response is significantly delayed, moreover; she seems to utter it well after the unknown woman has disappeared into the house, well after (one might suppose) she has gone out of earshot, for immediately after that utterance (or so it would appear), Lucie perceives the "vêtement jaune" on the second floor of that house.

If Lucie's response, and the recognition of sorority that it articulates, is not based on pure courtesy, what does account for it? Why should she insist upon Isabelle as her "véritable soeur," when they seem to be linked merely by effects of contiguity and situation, rather than anything more profound? Is there a kind of mirror-effect at work here, does Lucie see something in this woman that reminds her of herself? Is it a similarity based merely on gender, or on something more distinctive still, such as ethnicity or race? Certain cues in the text, like the notion that this neighborhood is inhabited by "familles émigrées," like the insistence on the "long vêtement jaune," suggest that the latter might be the case. If so, it is not astonishing that Lucie might be troubled, because, as Michael Sheringham has pointed out, the question of race is one that makes the people in Marie NDiaye's fictional worlds extremely wary, one which they approach obliquely, if at all.[10]

Despite Lucie's hesitation, and despite the chariness that the encounter inspires in her, there is something in the stranger, and in the manner of her salutation, "si agréable, sûre d'elle et désintéressée," that Lucie finds deeply appealing, indeed attractive. Does it reside in that "voix vive et gaie," that quick good humor, immediately reciprocated by a "grand rire de fillette"? Or does it reside in the way that this stranger understands the sorority the she and Lucie share, "d'une façon ou d'une autre," so readily, while Lucie herself remains unenlightened?

In short, everything plays out as if there were some sort of backstory here, one of which Lucie is absolutely ignorant, but which her virtual sister takes for granted. Something is lacking, in other words, something that would serve to explain these events, rationalize them, normalize them, and enable them to take their place in a well-made tale. We recognize, of course, that telling a well-made tale is perhaps not the first among Marie NDiaye's priorities; yet we inevitably recognize, too, that she plays upon our nostalgia for well-made narration, exploiting it and turning it to her advantage in key ways.

That dynamic is very much in evidence in *Autoportrait en vert*, most notably when NDiaye puts the "femme en vert" on stage. NDiaye sketches that latter gesture in increments, which heightens the strangeness of that female figure, for in the first instance she seems more like an apparition than a real human being. Despite the fact that she passed by the woman's house several times a day, the novel's narrator mentions, "il m'a été longtemps impossible de distinguer entre cette présence verte et son environnement" (9). The epithet is a telling one: "cette présence verte" serves neatly to camouflage this figure, whether the backdrop be the banks of the Garonne or the textual economy of *Autoportrait en vert*.

> Je passais donc devant chez elle quatre fois par jour. Et je la regardais et ne la voyais pas, et cependant une obscure insatisfaction m'obligeait à tourner la tête de ce côté, pourtant je ne remarquais rien, jamais, qu'un beau bananier insolite. Je freinais devant cette maison. Je roulais presque au ralenti et pas une seule fois mes yeux n'ont manqué de se poser sur la silhouette immobile, aux aguets, de la femme en vert debout près du bananier largement plus imposant qu'elle, et cela je le sais sans doute possible. (9)

In the first instance, then, the problem devolves upon a failure to *see*. Shirley Jordan has argued that that problem is a common one in Marie NDiaye's fiction, one that moreover inflects the reader's efforts to come to terms with the fictional world in significant ways.[11] In this case, the narrator's failure to see prevents us from seeing; her lack of understanding ensures that we, too, should be very much at a loss to understand. She senses that there is something which draws her to this site in exceptional ways, but she cannot find words for that something:

> Car j'avais, quatre fois par jour, le coeur étreint par quelque chose d'innommable quoique pas absolument mauvais, dès

que j'avais dépassé la ferme au bananier solitaire dans sa cour grillagée, et il avait encore après, sur la route de l'école, dans toutes sortes de jardins de nombreux bananiers sur lesquels mon regard se portait avec la plus grande indifférence. (9)

The fact that the narrator cannot name the phenomenon that grips her underscores its uncanniness, and suggests that there is something subtending it which she has failed to grasp. That anomia continues to afflict the narrator even after she has realized that her gaze had all along been attracted to a "femme en vert" standing next to the banana tree. She wonders if her inability to understand is based, in fact upon an inability to *name*: "Mais j'ai le goût des noms et croyant que mon trouble venait de ce que j'ignorais comment s'appelaient les habitants de la ferme, je me suis renseignée. On m'a dit: 'Oh, là-bas? Ce ne sont que les X . . .'" (9-10). The other people in the village, quite clearly, do not share the narrator's dilemma. They have no trouble discerning the woman in green, nor in naming her. Indeed, for them, she is an unremarkable part if the landscape—a consideration that comments wryly upon the narrator's initial failure to disintricate her from that landscape. Yet the name itself does not serve to enlighten the narrator, for she finds therein nothing that might help her to explain what she cannot grasp: "Il n'y avait rien à en tirer, rien à apprendre, d'un nom comme celui-là" (10). Moreover when, eventually, the woman herself tells the narrator her name, the latter remains mired in skepticism: "Je crois que la femme en vert, qui m'a dit s'appeler Katia Depetiteville, n'est pas Katia Depetiteville" (27). If even the proper name, which Roland Barthes describes as "le prince des signifiants,"[12] cannot be trusted, what remains to the narrator as she labors to discover who this woman in green might be?

It is important to recognize that she is the only one for whom this woman constitutes a problem. Others recognize her easily, and indeed trivially (like her neighbors), or they fail to perceive her at all (like the narrator's own children). Neither the ones or the others are troubled by that woman; in other words, she is the narrator's problem alone. Yet we readers share that problem, inevitably, because we apprehend this fictional world through the narrator's perspective, and because Marie NDiaye has placed this obstacle squarely in our path in the very beginning of her novel, casting it such that our entire reading of the latter be conditioned by that initial interpretive impasse.[13] NDiaye confronts us with something that she challenges us to understand, yet she withholds the narrative tools essential to such an understanding.

The way the narrator labors to understand the woman in green resembles our own efforts, and that analogy is vexed by ironies of different sorts. The questions that she asks herself about that woman are stylized variants of ones that we ourselves might ask. Does the woman in green recognize the narrator when she passes by in her car? Does she wait for her to appear? Is she there, in her yard, when the narrator herself is nowhere near? Is she to be understood as a living, breathing person, or rather as a phantasm serving primarily to make it impossible for the narrator to come to terms with her world? Those questions, and others like them, hover closely around the narrator, and around we readers, too. They cannot be adjudicated in any satisfactory way, and in fact everything points to the impossibility of their resolution. If one is convinced of NDiaye's seriousness of purpose (and I think that conviction is inescapable now, granted the profile of her work as a whole), one is left to conclude that she wagers upon a refusal to tell as a principal clause in the contract that she offers her reader.

A moment at the very end of *Autoportrait en vert* emblematizes that strategy of negative narrative in a lapidary fashion. Gazing out of the window of her house, the narrator sees a group of children in the street, among whom figure two of her own, huddling around something that she cannot initially make out. As she looks more closely however, she sees "une forme sombre, mouvante, nerveuse" (93) in their midst. That sight suffices to throw her into a panic, and she rushes down the stairs and into the street, praying that she will get there in time to avert a disaster which she feels to be imminent. When she arrives, the thing—whatever it may be—has fled, and the children exclaim, "Il était tout noir! Il s'est enfui, il est rapide!" (93). The resolution of that incident makes it clear that we have witnessed a very curious event indeed:

> Les enfants me demandent si je l'ai vu, si je peux leur donner le nom de ce que j'ai vu. Ils tournent vers moi leurs petites figures ensorcelées. Certains ont l'air repus, fatigués, comme des lionceaux après le festin.

>—Il faut rentrer à la maison, dis-je en frissonnant. Non, je ne sais pas comment ça s'appelle. Je crois, dis-je, que ça n'a pas de nom dans notre langue.
> Comme ils se taisent, je reprends:
> —En vérité, je n'ai rien vu, rien du tout. De quoi s'agit-il?
> Alors les enfants se regardent les uns les autres avec sérieux. Leurs lèvres sont très rouges. Sans se consulter davantage, ils prennent le parti de rester silencieux. (93)

Yet in what sense can it be said that we witnessed that event? And what, if anything, has been resolved here? Viewed as a narrative integer, the incident as a whole is vexed by a refusal to tell, a feature which guarantees its aporetic character. Several other considerations are worthy of remark. The uncanniness of the incident is heightened by the fact that it is played out against the backdrop of the familiar, of the everyday. This thing, this *horla*, has appeared precisely where one might least expect it, and that in itself is deeply troubling. The children's bewitched faces and the way the narrator shivers make it clear that something very exceptional has occurred, something well outside of our ken. The unnamable nature of the little beast (if such it be) is the very signature of its otherness, for the fact that language cannot provide a means of designating it ensures that it should escape from us entirely. Moreover, in quite the same perspective, the silence that the children adopt speaks eloquently: clearly enough, speech will not avail here, and some things just cannot be *said*.

It is legitimate to ask why Marie NDiaye might choose to end her novel on a note like this one, which frustrates our desire to *know* in such dramatic fashion. One feature of the incident seems to me unavoidable: if we cannot know, it is quite simply because we have not been *told*. Moreover, that failure to tell is an effect that recurs frequently in NDiaye's writing, a singularly privileged tool in her narrative repertory. In other terms, we may imagine the unnamable little beast that so appalls the narrator in *Autoportrait en vert* as skittering through all of NDiaye's fictions, in a variety of other guises. In each instance, it interrupts patterns of logic and causality, it escapes significantly from reason, and it confounds people's efforts to come to terms with it. Like the weird change of season or the politeness of the townspeople in *Un temps de saison*, like the witchery or the unknown woman who greets Lucie so familiarly in *La Sorcière*, or like the "femme en vert" herself, it is unexplained and unexplainable. Stretching a point, one might suggest what it is not, but what it might actually *be* is anyone's guess. Yet therein, in its patent negativity precisely, lies its power, for it obliges us to approach these texts in new ways, continually reminding us of the way they claim a newness for themselves, encouraging us to see them not only for what they are, but also—and crucially—for what they are *not*.

Marie Cosnay's Characters

CONTEMPLATING the name "Valdemar" in Edgar Allan Poe's "The Facts in the Case of M. Valdemar," Roland Barthes remarks, "Un nom propre doit être toujours interrogé soigneusement, car le nom propre est, si l'on peut dire, le prince des signifiants; ses connotations sont riches, sociales et symboliques."[1] His point is well taken, for the proper noun—and more particularly still the anthroponym—is always overdetermined in fiction, always heavily invested with cratylic value. That being true however, does the anthroponym deserve the honorific that Barthes bestows upon it? For the real "prince of signifiers" is not the anthroponym, I believe, but rather the individual whom that anthroponym identifies, that is to say, the *character*. More than any other element of a fictional world, it is the character who mediates that world for our benefit, who calls out to us, engages our attention, and encourages us to inhabit that world, either briefly or in a more enduring manner. That character mirrors us in strategic ways. He or she is deeply conditioned by everything that we know—and everything that we *think* we know—about human beings in the real world.[2] Certainly, a character is a writer's construction; yet Philippe Hamon points out that a character is also reconstructed by the reader.[3] We may choose to read a character in a variety of ways, our choice devolving both upon local textual features and upon our own desire for meaning.[4] Whatever tack we may take, character remains the surest guarantor of textual accessibility, the one integer in the text that, more than any other, welcomes us and persuades us that we have found a home therein.[5]

In view of those considerations, how curious it is that any writer should fail to exploit the semiotic potential of character to the fullest degree possible. Yet anyone who pays attention to contemporary fiction will be forced to recognize that character is a very embattled and precarious notion these days. Not in every novel that one reads, undoubtedly, but in enough of them to confirm that something is indeed afoot. I do not mean to suggest that the phenomenon is an utterly new one. Even in the early, postwar works of writers such as Nathalie Sarraute and Samuel Beckett, for instance, character was a fragile and tenuous idea.[6] One remembers, too, the way that Edmond Jabès progressively erases character from the world that he creates, and the way that character loses its pertinence in the work of Pierre Guyotat. In the last few years however, the reconsideration of fictional character has attained surprising proportions, and it has manifested itself in a variety of ways. One thinks, for instance, of the kaleidoscopic multiplication and consequent impoverishment of character in Régis Jauffret's *Microfictions*.[7] Or the way that Patrick Deville, in his "equatorial trilogy," has insisted principally upon place, rather than upon person.[8] Or the deliberately, indeed transparently thin representations of humanity who people Antoine Volodine's recent novels, figures like Dondog and Mevlido.[9] Undoubtedly, that phenomenon is not ubiquitous in contemporary fiction, but neither is it merely anecdotal. It limns one of the tactics the novel may exploit as it evolves in our time, and thus it demands that we account for it in some fashion. For my own part, I would like to make a couple of gestures in that direction, concentrating on a novel by Marie Cosnay entitled *Villa Chagrin*.[10]

The incipit presents a world perceived in uncertain focus: "Le 15 novembre je suis restée à la maison, évitant la brume sur l'Adour et le flot cotonneux aperçu la veille vers sept heures quarante cinq quand j'allais dans l'invisible, roulant vers le lieu le plus familier de la ville" (9). The evocation of the fog, the cottony flood, and the invisible suggests that narrative technique will wager on imprecision for effect—and indeed what follows confirms that notion. Chief among the features inflected thereby is character. The humans whom we encounter in *Villa Chagrin* are significantly approximate ones; they are distant from us in time, or they belong to unfamiliar worlds, or they are simply undetailed. Try as one may, it is impossible to *reconstruct* human beings with flesh on their bones here, and our readerly efforts in that direction are blocked at every turn. In fact, it might be argued that the main character of this text is not a person, but rather a river, the Adour, whose very fluidity provides a model of narrative strategy: "Déplacer avec soi quelque chose, aller d'une idée à l'autre, d'une ville à une autre. La mienne: ville où la rivière joint le fleuve qui sur deux cents kilomètres a parcouru jusque-là les monts rougis de bruyère" (10).

Just like the Adour, *Villa Chagrin* follows a meandering course, one that seems inevitable only in retrospect. It is a "loiterly" text, to borrow a term that Ross Chambers coined,[11] one that takes its time, playing out a logic that wagers on the dilatory. Also like a river, the text is composed of multiple currents, some more powerfully narrative than others, some less, some more precisely defined, others more amorphous. Voice is reassuringly singular here: one person says *je* from first page to last in an intercalated narration. We cannot say with any degree of confidence who that speaker is, though textual indices make it clear that she is a female. Other features in the text encourage us to abandon our skepticism outright and identify the narrator with the author. In the interest of theoretical rigor, I feel that it is unwise to do that; and more pragmatically, maintaining the distinction of author and narrator may provide a broader range of interpretive possibility.

If it is difficult to say precisely *who* speaks, the *where* of that speech is relatively easy to locate. It emanates from the right bank of the Adour, in the quarter of Bayonne known as Saint-Esprit, near the prison that lends its name to the novel. Or rather, not so much *near* as *not far*, in a triangulation whose terms are the prison, the Adour, and the narrator's home. "Non loin de la villa Chagrin, à Saint-Esprit, je regardais l'Adour," mentions the narrator (35), adding, a bit further along, "Je viens au coin des boulevards Alsace-Lorraine et Jean-Jaurès, non loin de l'Adour et non loin de chez moi" (56). The distinction between *near* and *not far* may seem overly fine on the face of it, yet I am persuaded that Marie Cosnay offers the "non loin" as a signpost in her text, one that may help us see her poetics of imprecision in a productive light, one that may also enable us to come to terms with the way that she puts traditional notions of literary character on trial. Let us now examine that latter effect in some detail, passing in review the various instances of character in the novel.

Casting about in *Villa Chagrin* for someone who might be thought of as a character, the figure who comes to mind most immediately is

Bram van Velde. Cosnay presents him to us in an offhanded manner, through one of his paintings, as if he himself were immediately and inevitably recognizable:

> *Femme au poteau de torture*, 1914. Bram de Velde. J'habitais dans la ville aux deux cours d'eau, l'un allait à l'océan. Sur le tableau, la femme au poteau de torture avait un corps nu et sombre, sans yeux ni parole. Des cheveux couvrant la face ou pas de face du tout. Un ventre à la lumière. (12)

The fact of the matter is that many people will not recognize Bram van Velde as a historical figure—and that many who do will not be able to situate him with any precision. Never as well known as certain of his contemporaries, such as Picasso, Matisse, or Chagall, Bram van Velde (1895-1981) is a largely forgotten painter by now. Marie Cosnay turns that forgetting to her own purposes, because one of the things that she puts forward in *Villa Chagrin* is an indictment of social and political amnesia. A key moment in the text occurs in 1938, when Bram is imprisoned in Bayonne for the crime of statelessness: "Arrêté à Bayonne, Bram passe devant le tribunal correctionnel. Sujet hollandais revenant d'Espagne, ou presque, sans papiers d'identité, il est condamné à quatre semaines d'emprisonnement" (63). In Cosnay's view, the scandal is absolute, and forgetting it is likewise scandalous—all the more so insofar as power is still free to behave scandalously in the narrative "now," and in particular with regard to undocumented immigrants.[12]

Undocumented immigrants, after all, are those people whose identities are judged to be too *thin*, and that very thinness means that authority can do almost anything at all with them, whether that means detaining them or deporting them, sending them either here, or there. Certainly that is Bram van Velde's fate in *Villa Chagrin*—and not only as an actor in the story that Cosnay tells, but also as an integer in the complex algorithm of storytelling. He bounces back and forth in this text like a pinball. We see him first in 1914, as the author of a painting; then in 1938, when he is arrested and imprisoned; then in 1932, when he and his first wife Lily first went to Spain; then in 1936, when Lily dies and Bram meets Marthe Arnaud; then in 1903, when he was a boy of eight; and again in 1977, 1949, 1895, 1958, and so forth, turn and turn about.[13] In short, authority in *this* text sends Bram van Velde here and there and back again in a strategically interrupted chronology, never focusing on him for very long, nor in one place. I say "strategically" because I am convinced that the apparently uncertain evocation of Bram van Velde serves Marie Cosnay's larger purposes very well indeed, and that he is emblematic of the manner in which she rethinks the principle of literary character.

As Cosnay's narrator gets ready to say something about Bram van Velde and Marthe Arnaud, she takes a moment and excuses herself in advance for being unfair: "il me faut cette pause, j'y ai quelque chose à dire à propos de quoi je sais que je ne serai pas juste car tous les deux, Bram et Marthe, savaient les accidents, les choses fortuites de la vie pas à pas et les choix même pâles et agonisants comme ceux que Bram fit" (54). Several questions might be asked here. Unfair to *whom*, for instance? And with regard to what set of norms? To whom is the narrator appealing in this particular instance? And what, precisely, is at stake here?

Questions such as those can be parsed only in a mobile fashion, that is, in the shift and flow of *Villa Chagrin*; and indeed I have argued that this text wagers heavily on the notion of mobility. One consequence of that wager is that we readers are called upon to appreciate the porosity of diegetic boundaries that we usually think of as far more impermeable. Cosnay invites us to imagine that different worlds collide incessantly here—the world of Bram van Velde, that of the narrator, the writer's world, our own world, for instance—and then recede from each other once again. The first sort of metaleptic gesture is a familiar one no doubt, but the latter sort is a bit more rare in the texts we read these days. And one of the effects that drives it is the deliberate thinning of character. No longer conceived as the convincing guarantors of closely guarded fictional worlds, characters now become shifters enabling the migration from one world to another. In that perspective, traditional features of character—psychological depth, for example, moral coherence, development over time, plausible disposition and motivation—are fundamentally otiose.

Marthe Arnaud is a case in point. Using just a couple of strokes, Marie Cosnay sketches her in an extremely summary fashion. Those two strokes are madness and disaster, the first being an intensely personal phenomenon, the second being broadly social and political. As Cosnay presents her, Marthe is a deeply troubled individual, one whose behavior goes well beyond mere eccentricity: "Marthe poussait parfois des cris étranges, saisie par les souvenirs d'Afrique. Là, devant la promenade et le pont, elle s'accroupit, fait un scandale" (14). More than anything else, it is her squattings in public places that define her, and that designate her as a person unlike others: "De Marthe Arnaud, on dit qu'elle s'accroupissait dans les galeries, en poussant des cris" (27). Cosnay makes it clear that Marthe's madness is not gratuitous; instead, it results from having been witness to a great deal of suffering during her time as a missionary in Africa. She underscores that point again and again in the early pages of *Villa Chagrin*, inscribing it repeatedly under the theme of disaster:

> Marthe avait connu le désastre, quelques formes de désastres. (14)
> Marthe est déjà passée par le désastre. (17)
> Marthe a déjà eu affaire au désastre. Elle revient de Zambie. (20)

Indeed, disaster is a kind of vocation for Marthe: "On peut penser, à propos de Marthe, qu'elle était douée de vie jusqu'au désastre" (27). And more than anything else it is that vocation which lies at the root of her madness.

It is important to recognize the mutual complementarity of the two character traits with which Cosnay endows Marthe Arnaud. In some sense, madness is to the individual subject what disaster is to a society, insofar as both are radical disruptions of the normal order, and both are radically irreducible, too. That analogy obviously intrigues Marie Cosnay, and it allows her moreover to present Marthe in shorthand, as it were. Let me be clear about this. Just like Bram van Velde, Marthe Arnaud was a real person who existed in the referential world. Like any other real person she left traces in that world. Some of those traces are in fact substantial ones. One can find certain of her books, including *Manière de Blanc*, in the catalogue of the Bibliothèque Nationale de France. One can find letters that Bram van Velde wrote to her in an edition of his correspondence prefaced by Jean-Luc Nancy.[14] Yet that referential consistency is not important for Cosnay, a fact that her narrator confirms beyond doubt: "Jusqu'à présent, je n'ai aucun renseignement précis sur Marthe Arnaud, son oeuvre, l'amour qu'elle donnait, la révolte, les accroupissements" (27). Just like Bram,

Marthe's role in this textual economy is merely to put the notion of *distress* on stage, and to make it perform.

Other characters in *Villa Chagrin* are less substantial still than Bram and Marthe. Shortly after introducing those latter figures to us, the narrator presents someone else: "Le 27 août 2003, Pierre M. s'est donné la mort dans son appartement de la rue Saint-Maur. Après un séjour en hôpital psychiatrique, il tenta de trouver le sang" (18). That presentation is a curious one, on the face of it. For one thing, it is extremely laconic. For another, the precision of the chronological reference stands in sharp distinction to the imprecision of the name, as if the one may be told, directly and unproblematically, but the other may not. Throughout *Villa Chagrin*, Pierre M. is a spectral, troubling presence. Indeed from the outset the narrator suggests that she is haunted by him: "Le 6 février 2005, vers 20 heures, le fleuve est éclairé par la lumière de la ville. Une mouette frissonne et le miroitement m'étreint. Sur l'autre rive je reconnais, de façon certain, la démarche de l'ami mort. Le bras gauche fait contrepoids au corps qui va de l'avant. La silhouette disparaît" (18).

We know very little about Pierre M., apart from his distress. One thing we do know is that he writes, and that he finds writing difficult: "Je ne peux pas écrire beaucoup, écrivait Pierre M. mon ami dans la nuit du 26 au 27 août, je suis trop fatigué. L'écriture tremblait. Il est mort au matin" (42). His appearances in the text are very rare (he is mentioned by name only three times, and the narrator refers to him on another occasion without naming him explicitly [15]), but clearly he means a great deal to the narrator. The epithets she uses to designate him—"l'ami mort," "mon ami"—confirm that abundantly. In fact, she identifies so closely with him that his death is bound up in her own. Shortly after seeing Pierre M.'s ghost, the narrator remarks, chillingly: "J'ai vu, concrète, ma mort" (18). All of those considerations notwithstanding, Pierre M. remains an extremely spare figure in the text, one whose claims to characterhood are flimsy at best.

Flimsier still are the claims staked by "Jean-Claude." He appears once and once only in *Villa Chagrin*, and I mention him as a limit case of the phenomenon that interests me here. "Jean-Claude a coupé les branches du mûrier qui poussaient chez les voisins," remarks the narrator in the liminal moments of her story (10). Where he comes from, we have no idea. And he sinks like a stone immediately thereafter, never to resurface. Is he merely part of the scenery? Is he bound up in some sort of *effet de réel* that comes and goes in the blink of an eye? Does he have any role to play, other than pruning the mulberry tree? In view of the kinds of questions that Jean-Claude's appearance elicits, and of the way that we thrash about in an effort to answer those questions, one thing that can most certainly be said about him is that he puts us on notice with regard to the fragility and the tenuous quality of character in *Villa Chagrin*.

Examples of intertextual allusion are very few and far between in Marie Cosnay's writing, and this text is no exception to that general rule. It is all the more surprising thus to see Ovid mentioned here on several occasions, and I wonder if it is not legitimate to consider him, too, in a discussion of Cosnay's poetics of character. Like most of the other characters, the narrator invokes him in the early pages of the text. "Le 18 janvier je marchais jusqu'au fleuve, de loin dans la brume j'ai cru des flocons de neige, les mouettes allaient d'un vol léger, écrirait Ovide, le ciel et la mer étaient des surfaces de miroirs vastes, lisses" (13). She mentions him on three other occasions, suggesting each time that Ovid would describe Bram van Velde as being deficient in "le suc du corps" (25, 38, 50). A couple of things might be noted here. On the one hand, the allusions to Ovid function as part of a phenomenon I noted a moment ago, the invitation to erase the distinction of author and narrator. Marie Cosnay is a classicist by training, and she has in fact translated Ovid's *Metamorphoses*. On the other hand, in each of those latter three moments the text focuses squarely upon how very disincarnate Bram has become, how emaciated he has become, how very insubstantial he appears. In other terms, if Ovid has a role to play here, it is one that seems to be involved in the interrogation of character.

When Samuel Beckett makes his appearance in *Villa Chagrin*, it is somewhat less surprising. Like Ovid, Beckett is explicitly affiliated with Bram van Velde. In this case, however, that affiliation is less arbitrary, because Beckett knew Bram van Velde personally, and admired his painting. He devoted several essays to Bram van Velde,[16] one of which Marie Cosnay quotes in the epigraph to *Villa Chagrin*. In the passage that Cosnay cites, Beckett complains of the difficulty he encounters when trying to write on the painting of Bram van Velde and his brother, Geer. Patently enough, that epigraph puts the reader on notice that writing and its vexations will be a major theme in the book; yet in a perspective a bit broader still, what is really at issue is the problem of representation. And indeed, in both of the instances when Beckett reappears, that problem is absolutely paramount. "Au sujet de Bram, à la place de Bram, Beckett écrit: 'Je ne peux voir l'objet pour le représenter, parce que je suis ce que je suis,'" says the narrator (61), remarking a bit further along, "'Que reste-t-il de représentable si l'essence de l'objet est de se dérober à la représentation?' écrivait Beckett à propos de Bram van Velde" (74). There is an interesting palimpsestic relation here, as writing is layered upon writing. But the real pungency resides in the vexed question of representation, and especially the representation of people. Few writers have practiced the thinning of literary character more programmatically than Beckett, and the fact that he should have a role to play here strikes me as utterly appropriate on a variety of levels.

Two other figures in *Villa Chagrin* bear mention, and both of them (unlike the ones I have discussed thus far) are anonymous. The first of them appears on the very first page of the novel, but in an extremely oblique manner: "Le 17 novembre j'en suis venue au vif du sujet. La question, je la poserai, ai-je dit en me levant du bon pied. *Il* est quelque part en Bulgarie (il a fallu que je regarde sur la carte où était Sofia exactement, de l'exact je n'avais qu'un enchevêtrement de routes, de noms oubliés), et je ne *le* vois pas" (9-10). We have no way of knowing who this might be, of course, yet the italicization of the pronouns leads us to suspect his importance and whets our curiosity. Thereafter, Marie Cosnay plays squarely upon our desire to know, causing her narrator to dole out information little by little. When the narrator remarks that she had come upon a photo misplaced by "l'homme que j'aime" (12), our tendency is to infer those two otherwise unidentified male figures are one and the same person. A bit further along, the narrator mentions him again: "L'homme que j'aime va de ville en ville. Il fonde les libertés sur le noyau des phrases, leur grammaire, sur le temps offert d'un mot à l'autre, sur le déroulement où mourir n'est pas" (15). But it is not until two thirds of the way through the text that the initial sighting of this character can be confirmed as such: "L'homme que j'aime traversait les ponts et les villes, Sofia, Kyoto, Moscou, Los Angeles, Bologne" (49).

The epithet by which the narrator designates this man is an eloquent one; yet it tells us more about the narrator than about the man himself, as if he were absolutely tributary to her. She is aware that she has not described him in any sort of detail—she admits as much, in fact. But as other elements of his very sparse portrait emerge, points of clear correspondence between them become apparent:

> Derrière la porte l'homme que j'aime se tient. Je n'ai rien dit de lui, si ce n'est pas qu'il fait le tour des villes suivant le ruban de l'eau entre les rues étroites ou bien contournant les grandes épingles des vastes surfaces bleues surmontées d'un pont inattendue, rouge, laid ou ancien, qui forme des arcs sous quoi vont les péniches. Si ce n'est qu'il affirme ce que peuvent les mots assemblés. Si ce n'est qu'il a vu une fois la femme. (29)

Like the narrator, he spends his time in cities traversed by rivers, he knows the value of words, he has *seen* a woman. He is almost never wholly and literally present, he is almost always elsewhere and separated from the narrator, whether on another continent or simply behind the door. There are only a few exceptions, including a moment when the narrator gazed into his eyes: "Il est arrivé que mon visage se reflète dans la prunelle de l'homme que j'aime. Cela m'est arrivé" (61). That moment confirms the idea that curiously specular relations prevail between the narrator and this man, for it is not him that she sees, but rather herself.

One wonders if that was not the very person she has been looking for all along. And perhaps that man provides the most reliable mirror that the narrator encounters. For her other engagements with mirrors serve merely to confound her or to alienate her from herself. "J'avançais pour sortir. Soudain, quelqu'un fut devant moi, avec toutes ses dents, j'hésitais sur le genre, c'était *elle*: elle était prête à mordre ou à bondir, elle venait sur moi, elle y était" (22). The other woman that the narrator sees, pure projection, is the final character whom I would like to examine. She is marked by her difference, a difference that survives largely intact, even when the narrator realizes that she has glimpsed herself in a mirror: "Puis je me reconnus dans ce miroir qui au fond de la pièce gigantesque semblait mener à la sortie. J'avais vu quelqu'un, presque une femme, laide et peut-être morte et grimaçante" (23). In each case, that other woman is marked by ugliness, or by death, or by both at once. That is true regardless of the specular vehicle, whether it be a home movie that her father took of her when she was ten years old, wherein she sees "une presque morte" who moreover carries the contagion of death (24), or in a photograph of her dressed as a clown: "de quelle laideur je suis, de quelle profonde laideur" (24).

Another incident provides a very troubling and uncanny confrontation with that other woman, reversing the terms of the mirror scene, as if in a looking-glass world. Contemplating some photographs, the narrator first comes upon images of the Adour, then a series of photos of a person she takes to be herself:

> 2 mars 2005. Dans une des chambres de l'homme. La photographie en noir et blanc du pont sur l'Adour qui rase le cadre. Les nuages sur l'image, au-dessus de l'eau, sont si blancs, on dirait qu'ils furent épurés. Je m'attache là, je m'attache à l'image, au ciel et au fleuve saisis et je sais ce qu'il va m'en coûter. Je soulève doucement l'image. Ponts, ciels, villes. Les quinze photos qui suivent sont des portraits de femme. Je la reconnais tout de suite, c'est bien moi, elle appelle, de la bouche, l'homme qui regarde. J'appelle. Je la reconnais tout de suite, elle est visible dans le cadre, les yeux sont grands ouverts, elle voit, elle est vue. C'est moi, dans le cadre le l'homme. (48-49)

As bracing and reassuring as that recognition may be, the narrator quickly realizes how deeply mistaken she is, because, quite simply, "*Il ne m'a jamais prise en photo, en portrait, quinze fois*" (49, emphasis in original). She is left to gaze at "l'image quinze fois répétée de moi qui ne suis pas" (50), with no means of resolving the dilemma, one way or another.

That moment is an emblematic one in the general economy of *Villa Chagrin*, and more particularly with regard to Marie Cosnay's poetics of character. First and foremost, it serves to remind us that in fiction it is *never* the "same person," it is *always* someone else, whether that "same person" be someone who exists (or has existed) in the phenomenal world, or someone invented out of whole cloth. Characters are arbitrary, consensual, and contingent; their existence depends upon our willingness to imagine them. They are matters of contract, a contract that we rarely examine, so obvious and self-evident it seems to us. In such a perspective, any character at all is inherently and necessarily "thin."

Yet something else is going on in this text, I think, something deeply involved with representation and its conditions of possibility. For despite their thinness, characters are also, I am firmly persuaded, the "princes of signifiers," exceptionally privileged objects among the many constitutive objects one might name in any literary text. Pondering the way that Beckett addresses the problem of representation in his essay on Bram van Velde's painting, and more especially Beckett's conclusion that he cannot *see* the object because he himself is what he is, the narrator turns the table and tries to imagine what the object might say: "L'objet dirait, lui: Je ne peux pas être représenté, car je ne suis pas ce que je suis, ou je suis le contraire" (61). Her remark opens onto a field of speculation toward which many other elements *Villa Chagrin* point, and none more urgently than the characters. For all of those characters, whatever other role they may be called upon to play, put in evidence an absolutely fundamental gesture of fiction, that is, the way it always directs us, either suavely or more brutally, either subtly or more overtly, from the *same* to the *other*.

Bernard Noël's Trips

BERNARD NOËL'S *Un trajet en hiver* (2004) presents itself as a travel diary, recounting a series of thirty-four trips on the train and one very brief visit to the Buffet de la Gare, in Lausanne. That simple description is reductive, of course, and perhaps not entirely faithful to the purposes that animate the text. For *Un trajet en hiver* is not strictly speaking a diary: there is no question of a *daily* practice of writing; there are no temporal indications prefacing the entries; and there is no effort to seize events of personal life that may have occurred apart from those train trips. Yet Bernard Noël is on record as claiming that all of his books may be read like fragments of a diary, whatever other appearance they may offer,[1] and this particular text flirts with that genre quite openly, in provocative ways. As to travel, that is perhaps not the most crucial concern of this book. In other words, it is not travel as such that interests Noël here, but rather the ways in which we choose to furnish the curiously suspended time of a train ride.[2]

For his part, Noël boards the train with plenty of material to occupy his time (newspapers, magazines, books), and with the best of intentions. Though he reads in the train, and his readings are often interesting ones (Peter Handke, Julio Cortázar, Jean Genet, William Burroughs, Francis Ponge, for instance), his mind quickly wanders. Sometimes, it's the physical landscape that distracts him, whizzing by at breakneck speed in contrast to his own immobility. More often still, it's the human landscape that grabs his attention, and more precisely the conversations of his fellow-travelers. Eavesdropping may be a guilty pleasure, but it's an undeniable pleasure nonetheless. It is difficult to resist in a confined, public space like that of a train, where one's own anonymity and that of others rub elbows. The temptation is particularly imperious when one begins to suspect that each conversation constitutes a story—and when the listener himself is someone who makes his living telling stories: "Difficile de rester dans ton livre quand il n'y a qu'à prendre un récit en train de se faire" (29). That latter phrase, *un récit en train de se faire*, with its conspicuous paronomasia and its equally obvious metatextual intent, articulates efficiently what is at stake in this text, wherein Bernard Noël issues an invitation to the voyage recalibrated to suit the spirit of what passes, *now*, for our own moment in time.

In one of the conversations that Noël overhears, a woman speaks about what is, for her, the chief pleasure of travel: "Ce que j'aime en voyage, c'est de me dire en regardant le paysage: y'a des gens qui vivent ici, moi pas, et ces gens n'auront jamais la moindre idée de l'endroit où je vis" (91). If Noël chooses to put that utterance to use in the explicit of his text, rather than any other, it is perhaps because it encapsulates much of what *Un trajet en hiver* has to say about travel and its uses. In the first instance, the landscape that one observes—both outside the speeding train and inside, importantly—is fundamentally *human*, rather than merely geographic. Furthermore, one is free to look without being seen. In corollary, one may comment abundantly upon what one observes, without divulging any more than one may wish about oneself. "Je n'aime pas les confidences, ni exhiber directement mon intimité," Noël remarks in a conversation with Jean-Marie Le Sidaner ("La Vie l'écriture" 163); and *Un trajet en hiver* is a text that does not easily surrender its "intimacy," its "privacy." Or at least not *directly*. Take the example of the woman whom Noël overhears: what she says about how she travels tells us more than a little, if *indirectly*, about who she is. By the same token, the details that Bernard Noël chooses to note in the account of his travels that he puts on offer tell us a great deal about who he is—yet we "overhear" those details for the most part, instead of being told about them more directly. In that sense, it is useful to recall Marc Augé's insight about travel in the Parisian subway system. Therein, he argues, we are largely anonymous beings; we constantly brush up against others, but never meet them; our experience of travel is shared with other travelers, without any real reciprocity. Yet that apparent lack of engagement with others masks a very real engagement with ourselves, Augé argues: "Surely it is our own life that we confront in taking the subway" (*In the Metro* 9).

Augé suggests moreover that people using the subway are especially attentive to time and space,[3] and the same can undoubtedly be said of train travelers. Often, those categories come into play in the tyrannical teleology of travel. For most travel is end-loaded: one travels in order to get somewhere, and the trip itself assumes importance principally through its end result. Bernard Noël is looking for another way to think about travel, one where the most ordinary reflections become a *train of thought*, something that serves to furnish time and space significantly. One such reflection occurs early on in *Un trajet en hiver*, as Noël eavesdrops on a fellow passenger:

> Tu as du mal à distinguer les derniers mots: l'effort de l'écoute t'a mis en retard sur la suite, qui est d'ailleurs perdue dans le bruit. Tu ouvres le journal acheté tout à l'heure, tu n'y trouves rien qui te retienne. Tu vois passer une colline, un clocher pointu à quatre pans, cinq vaches blanches avec des taches noires, des maison basses et si petites qu'on dirait des cabanes, sept vaches rousses, des haies ébouriffées, un château avec deux tourelles, des files d'arbres, une chapelle en ruine dont le clocher décapité est assailli par le lierre, un feu dans un champ, un gros nuage, le coude d'une rivière, le train s'engage sous un pont à l'instant où une camionnette passe dessus. . . . (8)

Time passes here, spaces passes too, and each inflects the other. Noël is bound up in that passing, of course, and the present tense of his narration testifies to the way in which he seeks to account for it. Yet that present is precisely what escapes from him: "Maintenant. La vitesse te prive de ton maintenant, car ce que tu regardes maintenant n'est déjà plus là, et il n'en reste rien. Ainsi la colline boisée qui est là n'est plus là quand tu écris son apparition" (43).

Clearly, the way the present escapes from us is something that we can observe in other circumstances, not merely during a train trip. But Noël suggests that the phenomenon is particularly evident during travel, granted the suspension of certain other activities and concerns that typically cause us to focus on something beyond the moment at hand. When we travel, we may be struck by fresh ways of looking at the present, as elusive as it may be. We may recognize, for instance, that we apprehend the present in an interrupted manner, rather than in what we assume to be a continuous flow.[4] And that is also true of the way we attempt to account for the present, grasping at chunks of it as it whizzes past, and recording them as best we may. Noël underscores that process, inscribing it in the very structure of this text: *Un trajet en hiver* is insistently interrupted, episodic, and fragmentary. It wagers upon accretion in its efforts to put on display a convincing account of ordinary human experience.

Curiously, it is the very banality of the experience he witnesses that intrigues Bernard Noël, and he focuses upon that phenomenon very closely indeed. That kind of sustained attention is required here, because daily life has a fundamental opacity to it, being so apparently obvious and familiar that we may fail to see it. Noël suspects that such familiarity masks things largely unanticipated, however: "L'habitude est un territoire sur lequel peut advenir un étonnement inhabituel," he suggests (49). Of course, he is not the first French writer to interrogate the banality of quotidian experience. One thinks of Georges Perec's interest in what he called the *infra-ordinary*; or of Jean-Philippe Toussaint's early books; or indeed of Christian Oster, who wrote a novel whose heroine was a common housefly.[5] Each of those writers seeks to shift traditional literary values such that importance might be found in the trivial, and that what we normally take to be the endotic might prove, upon very careful inspection, to be exotic. The originality of Noël's approach lies in an intense theatricalization of the quotidian, in the way that he puts everyday life on stage and causes it to perform.

The conversations that Noël overhears are an important part of that process—and of course their dialogical structure corresponds closely to theater's fundamental form. Moreover, he invites us to consider those conversations much like spectators at a theatrical performance consider a play, insofar as the way that he listens to what others are saying is always framed by the gaze that he casts upon them. So much so that it is difficult to distintricate listening and seeing.[6] The conversations hinge upon many things: politics, sex, money, gossip. They are the kind of idle chat we engage in to pass the time, in order not to feel time passing; and they are too ordinary to leave a trace in the normal course of events—unless one happens to be sitting next to a writer. Noël is intrigued by the way in which these brief glimpses of individual lives suggest far broader panoramas of life, adumbrating inferential possibilities that ramify almost infinitely, and allowing him to exercise his writerly imagination. He ponders the paradoxes of distance and proximity that train travel offers, how one is both close to one's fellow travelers and apart from them, how one can engage with them without really becoming engaged. Most of all perhaps, he is seduced by the ease and apparent naturalness of his own listening and looking: "Tu entrentends comme tu entrevoies" (41).

Upon occasion, the narrative interest of these conversations is not immediately apparent. Such is the case, for instance, when he overhears people talking about buying televisions and washing machines (8). At other times, the brief chunks of conversation that he seizes suggest that they have been abstracted from far vaster and more compelling stories, as when Noël overhears a young woman talking about an older man who had raped her when she was a teenager (29). Still other instances devolve upon events that are ordinary enough, but that cause Noël to reflect upon literature and its uses, generally in an ironic mode: "La seconde préfère dormir que lire," remarks one passenger to another. "Je l'oblige à lire une heure par jour. Hier, je l'envoie lire dans sa chambre et, un moment après, voilà qu'elle me crie; Maman, qu'est-ce que ça veut dire, orgasme?" (13). There is something for everyone here, including us academics—though we may find that the portrait of an academic that Noël limns cuts a bit close to the bone:

> Tu ne vois pas ton voisin de devant, mais sa voix déborde, envahit ton espace. On dirait qu'il tient une conférence alors qu'il ne s'adresse qu'à son voisin—ou sa voisine.
>
> —L'homme n'a rien produit d'immortel. Dans ce qui a survécu le plus longtemps, mais ça n'est que cinq ou six millénaires pour les monuments, beaucoup moins pour la littérature, oui, même dans ce qui a survécu, quelque chose est mort, qui est le sens. Et voilà ce qui nous retient, cette mort, car elle s'alimente de notre volonté de retrouver le sens, c'est-à-dire la circulation, c'est-à-dire la vie. . . .

> Le train démarre avec des crissements métalliques qui couvrent la voix, ou plutôt qui en couvrent le sens. Tu comprendras plus tard que ce monsieur va faire une conférence à l'université. (73)

That narration in the second person singular fosters an illusion of intimacy and complicity. For the *tu* is in a sense transparent: we realize that the narrator is speaking to himself, but we allow ourselves to imagine that he might as well be speaking to us. Moreover, the interrupted, dilatory rhythm of the narration is also nicely calculated to put us at ease. *Un trajet en hiver* is an example of what Ross Chambers has called a "loiterly" text.[7] Bernard Noël takes care to call our attention to the loiterly character of his project, foregrounding it from time to time in the conversations that he surprises and in his comments thereupon. "Le temps change de forme quand on n'est pas pressé," says one woman whom Noël overhears (90), and what she remarks about the trip in the train might equally be remarked about the writing of this text—and indeed about our reading of it, as well. Chambers argues that the choice to favor the dilatory, or the digressive, is in fact a critical gesture with regard to a more conventionally linear narrative technique (15), and Bernard Noël underscores the critical dimension of his own project again and again, sometimes subtly, sometimes more imperiously.

A good deal of that critical discourse is bound up in a meditation upon words and things. Through the gaze that he casts upon the landscape passing by, Noël becomes conscious of the way words enable us to come to terms with things: "Je vois tout, penses-tu, mais l'attention se limite aux choses que j'ai le temps de nommer. Le monde est trié par les mots" (8). Indeed, he decides, it is the verbal that enables the phenomenal to come into being—at least in the way that we perceive and understand the phenomenal. "Le monde n'est le monde qu'à force de choses nommées," he muses, "autrement il ne serait qu'un entrepôt" (12). That notion is a crucial one for him, because it allows him to focus on the quiddity of words themselves. Listening in on a conversation between a man and an elderly woman, it is that aspect of words which strikes Noël:

> Le mot "dedans" te fait dresser l'oreille.
> —On ne voit pas de bestiaux.

—Ils sont dedans.
Ton attention ne s'est éveillée qu'à ce dernier mot, mais tu avais enregistré son contexte. L'étrange est que, tout de même, ayant associé "bestiaux" et "dedans," tu as cru que ce dedans désignait l'intérieur du train. (75-76)

This moment is interesting for a variety of reasons; but perhaps its most interesting feature is the way that it highlights the tension between words *as things* and the ways words represent things. On the one hand, it is the word *dedans* itself that strikes Noël, in its very quiddity. On the other hand, it is the referential function of the word that strikes him. The former is perhaps more immediately reliable than the latter, because Noël is quick to point out the way he misinterprets the word's referent, and the strangeness of that misinterpretation. Yet that misinterpretation may lead to another consideration, likewise devolving upon words and the way we use them to locate ourselves in the world. For what is *inside* and what is *outside*, here? More particularly, where is Bernard Noël during the trip he takes on the train? Is he inside, by virtue of being in a train car, gazing out at the passing landscape? Is he outside, with regard to the conversations that he overhears and the lives to which those conversations testify? Is he both at once, or one after the other, in function of shifting perspective? However one chooses to answer those questions, it quickly becomes apparent that much of the problem is bound up in language and its uses. It also becomes clear that Noël regards writing—in one of its aspects, at least—as the process of creating a particular space, one with recognizable boundaries, defined by language.

Un trajet en hiver deals significantly, thus, with language as a daily practice, one that we take for granted and consequently rarely examine. It draws our attention to what we hear when we're not listening, or barely listening. Yet it also focuses upon writing, and particularly upon writing as a daily practice, as a habit, as a discipline. Noting down the conversations he hears around him, Noël thinks about his own motivations, about what impels him to write, rather than to read or to stare out of the window, for instance. He wonders, too, if his gestures are literary in character, or if they're merely, well, *writing*. He is convinced that writing, in our time, is a useless activity, one that people pay very little attention to, "Mais que devient cette inutilité, quand elle est un travail ordinaire?" (69).

Reading Peter Handke in the train, Noël comes upon a passage where Handke mentions that he is about to undertake "un travail littéraire, comme d'habitude" (9). That formulation strikes Noël as very curious indeed, something that demands to be closely examined and parsed with regard to his own circumstances:

> Tu relis les six lignes, tu les relis encore et toujours tu t'arrêtes à "comme d'habitude."
>
> Tu ne penses qu'à ça, ce qui veut dire que si tu penses, c'est aussitôt à cela que tu penses. . . . En fait, ton voyage est à présent aimanté par ces mots-là au point que tu te regardes voyager pour voir comment, peut-être, agit dans cet exercice la contamination de l'habitude. (10)

He will return to that notion again and again in *Un trajet en hiver*, understanding it in different ways and putting that understanding to different purposes. Traveling is clearly a habitual behavior for him, and that habit is reflected in the iterative, accretive structure that he has chosen for his text. Yet habit, just like banality, has a tendency to render experience transparent and insignificant, making it difficult to assess. All the more crucial, reasons Noël, to focus precisely upon the way that habit itself colors habitual behavior. Being a writer, the tools most readily available to Noël when he undertakes that examination are those of writing—and there, his meditation becomes considerably more complicated, because writing, for him, is yet another habitual behavior. More complicated, but richer as well, because that is where this text takes on its greatest pungency, as Bernard Noël turns the notions of habit and writing back upon themselves in order to understand what it means to be a writer.

Traveling in the train, he watches himself carefully, recording his impressions in writing, and focusing at the same time precisely upon that writing as habitual behavior. "Mais qu'est-ce que l'habitude quand on écrit?" he asks himself. "Est-elle ailleurs que dans le geste, la posture, puisque l'enjeu n'est jamais le même . . ." (10). In a dynamic of extraordinary cathexis, every other aspect of his experience turns toward that writing and the inquiry that impels it. That is even true of phenomena in the world outside of the train. On one occasion, for instance, observing that it is snowing outside,

Noël remarks, "Tu aimerais que neigent des mots, plutôt que de te demander encore et encore ce qu'est 'un travail littéraire, comme d'habitude'" (17-18). Yet in a real sense, it is snowing words *inside*, as Noël grapples with writing and habit. On certain other occasions, his thoughts are prompted by considerations that are more obviously logical. Reading Julio Cortázar, for example, Noël registers the way that writer stakes a claim as an "amateur" of literature, while nevertheless admiring literary "professionals." That passage enables Noël to view his central concern in sharper focus. "Le professionnel," he muses, "est évidemment celui qui est capable d'entreprendre un travail littéraire, comme d'habitude" (20).

All of this serves to create a texture of unrelenting specularity in *Un trajet en hiver*. During his trips in the train, Bernard Noël takes the opportunity to ponder writing *as writing*, that is, in its raw form, as a behavior, largely apart from the purposes one usually imagines for it: "Ces notes ne sont ni pour penser ni pour se souvenir," he remarks. "Elles ne s'accompagnent d'aucune représentation. Quand tu notes 'maison,' c'est la forme d'une maison. Sans plus" (41). In that very perspective, when Noël overhears a woman speaking nearby, he seizes her words in a largely decontextualized manner, for he has become aware of her speech in midstream. He is not aware of what she is speaking about, but he recognizes nevertheless that what she says is closely attuned to the way his own thinking is developing:

> Derrière toi, une femme parle depuis un bon moment. Ton oreille a dû s'accorder peu à peu à sa voix si bien que tu distingues ses mots après n'avoir entendu qu'une rumeur:
> —J'élimine, je crée les conditions du rien et dans ce rien, j'attends. Il y a trop de choses. Faut déblayer. Déblayer tout ce qui a l'air d'avoir un sens, mais qui n'en a que l'apparence. Je le cherche, le sens. Je sais bien que la parole ne peut surgir que quand il n'y a plus rien. (26-27)

The fact that the woman's remark hinges on the notion of the *rien* adds pungency to this moment, because, like Mallarmé, like Beckett, Bernard Noël is fascinated by nothingness, by emptiness, and by the manner in which we struggle to represent that topos in language that often seems unequal to our expressive needs. Not to put too fine a point on it, what Noël hears is a reflection of his own reflection.

That doubly specular effect is moreover an insistent one in this text, just as if Noël were traveling in a carnival funhouse instead of a train. Because one thing always mirrors another here, wherever one turns. Sometimes those moments are framed explicitly and apparently simply, as when an elderly woman extracts a compact mirror from her handbag and looks at herself in it. Yet the simplicity of that gesture reveals itself as substantially more complex when one realizes that the way Noël looks at that woman gazing at herself is precisely analogous to the way he invites us to look at *him* as he asks himself what it means to be a writer. At other times those specular moments, though brief, are patently a bit more complicated. "Ta voisine se lève," notes Noël at the end of his account of a trip from Paris to Toulouse, "elle est moins belle que son reflet" (73). The counterintuitive character of his remark is striking, but it is also powerfully suggestive in its promotion of *reflection* as a manner of seeing and understanding.

Perhaps that is the chief advantage of these trips in the train, the way they enable Noël to see things in reflection, and thus in reciprocity—that is, in the way the reflected image comments upon what it reflects. "Dès que le train sort de la ville, il entre dans la nuit. La vitre devient aussitôt un miroir dans le fond duquel s'agitent parfois des lumières. On dirait qu'il y a dans ce miroir un plafond, qui reflète l'intérieur du wagon en mettant son contenu sens dessus dessous. Cela t'environne d'un état de suspension que tu voudrais prolonger . . ." (82). Travel provides such a state of suspension, of course, as long as one travels with an open mind and a loiterly spirit. Yet so does writing, Noël argues, when one considers it very closely indeed, focusing on it as a behavior, rather than upon its notional purposes. To his way of thinking, that insight is a crucial one for a writer, and a liberating one, too. Looking over his shoulder as it were, watching him reflect upon writing throughout *Un trajet en hiver*, watching the way his writing mirrors him too, we readers may come to understand that Bernard Noël is offering us a state of creative suspension closely similar to the one that he enjoys. Among the many reciprocities that he limns here, that is surely the most profoundly invigorating one, and the most deeply reflective.

Jean Rolin's Mourning

A TASTE for lands far from Metropolitan France marks Jean Rolin's writing, whether it be the Congo (*L'Explosion de la durite*, 2007), Turkmenistan and the Australian Outback (*Un chien mort après lui*, 2009), the Strait of Hormuz (*Ormuz*, 2013), or the Caroline Islands (*Peleliu*, 2016). He indulges that taste in *Savannah* (2015), an account of a trip he took to that American city in remembrance of a previous trip in the company of his friend, the photographer Kate Barry. An elegiac tone echoes throughout the book, for between those two trips, Kate Barry died. The gaze that animates *Savannah* is a curious one insofar as it is always double, for Rolin is constantly reading his new experience through his former experience, reinterpreting the latter in the light of his new circumstances. He puts memory to the test as he revisits a place where he had been happy, without realizing it at the time. He now considers that happiness well after the fact, as something that *must have been*—an effect that serves to confirm Rolin's reputation as a "melancholic" writer.[1]

Rolin deliberately retraces his former trip in his present one; and he is careful to link the second trip to the first through precise temporal and spatial references, as if the only way to guarantee the authenticity of his present experience were by virtue of its fidelity to past experience. Thus, he mentions that in the plane during that first trip, Kate was reading a copy of *Libération* dated August 26, 2007, and shortly thereafter he remarks that seven years after that, "presque jour pour jour," he once again takes a flight from Paris to Atlanta, en route for Savannah (15-17). Thus too he remarks, "Le mercredi 27 août 2014, à l'aéroport d'Atlanta, j'ai pu changer ma réservation pour le trajet suivant et emprunter presque aussitôt un vol à destination de Savannah" (18), carefully certifying that date, as it were, further along in the text when he mentions that Kate had signed a guest book in Milledgeville, Georgia with the notation "27 August 2007" (85).

As to spatial references, Rolin visits and remarks upon several different places: Atlanta, for instance, and Macon, and Milledgeville in Georgia, and Hilton Head Island, in South Carolina. But Savannah is clearly the place that is the most important to him, the most heavily charged with memory and meaning. He recalls in particular the moment when he and Kate arrived at their motel, a moment that Kate had filmed. Indeed, she had filmed more or less constantly during their trip, and a bit compulsively, as Rolin suggests early in his text (8). Later, he speculates that she behaved that way neither for the pleasure of it, nor in view of some future film project, but rather in response to a psychic impulse that was, for her, irresistible (103). Whatever her motivation, the film record that Kate left now provides Rolin with a map of their trip to Savannah in 2007, a map that he follows very closely in this second trip. Or as closely as he can, for it shortly becomes apparent to him that many things have changed between then and now:

> Lorsque après la mort de Kate j'ai décidé de retourner à Savannah, je me suis efforcé de retrouver sur Internet les coordonnées du motel où ces images avaient été filmées. Mais de cette recherche, il ressortait qu'il avait disparu, entre-temps, sans laisser d'autres traces que les commentaires nettement défavorables de ses derniers usagers, plusieurs années auparavant.
>
> Sur place, il s'est avéré que l'établissement le plus proche du précédent, et celui qui présentait le plus de ressemblance avec lui, était le motel Best Western situé à l'intersection de Bay Street et de Martin Luther King Jr. Avenue. (23)

Change is often vexatious, of course, but most especially so when the place that *should have been there* can no longer be found, and thus cannot testify to that which *was*. The rule of the game insofar as place is concerned is a fairly simple one: if the remembered place has disappeared, one will choose to visit the place that seems to be the closest to it, both spatially and affectively. Thus, throughout Rolin's account of his new visit, he notes a series of *displacements*, clinamens of a sort which serve to remind us that change is inevitable, however fervently one might wish it were not so. In the general economy of the text, those moments would seem negligible, were it not for the fact that they underscore, indirectly and mutely, the principal change that has occurred between the first visit to Savannah and the second: the fact that Kate has died.

Time and space provide Rolin with reference points as he charts his new itinerary through the American South, then, and so do the films that Kate took. Yet there is still another thread that he follows, one provided by "le goût de Kate pour la personne et l'oeuvre de Flannery O'Connor" (11). Rolin recalls that soon after meeting Kate, he had read her one of Flannery O'Connor's stories, and he muses that it was perhaps O'Connor's spiritual faith that Kate found most attractive (13). Rolin rereads O'Connor in the narrative "now" of his second visit, reading her as he imagines that Kate did, in a sense, trying to recapture the enthusiasm that she felt for O'Connor's work. He revisits "Andalusia," O'Connor's family home in Milledgeville, Georgia, retracing his first visit there with Kate, attempting to see things through Kate's eyes, and trying to register those impressions in his narrative. Back in Savannah, he rereads Flannery O'Connor's letters, in a volume heavily underlined in pencil by Kate, in essence reading *her* reading of O'Connor. In the bus from Atlanta to Savannah, Rolin notices "au moins trois passagers dignes de figurer dans une nouvelle de Flannery O'Connor" (100). That uncanny metaleptic moment holds a strange and fragile promise for him, because if fiction can contaminate the real in such a convincing manner, so perhaps can past event be reclaimed in the present.

The web of references to Flannery O'Connor that Rolin constructs in *Savannah* takes its place in a broader strategy, a discourse of mourning whose most characteristic gesture is the sustained retrospective glance that characterizes Rolin's text from first page to last. He calls upon O'Connor to authorize that strategy in a metaliterary manner, and he sees her, more broadly, as someone who voices the mythology of the American South. That mythology, in its most stereotypical form, comes ready-made with the kind of effects that Rolin seeks to exploit in his own text: a suggestion of the belatedness of all things; an insistence upon looking backwards; a nostalgia for the way things once were, and can never be again; a particular prominence accorded to death and grief. In *Mémoires de l'oubli: William Faulkner, Joseph Roth, Georges Perec et W. G. Sebald* (2017), Raphaëlle Guidée, borrowing a term from Patrick Boucheron and Mathieu Riboulet, invokes the notion of "parler après que la mort est passée," arguing that this *parler après* takes its place in a venerable tradition "qui assimile l'écriture à un rite d'enterrement" (11). In that light, it is legitimate to see in *Savannah* a kind of *tombeau*, in Mallarmé's sense of the word—and it is certainly not for nothing that Rolin tells us that one of Kate's favorite things to do when traveling was to visit cemeteries. Other effects that he puts into play are nearly as undisguised, for example when he mentions that Kate, during her visit to O'Connor's estate in Milledgeville, had filmed a vulture soaring over her head (93). As uncomplicated and transparent as that image may seem to us, it should be noted that it wagers upon the kind of *retrospective prospection* that colors *Savannah* throughout, as if the decision to model present behavior on past behavior were not a matter of choice, but instead a question of vital necessity based in fact.

Feeling the way he plainly does about past experience, one may be struck by Rolin's curiously flattened narrative style. His description of a visit to the Laurel Grove Cemetery in Savannah, for instance, is baldly phenomenal and declarative. Rolin points to *things*—"pelouses, stèles éparses, arbres auxquels pendaient de longues barbes de mousse" (108-09)—rather than to the thoughts and emotions they might call forth. Even when it is a question of the people he meets, Rolin stays mostly on the surface, describing their way of walking or their way of dressing, rather than their affect. At the same time, he recognizes—and confesses—that he is not particularly suited to cultivating relations with people encountered by chance, and that he was always impressed by Kate's ability to do so. Speaking about a taxi driver named "Lionell" whom he meets in Savannah, he mentions that he would have liked to have the same easy rapport with him that he and Kate had had in 2007 with another taxi driver named "Willy": "peut-être avais-je imaginé reproduire avec lui la relation que nous avions établie avec Willy, ou une relation du même genre, oubliant simplement à quel point Willy était un type spécial, et à quel point Kate était plus douée que moi pour se lier avec des personnes de rencontre" (109). One of the possibilities that Rolin limns, in other words, is that the narrative impassivity in his account is a matter of personal constitution rather than style.

As flat as his account may be, Rolin's mourning for his friend is everywhere apparent. One of the ways that it manifests itself is the melancholy gaze that he casts upon people and things. Freud famously distinguished melancholy from mourning, characterizing the latter as normative behavior, and stigmatizing the former as pathological.[2] In the interest of transparency, I should note that I will not rely upon that distinction in my reading of *Savannah*. On the one hand, I believe that "melancholy" comes in a lot of different stripes; some of them may be pathological, some of them are clearly not. On the other hand, I do not feel that a characterization of Rolin's own melancholy outlook as "pathological" is significantly productive of meaning. A moment ago, I mentioned that Jean Rolin has established a reputation as a "melancholic" writer. *Savannah* certainly confirms that reputation, but I believe that something else, something more precise, is going on in the book. Here, Rolin recognizes his tendency toward melancholy and puts it to work: he comes to terms with it, hones it, and enlists it in the service of his mourning. Thus, while *Savannah* touches on topoi that he has exploited frequently in his other books, his way of using them here is more organized and pointed.

One of those topoi is the notion of the *zone*, of the neglected, insignificant, and largely undefined site on the margins of our more habitual spaces. Many critics have noted Rolin's predilection for sites of that sort,[3] and indeed certain of his books (both *Zones* and *La Clôture* come to mind) take those sites as their very setting. In *Savannah*, Rolin walks along the largely disaffected banks of the river, noting "le remorqueur *Florida*," for instance, or "le transporteur de voitures *Tugela* de l'armement Wallenius-Wilhelmsen" (41). During their 2007 trip, Kate had filmed the route the two of them took between their motel and the river, noting along the way a seedy watering hole called "Malones," distinguished by a sign proclaiming, "Where the girls dance on the bar" (43). She had also noted a power plant illuminated by dystopic sodium lights. "Kate était devenue familière de cet éclairage," Rolin remarks, "à cause de tout le temps qu'ensemble, à Saint-Nazaire, Dunkerque ou Le Havre, nous avions passé dans des ports" (43). At one point, Rolin recalls a trip prior to 2007 that he and Kate had made to New York, during the course of which they had gone to Staten Island to visit a wrecking-yard for ships. "Parfois je m'en voulais d'infliger à Kate mon propre goût pour les terrains vagues ou les friches portuaires," he confesses (35), seemingly not recognizing that he is performing the same gesture with regard to his reader. Yet this time the gesture is strategic, for the evocation of these places is deeply bound up in the way that he mourns his friend, in the way that he remembers her, in the way that he represents her to us.

Rolin invokes a variety of other sites in much the same perspective. He speak lyrically, for instance, of a highway ramp and its landscape, calling it "un paysage de désolation, celui d'un mall démesurément étendu et de ses métastases" (88). He is particularly fascinated by low-end motels, savoring the bizarre exoticism that they exude. It is true that, to a European imagination, motels have incarnated a certain kind of American exoticism, at least since Nabokov; but Rolin distinguishes himself by the depth of his devotion to them. Speaking about the Best Value Inn in Milledgeville, for instance, he remarks, with superb understatement, "on n'est pas reçu dans un Best Value Inn à Milledgeville comme dans un Four Seasons à Washington" (89)—and it is clear that he chalks that effect up to the Best Value Inn's credit.

Another familiar topos of melancholy in *Savannah* is the notion of solitude. During his second trip, even when he is among other people, Rolin describes himself as being fundamentally alone. He is alienated because of circumstance, certainly, but his solitude is undoubtedly rooted in considerations deeper than that. Most obviously, his present solitude offers a point of stark contrast with his first trip to Savannah, when he was constantly in the company of Kate; and as such, Rolin's evocation of his solitude participates in the process of mourning that his book enacts. Interestingly enough, while he speaks frequently about his own sense of being apart from other people, he also points on several occasions to another figure who seems to be still more alienated than he is. The first of those occasions occurs during a stroll that Rolin takes along the river in Savannah, and the way that he sets the stage for that moment deserves attention. He mentions that one of the paths he walks along is sandwiched between an abandoned motel and the power plant I mentioned earlier, now likewise abandoned, remarking about the path that, "il est possible, aux heures où personne ne l'emprunte, d'y éprouver non seulement de la mélancolie mais une certaine angoisse, liée sans doute à des réminiscences littéraires ou cinématographiques: dans un roman, ou dans un film, ce serait un lieu très propice au crime, et donc peut-être aussi dans la réalité" (39). The way he stresses his solitude, the mention of melancholy and anxiety, the notion, once again, that our experience of fiction shapes our perception of the real, all of this works in concert to clear the way for something exceptional. And indeed Rolin does not disappoint. "C'est dans cet état d'esprit," he continues, "que pour la première fois j'y ai observé un personnage étrange, que pendant la durée de mon séjour à Savannah je devais rencontrer encore à plusieurs reprises, et qui était un sans-abri, noir, âgé peut-être d'une trentaine d'années" (39). He remarks that this man radiates "une aura de démence et de solitude," and that he inspires in Rolin himself "une appréhension très vive, irraisonnée" (40).

He will encounter that man again and again during his stay in Savannah,[4] and he will gradually come to terms with him, noting toward the end of his visit that the man had ceased to frighten him (131). That anonymous man serves as a kind of double for Rolin, I think. Rolin sees in him reflection of his own alienation, his own solitude, exaggerated and a bit carnivalized. More than anything else, that is what frightens him, because the anonymous man presents to Rolin an image of what he might become if he fails to check his own inclinations toward melancholy and solitude. And the fact that he eventually comes to terms with that man is emblematic of the way that he comes to terms with his inclinations: through conscious mourning, that is, and through the deliberate expression of that process in this book.

Like melancholy, mourning comes in many different stripes. Lionel Ruffel has written about how contemporary French authors mourn the death of modernity, for example.[5] More recently, Raphaëlle Guidée has reflected upon how writers come to grips with historical disasters.[6] Jean Rolin's purpose is both more local and more modest. It is the loss of one individual that afflicts him; and, unlike the way that Mallarmé mourns Poe, for example, Rolin's grief is intensely personal. What interests me most particularly is the way he takes that deeply personal dynamic and renders it public, in *Savannah*. We can assume, I believe, that one of the ways he comes to grips with his grief is through the exercise of his writerly imagination. And indeed Julia Kristeva, among others, has argued that mourning can stimulate the creative impulse instead of stifling it.[7] In its most heavily charged passages, *Savannah* presents a discourse of mourning focused centrally on Rolin's attempt to represent how his friend Kate Barry *was*, as he reflects upon those moments when she astonished him the most. Let us briefly consider three of those moments.

The first of them occurs when Rolin recalls the way that Kate engaged three total strangers in conversation, during their 2007 trip to Savannah. Rolin suggests that his reaction at the time was less than generous—ungenerous enough, in any case, for Kate to ask him if he was annoyed. He mentions that in fact he had been staggered by the natural, friendly way Kate had of addressing strangers. Reflecting upon that encounter well after the fact, he sees that it reveals a fundamental truth about his friend—and about himself, as well:

> D'une manière un peu stupide, ou vaine, ou inappropriée, ou me paraissant telle parce que Kate est morte entre-temps, j'ajoute, lors de cet échange, qu'elle présente au plus haut point des qualités dont il me semble que j'ai toujours manqué, et qui lui auraient permis d'exceller, l'eût-elle souhaité, dans le reportage aussi bien que dans la drague, deux des activités auxquelles je me suis moi-même exercé. (49)

Another such moment that deserves our attention occurs when Kate, deciding to visit all of Savannah's cemeteries, enlists their taxi driver, Willy, in that enterprise. Recalling Willy's initial surprise, Rolin remembers that Kate won him over immediately by virtue of her humor, her ease, and her grace. What would have been an absurd and maudlin project in any other hands became, under Kate's aegis, something quite different, prompting Rolin to muse, "c'est une chose qui m'a toujours frappé, même dans les moments les plus tumultueux de notre vie commune, que Kate, si elle pouvait se rendre odieuse, comme tout le monde, n'était jamais ridicule, ni disgracieuse" (106). That realization also causes him to wonder if he visits (or revisits, more exactly) cemeteries in quite the same spirit—and the implications of that question echo throughout *Savannah*.

The third and final moment of that sort comes when Rolin recalls that Kate often reacted badly when he spoke of sad things: "Et il me revient aussi que lorsque je m'exprimais sur un ton solennel, par exemple au sujet de la mort déjà ancienne de quelqu'un qui m'avait été particulièrement cher, elle me reprochait de 'parler comme un camembert,' quelle que soit l'origine de cette expression—peut-être 'ferme ta boîte à camembert'?—dont il me semble qu'elle lui est propre" (101-02). Kate's remark, and Rolin's account of that remark, should be considered broadly, in terms of what it implies for Rolin's project in *Savannah*. If his purpose—or a large part of his purpose, at any rate—is to remember and memorialize Kate, he is obliged by her very memory to avoid speaking like a camembert. Perhaps that consideration accounts, in some degree, for the flatness of his narration. Most certainly, it explains why Rolin so stoutly and consistently eschews the most hackneyed tropes of pathos.

It is principally a question of fidelity, after all, of fidelity to Kate's memory and to her way of being. More than anything else, Rolin relies upon the *image* to ensure that fidelity, and particularly, the images that Kate herself had filmed. I mentioned earlier that those images provide a map of their 2007 visit that Rolin follows as closely as he can in 2014. Yet it is important to recognize that their function is not limited to that mapping. They also serve to stimulate Rolin's memory of that trip, especially his affective memory, and to guarantee the authenticity of what he remembers. When he remarks, early in his account, that shortly after arriving in Savannah on his second visit, he sets off "à la reconnaissance de certains des lieux par lesquels nous étions passés en 2007, et que les images de Kate m'avaient remis en mémoire" (24), that remembrance is not merely topographical. For the image is heavily charged with affect, as well; and that undoubtedly constitutes its principal value for Rolin. In other terms, what is crucial about these images is less what they *present* than what they *represent*. The things one may see in them—a riverbank, a cemetery, an abandoned power station, for instance—are inevitably colored (and effectively overwhelmed) by the fact that Kate chose to focus her camera upon them. That is, as Roland Barthes noted about still photography, these images testify first and foremost to Kate's *presence*.[8]

Rolin recognizes moreover a curious phenomenon regarding these images, and he articulates it in terms that comment eloquently upon his own representational strategy in *Savannah*:

> Quand les images filmées par Kate montrent quelque chose d'intéressant, et c'est le plus souvent, on peut s'attacher à ce qui est montré, momentanément, et oublier le reste. Quand elles ne montrent rien, comme dans le cas du Kevin Barry's Pub, on n'y voit qu'elle—même si elle est absente de l'image—et ce qui obscurément, impérieusement, l'inclinait à filmer ce presque rien. (128)

Insofar as there is very little in the images to capture and hold his attention, to that same extent he focuses his attention upon Kate. Can a similar effect be noted in *Savannah*? That is, does the banality of the images Rolin offers to us—a riverbank, a cemetery, an abandoned power station, for instance—serve to focus our attention upon Rolin's mourning? Such would seem to be the case when he describes a sequence that Kate had filmed in a restaurant, noting as if in passing the wrenching effect it has upon him:

> Si étrange, ou ridicule, que cela puisse paraître, la scène qui suit, de toutes celles que Kate a filmées pendant ce voyage, est pour moi une des plus déchirantes, bien qu'elle ne montre en apparence que des bacs remplis de nourritures insipides: sans doute parce que dans la façon qu'elle a de désigner, parmi ces nourritures, celles de son choix [. . .], Kate est plus présente, plus tangible, que dans aucune autre des séquences filmées, à l'exception peut-être de l'une des premières. (69-70)

Presence and tangibility: those are two things that memory alone can never really achieve. And they are also two things that we nevertheless infallibly seek in the photographic image, bound up as it is in its familiar, reassuring mythology.

That very dynamic becomes massively apparent in the instances where Kate's images include herself and Rolin.[9] At the simplest level, one would be tempted to claim that these images guarantee their presence, together, as something that *was*. Yet something a bit more complicated is involved here, I think. For while some few of those images involve Kate filming Rolin directly, in most of them Kate films her reflection, or their reflection, in a mirroring surface: a window, a puddle, a glass door, and so forth. Rolin takes care early on in the text to prepare us for moments like that, suggesting their importance. He tells us that Kate would mostly film the feet or the legs of the person with whom she was in conversation at any given time, the only exceptions to that general practice being "lorsque Kate filme son reflet, ou nos deux reflets conjugués" (8). One of those events comes when Kate films in a cemetery. "Kate s'immobilise," comments Rolin, watching the film seven years later, "et l'image avec elle, au-dessus d'une flaque d'eau dans laquelle elle fait signe à son reflet, agitant sa main droite, doigts écartés, avant de m'inviter à la rejoindre et à saluer comme elle de la main" (51).

The specularity of such moments is obvious, and even ostentatious. Moreover, they flirt dangerously with triteness, an effect that Rolin clearly recognizes, for he feels himself obliged to append a parenthetical remark to the passage I just quoted, assuring us that "Les potentialités de niaiserie de cette image ne m'ont pas échappé" (51). Yet those moments are nevertheless quite patently overdetermined ones in the textual economy of *Savannah*, and consequently they deserve our special attention. And a bit of skepticism as well, because as much as these events would seem to affirm the principle of presence, they inevitably serve to put that principle on trial. Their specularity is double, after all, for what those images put on display is a reflection of a reflection. They are in that sense doubly removed, or distanced, from the reality that they purport to represent, and to certify. In just that perspective, too, they perform a critique upon Rolin's purpose in this book, upon his own *reflections*, in other words.

For whether they be conceived literally or figuratively, reflections are always fragile things. Just as memory is fragile, just as the image is fragile. Just as the photograph is fragile, too, because although the photograph indisputably records what *was*, it no less surely records what *no longer is*. In *La Chambre claire*, Barthes thinks long and hard about the paradoxical message of photography, about the manner in which, while it guarantees presence, closely scrutinized, it also calls our attention to the passage of time, to distance and death.[10] J.-B. Pontalis is also struck by that paradox. "Étrangement, une photographie, même celle d'une personne vivante, est porteuse d'une disparition," he argues. "Cet enfant cessera bientôt de l'être, ce jeune homme rieur qu'était mon père est mort, cette maison que j'ai tant aimée n'est plus" (31). Just as memory fades, so too does a photograph fade. And if the latter is cast in a prosthetic relation with the former, any sustained inquiry into that relation will put its fundamental fragility into evidence. In that light, the vexations that we encounter when we interrogate the image are closely analogous to those that bedevil us when we attempt to remember the past. "Incapable d'oublier," writes Raphaëlle Guidée, "le mnémoniste éprouve la présence du passé comme un fardeau, mais ne cesse, dans le même temps, de se confronter douloureusement à la perspective de sa disparition" (162).

Such is the very uncertain terrain that Jean Rolin proposes to cultivate in *Savannah*. In the first instance, it is to forestall the inevitable process of forgetting that Rolin conceived his project. Let us remember that his project is closely derivative of Kate's own initial project—even if their purposes were very different. Moreover, both projects are marked by failure. Kate Barry never finished the film she wished to make on Flannery O'Connor. And failure characterizes Rolin's project from beginning to end. Early in his account, he confesses that he has never understood what drew Kate so powerfully to O'Connor:

> Je n'ai pas de réponse à cette question [. . .] je ne suis pas parvenu à déterminer exactement pourquoi elle s'était prise d'un tel amour pour cet auteur, au point d'envisager de réaliser un film sur elle, et auparavant de m'entraîner en 2007 dans un voyage à Savannah, où Flannery était née, et de là à Milledgeville, dans le fin fond de la Géorgie, où elle avait vécu la plus grande partie de sa vie, brève, et composé la quasi-totalité de son oeuvre. (11)

Rolin launches his own project, thus, in benightedness and doubt. He remains extremely attentive to the structure of the project—to the way that he will attempt to imitate, as closely as possible, the trip that he and Kate took in 2007—as if that attention could guarantee a fidelity to the memory of his friend. He documents the way that he repeats their trip with a great deal of care; yet he also mentions those moments when he failed to do so, pleading force of circumstance beyond his control, but nonetheless clearly feeling delinquent: "Il me semblait qu'en évitant Dublin—dans la mesure où les bus Greyhound qui desservent Macon n'y marquent pas d'arrêt—, je ne m'acquittais pas complètement du programme que je m'étais fixé, qui devait consister à retrouver tous les lieux, sans considération de leur intérêt ou de leur accessibilité, par lesquels nous étions passés en 2007 et que Kate avait filmés" (86). At other times, in moments still more telling, he reports instances where, rather than doing *less* than what he and Kate had done, he does *more*. One such passage occurs during his stay in Milledgeville, when he remarks that he regrets not finding the mule that he and Kate had seen. "Et pas plus que celle-ci," he says, "je ne revis de cardinaux, ces magnifiques oiseaux rouges, auparavant nombreux, sur lesquels j'avais attiré avec succès l'attention de Kate. Bien qu'en règle générale mon projet impliquât de ne pas en faire plus que ce que nous avions fait ensemble, je m'enfonçai un peu plus dans les bois entourant la maison, mû par le désir, qui ne devait pas être exaucé, d'apercevoir au moins l'un de ces oiseaux" (92).

In all of this, it is the question of the coherence of his project that concerns Rolin, whether his project is consistent and logical, at least insofar as its shape is concerned. Initially, that question is one which he addresses to himself; but insofar as he wishes to write about his project, he will be obliged to ask other people to consider it, too. Thus the issue of communicability arises, and it is a matter that Rolin contemplates with a great deal of circumspection. In that perspective, one notes in *Savannah* an interesting disjuncture between two sorts of Rolin's interlocutors: on the one hand, the people whom he meets during his trip, on the other hand the readers to whom he addresses his account. He mentions meeting Elizabeth Wylie, the Executive Director of the Andalusia Foundation, remarking that she is "[é]videmment ignorante des véritables raisons pour lesquelles j'avais entrepris ce voyage" (96), imagining that he is motivated by his own enthusiasm for Flannery O'Connor. The adverb he uses is curious, as if Wylie's lack of insight were something to be taken for granted. And it may be just that, in view of the fact that Rolin has said nothing to her about his project. But her lack of understanding stands in ironic distinction to the perspective that we readers enjoy, and it is one of the techniques that Rolin deploys in order to enlist us in his purposes.

Another passage invokes that same distinction, but in a different way. It concerns "Willy," the taxi driver whom Kate and Rolin had frequented in 2007, and whom Kate had befriended. Rolin mentions that during his subsequent trip, he had not sought to get in touch with Willy, dreading the responsibility of telling him about Kate's death, "au risque de laisser paraître un chagrin qu'il ne pourrait partager, ou pas au même point" (64). But of course we readers are aware that Kate has died, just as we are aware of what prompts Rolin to visit Andalusia. That being the case, the question of tact is rather different for us, granted that we had no personal connection with Kate. Furthermore, it is largely for *himself* that Rolin fears with regard to Willy, imagining that he might reveal too much of his own grief. The way that passage plays upon what is fundamentally at stake in *Savannah* is both canny and intriguing. How much is Rolin willing to reveal in his account? How much does he feel bound to withhold from us? Those questions would likely seem otiose, were it not for the fact that Rolin frames them so deliberately and programmatically in his text. Upon occasion, moreover, he takes pains to point out the limits of our knowledge, and toward the kinds of things that he is unwilling to reveal. "De la cause réelle, profonde, des disputes qui survenaient quelquefois entre nous," he remarks, "particulièrement lorsque nous étions en voyage, je ne dirai rien ici: ça nous regarde" (125).

Several related things are at issue in this discourse on communication and communicability: what Rolin can tell, most obviously, but also what he is willing to tell; to whom he chooses to disclose what order of things; what he himself understands, and what we may be expected to understand; what his project may put in evidence, and what we may infer from that evidence; and so forth. As Rolin wields all of these things, rubbing them against each other in order to see what sparks might fly, he remains persuaded that his project is flawed and consequently doomed to fail. As he sees it, that failure devolves both upon a fundamental misapprehension on his part and on his inability to work through his project toward a better understanding of his friend:

> Que Kate m'ait toujours donné l'impression d'être petite, ce qu'elle n'était pas, qu'elle ait été frêle, en revanche, avec une silhouette presque enfantine, et douée cependant, par moments, d'une force incroyable, que son visage—yeux marron-vert, nez imperceptiblement brusqué, oreilles dont l'une présente une curieuse irrégularité, comme si une souris en avait grignoté un petit bout—, que son visage ait été le plus expressif de tous ceux que j'ai connus, parce qu'elle éprouvait

joie ou peine plus vivement que quiconque, voilà, parmi beaucoup d'autres choses, ce dont tout ce qui précède ne donne à peu près aucune idée. Et de même ai-je échoué, pour l'essentiel, à démêler ce qui l'attachait si particulièrement à la figure de Flannery O'Connor, écrivaine catholique affligée d'une maladie incurable et éleveuse de paons. (132-33)

The game Rolin plays here might be described as "loser wins," a strategy that Michel Beaujour has identified as a classic technique of the avant-garde, on a reconfigured cultural horizon where winning outright is no longer possible.[11] In just such a light, the last gesture that Rolin offers in *Savannah* may seem a bit more clear, a bit less confounding and gratuitous. "En sortant de la messe," writes Rolin in his final sentence, "je me suis rendu dans une librairie proche de Madison Square pour y acheter *The Sibley Field Guide to Birds of Eastern North America*, illustré de la main même de David Allen Sibley, et c'est la dernière chose, ou du moins la dernière chose notable, que j'aie faite avant de quitter Savannah" (135). One of the things he will find in that volume, of course, is an image of the cardinal, the bird that eluded him despite his best efforts during his trip to Milledgeville. The moral of this dimension of his story is that in the absence of the thing itself, one instinctively turns toward the representation of the thing. Plainly, *Savannah* puts that very same dynamic on stage, but with regard to Kate, rather than a bird. "Every mourner tends to simplify his task by building up a kind of substitute object within himself after the real object has departed," argues Otto Fenichel (394), and such is the real sense of Rolin's project.

Among the many other concerns to which it attends, *Savannah* puts on display a parable of mourning. That process, as Rolin describes it, is very intense indeed, fueled as it is by the scandalous fact of Kate's absence. Allusions to that absence abound in the text, manifesting themselves in different ways: evocations of emptiness, for example, or insignificance, or lack, or insufficiency, of nothingness.[12] Rolin is patently and abundantly aware that no effort on his part can repair the unforgiving order of things in such a way that Kate should be somehow restored to him. Yet one of the lessons that *Savannah* evinces is that mourning is not about nothing—and nor is it *for* nothing. To the contrary, in Rolin's view, mourning is both significant and productive: it means something, and it makes something. Mourning certainly cannot revivify Kate in any meaningful way, but it can call a "Kate" into being. The latter is of course sadly incommensurate with the former, but the point of Rolin's gesture is perhaps elsewhere. Though mourning is undoubtedly condemned to failure when one expects it to achieve the impossible, if one is willing to adjust one's sights a bit in order to allow for a legible displacement, mourning can demonstrably produce something *else* imbued with some consistency, some heft, some meaning.

Jacques Serena's Fever

THERE ARE writers who work very hard at their craft, producing interesting, estimable texts year after year, but who for whatever reason do not achieve the kind of recognition that their writing warrants. Jacques Serena is one of those writers. He inaugurated his career at the Éditions de Minuit in 1989 with a novel entitled *Isabelle de dos*. Other novels soon followed, mostly (but not exclusively) at Minuit, including *Basse Ville* (1992) *Lendemain de fête* (1993), *Voleur de guirlandes* (2000), *Plus rien dire sans toi* (2002), *L'Acrobate* (2004), and *Sous le néflier* (2007). He has written quite a bit for the theater, texts such as *Rimmel* (1998), *Gouaches* (2000), *Quart d'heure* (2000), *Clients* (2000), *Velvette* (2001), and *Jetée* (2001). He has written essays about plastic art, including *Fleurs cueillies pour rien* (2001), on Gustav Klimt, and *Diotima* (2008), on Serge Plagnol. More recently still, he has participated in the Publie.net experiment, an online (and now hardcopy) publication platform launched in 2008 by François Bon, and originally conceived as a writers collective. There, Serena has published shorter texts, such as *Artisans* (2009), *Wagon* (2011), *Elles en premier toujours* (2012), and *Musaraignes* (2013). Briefly stated, Jacques Serena is an individual of significant accomplishment, and a writer whose books deserve more sustained attention than they have thus far received.

Among those books, *L'Acrobate* recommends itself as an intriguing study in psychology, as a meditation on the uses (and abuses) of imagination, and by virtue of the uncompromising gaze that it casts upon the process of writing. I would like to consider those aspects of the novel, beginning with a close examination of the narrative strategies that Serena deploys in the early pages, as he sets the stage for the principal acrobatics of this text. Those acrobatics play upon topoi such as gender construction, illness and contagion, the seductions of fiction, the precarity of interpretation, to name just a few, and they cluster squarely around the notion of *fever*.

The novel's incipit plunges us into an unfamiliar, quirky world, in the middle of a situation we have no means of understanding: "J'entends Lagrange passer sous ma mezzanine. C'est dérangeant mais, neuf fois sur dix, il suffit que je me penche sur mon travail en fronçant les sourcils pour qu'elle ne fasse que passer. Qu'elle renonce à monter me voir. Ou à me parler d'en bas" (7). Putting things in motion in this fashion, Serena sets the terms for his novel, and for our encounter with it. This incipit deserves special attention, because it describes a clearly vexed relationship—and at least since Tolstoy, one understands that the evocation of a vexed relationship is a very efficient way to launch a novel.[1] Serena invests heavily in what Roland Barthes famously called the hermeneutic code, wagering upon his reader's curiosity, upon his reader's desire to *know*.[2] For this initial sentence raises several questions. First and most obviously, who is speaking? What is the nature of the work upon which that person is engaged? Who is "Lagrange"? What are the relations between Lagrange and the narrator? And so forth. In this incipit and in what follows, Serena creates the impression that information is being withheld—and nothing is more apt to whet a reader's curiosity than that.

Insofar as the first question, the identity of the narrator, is concerned, we learn rather little in the novel's opening pages. In a brief conversational exchange with the narrator, Lagrange mentions that he is an artist, that he never leaves the house, and that she's worried about his psychological balance (9). The narrator himself confirms that he is a published author, and that he never leaves home these days. Such was not always the case, however, he remarks. For it used to be his habit to go out every night in search of young women. But not just any young women; his own desire drove him toward women whom he terms "fiévreuses": "Autrement dit en situation limite, dernière chance avant la radiation" (9-10). It quickly becomes apparent through those remarks that the narrator (who remains nameless throughout) regards himself with a considerable degree of irony,[3] an effect that necessarily complicates the reader's efforts to come to terms with him. Throughout this text, Serena puts a significantly divided subject on center stage. The narrating self and the narrated self (the one who appears in the account that the narrator provides of his circumstances) are continually at odds, and the tension generated therein is a significant source of textual efficacy. Serena's strategy with regard to that divided subject is both canny and highly calculated. At certain times, he amplifies the effect, pointing out how very vexed are the narrator's attempts to understand his own behavior, how alienated he is from himself. At other moments, he exploits the force of contrast, comparing the narrator to other people, more "normal" folk who are largely untroubled by questions of personal identity.

Lagrange incarnates the very image of the latter sort of person. Indeed, it is her fundamentally uncomplicated nature that defines her for the narrator—and that exasperates him, as well. We don't know much about her, other than the fact that she shares the narrator's living space, and undoubtedly his life too, more broadly speaking. The fact that she has a name clearly distinguishes her from the anonymous narrator, even if her name is, on the face of it, curious and starkly impersonal. "Je dis Lagrange, elle a certainement un prénom, mais pourquoi faire, un prénom," says the narrator (8), as if that datum were trivial and unworthy of mention. The dispassionate manner in which the narrator refers to his companion speaks volumes about the way he conceives his relation with her, and the way he wishes to present her to others. The eschewal of the first name suggests that she does not deserve our attention as an individual; rather, she serves as a kind of narrative prop.[4] Lagrange is calm and optimistic by nature, qualities that merely irk the narrator. He confesses that he has less liking for her than for a cat, a hamster, or a chicken. He formulates his most inexorable denunciation of her with an epithet that is as indisputable as it is devastating: "Lagrange, appelons un chat un chat, Lagrange est bel et bien une épouse" (116). That word is a totemic one in this novel. It connotes a specifically female domesticity colored by bourgeois satisfaction, sanguine disposition, incuriosity, pragmatism of spirit—in short, every character defect that the narrator sees in his wife. Clearly, for the narrator, an *épouse* is a person beyond any possibility of redemption.

One might well ask why he has chosen to make his life with Lagrange, in view of everything with which he faults her. Fairly early in his account, the narrator anticipates that question, and addresses it: "Mon but, en me mettant à vivre avec elle, était bel et bien, dès le départ, et reste toujours, d'oublier tout ce qui pourrait me faire retomber dans les profondeurs" (26). More than anything else, then, Lagrange represents a bulwark of sorts, something that stands between the narrator and the kind of destructive behavior he has manifested in the past. The metaphor that he chooses to describe that behavior is interesting. It hinges upon a vertical vision of things, and his own verticality is a normally point of honor with the narrator. He opposes that character trait to Lagrange's horizontality, her superficial manner of being, the way that she remains (in his view at least) on the surface of existence. Yet the nether end of the narrator's verticality is obviously something that threatens him in the extreme: falling into those depths is an eventuality that he seeks to avoid at all costs—even if those costs should be incurred through the daily frequentation of Lagrange.

As clearly scripted as that role seems to be for Lagrange, she may have yet another function with regard to the narrator, and with regard to the story that he tells. "Quand je n'ai pas pu l'empêcher de me parler, je lui réponds n'importe quoi, exprès," he remarks. "Et la voilà qui essaie de comprendre, qui n'y parvient pas mais essaie. Ne lui viendra jamais l'idée qu'on lui dit n'importe quoi. C'est qu'elle ne doute jamais de moi, Lagrange, ni d'elle, ni de la vie, de rien" (7-8). It is principally Lagrange's credulous inclination that is at issue here, for the narrator. She is trusting, certainly, and naive, undoubtedly; granted that, she serves as a foil for the narrator's own skepticism, for his constitutional reluctance accept things as given. He recognizes that he can say *anything at all* to her, and she will believe him, even if she understands nothing of what he says.

Stepping back just a bit from this textual moment in order to see it in longer focus, one may recognize in it a kind of parable of interpretation. On the one hand, there are people who takes things at face value; on the other hand, there are the doubters. The former are content to play a role that is largely passive; the latter insist upon a more active role, feeling that there must be room for them to *do* something.[5] The former believe what they are told, but fail to understand; the latter doubt everything, yet through that very skepticism they come to understand. The former are horizontal and unitary; the latter are vertical and divided. Implicitly but nonetheless surely, the narrator asks his narratee what sort of interlocutor he or she may be. And through the same gesture, Jacques Serena asks that question of his reader. But the question itself has a performative value. That is, the manner in which it is posed encourages us to take our place on one side of the issue, rather than the other. That dynamic is part of a strategy that Umberto Eco has termed "constructing the reader," a process whereby an author attempts, through flattery, enticement, or coercion, to mold the reader into the kind of collaborator he or she seeks to have.[6] The reader is called upon here to be a sort of anti-Lagrange in effect, exercising skepticism and intellectual mobility in the business of interpretation.

The gender binaries suggested by such a dynamic would seem to be sharply and tritely familiar, were it not for the fact that they are blunted by another kind of female, the kind of woman whom the narrator calls a *fiévreuse*, who stands in stark opposition to the kind of woman that Lagrange represents. The ideal *fiévreuse*, as the narrator describes her, is a woman who is poor, thin, and ill; she occupies a very marginal position in society, and her existence is tenuous in the extreme. The narrator cannot say what it is that draws him to that sort of woman, beyond the fact that it is their very "fever" which attracts him. "Voilà ce que je voulais, retrouver la fébrilité," he remarks. "Moi, c'est ce genre de corps qui me la provoquait. Comme jamais les corps bien ronds des femmes bien saines" (35). The precise nature of that fever is ill-defined; yet it does not seem to be contagious, for despite all of his efforts, the narrator does not contract it. Perhaps it is more metaphysical than physical, a matter of fundamental constitution. Yet there is a marked moral dimension to it as well, in the narrator's eyes: "ça restait de la fébrilité honteuse, voilà le problème," he says (36).

Clearly enough, that problem is his, rather than that of these young women themselves. That is, he reads his attraction to the *fiévreuses* as something shameful. He sees it moreover as a kind of betrayal of himself—"on s'arrange pour se trahir," he mentions at one point (31)—and he strains to rationalize his behavior. He suggests, for instance, that his interest in the *fiévreuses* is principally professional, citing his "curiosité d'auteur pour ce parler d'elles" (20), and noting the fact that he sometimes copies down their utterances. But that excuse rings false, even to him. On several occasions, he wonders why the men he calls his "confrères," writers and artists, are drawn toward more conventionally attractive women, and seem quite proud of that fact, while he is so strongly captivated by the *fiévreuses*, and obliged for the most part to hide his predilection. He sees that predilection as a central given of his character; he experiences it as powerfully engaging, certainly, but also as an affliction.

There is no doubt that Jacques Serena sees this fascination as the crucial trait of his protagonist—and indeed as the principal source of narrative interest in his novel, as well. Asked by Jean-Baptiste Harang to provide a brief description of his book, Serena responds thus: "Voilà, l'histoire, c'est quelqu'un qui est attiré par une sorte de femmes qui n'est pas réputée attirante. Je les appelle 'les fiévreuses,' c'était le titre du livre avant qu'on le change" ("Serena sur un fil"). It is difficult, moreover, to imagine that dynamic as being safely and reassuringly contained within the boundaries of a fictional world when one realizes that Serena claims the same sort of predilection as his protagonist. In 2005, the year after *L'Acrobate* appeared, he published a text entitled *Les Fiévreuses* at the Éditions Argol. There, speaking in what is apparently his own voice, he mentions that he met his first *fiévreuse* when he was sixteen years old, and living among young people on the edges of society, at loose ends (7). In the course of the book, Serena tells several stories about the women who fascinated him over the course of his life, each of whom conforms to the type he describes as the *fiévreuse*. As he conducts his narrative, leading it out of the distant past and into the narrative present, Serena is careful to cast his fascination for the *fiévreuses* as a durable, lifelong obsession: "entre moi et les fiévreuses d'étranges connections existent, comme ça, une nuit, des nuits, des attirances comme aveugles, soudaines" (83). His book is illustrated with a series of black-and-white photographs of women; yet those images are curiously lacking in focus. The same might be said of Serena's prose, as if the intent behind both kinds of image, verbal and photographic, were to provide a minimum of real *resolutio*n.

One consideration that is absolutely unmistakable in *Les Fiévreuses*—and in *L'Acrobate*, too, for that matter—is a kind of straining on the part of the subject toward someone as different from himself as it is possible to imagine. Pierre Bayard has noted a similar dynamic in Éric Chevillard's work, and he argues that such a yearning to know an *other* is bound up in the subject's desire to know himself:

> Si ce qui est radicalement Autre m'enrichit, c'est qu'il me fait accéder à des parties ignorées de moi-même qui se dissipent dans la fréquentation du même. En cela, loin de me faire perdre ma singularité, le différent la renforce. L'Autre, par son hétérogénéité, me fournit une forme de langage pour accéder à moi-même, là où le langage commun se révèle impuissant à m'exprimer. ("Pour une nouvelle littérature comparée" 111)

Yet for Bayard, such a gesture is not exclusively and fatally narcissistic. To the contrary, it testifies also to the subject's urge to get outside of himself. In *Aurais-je été résistant ou bourreau?* Bayard speaks of "la capacité à se déprendre de soi et de ses intérêts propres pour s'intéresser à l'Autre, c'est-à-dire à traverser la frontière qui nous isole du monde" (81). This is yet another manifestation of the divided subject I mentioned earlier, an individual who is significantly torn between the *within* and the *without,* and who sees the world and his own position therein in monochrome, that is, principally in terms of *difference.*

In *L'Acrobate*, that difference is postulated in the first instance—indeed in the first sentence—by the vexed relationship of the narrator and Lagrange. Throughout the novel, the narrator examines the terms of that relationship again and again, yet that process serves only to exasperate him further. As much as anything else, it is Lagrange's body that irritates him: "Corps moelleux, généreux, bien plein comme il faut. Tout bien en place et coloré comme il se doit. De quoi remplir la main d'un honnête homme, comme on dit. Comme ont dit les confrères. Et c'était le but. Que tout en elle témoigne aux yeux de tous de mon bon goût en matière de femme" (46). The conflation of the physical and the moral in these remarks is interesting. On the one hand, Lagrange's body is soft; on the other, it is generous: both of those terms, one quickly understands, are anathema to the narrator. The expressions "comme il faut" and "comme il se doit" are equally telling, insofar as they appeal to a norm that is usually unquestioned—yet it is the very notion of the norm that sets the narrator's teeth on edge. Once again, the narrator invokes his "confrères," as if the way he imagines Lagrange were necessarily mediated by the gaze of his colleagues. The figure of the "honnête homme" is likewise an abomination to the narrator, but it nicely incarnates the gravest threat that Lagrange poses, that of turning him into an ordinary fellow, someone just like everyone else.

In all of this, the game that Serena plays gradually becomes apparent, as one comes to recognize that Lagrange's difference is a highly constructed effect. While that may be obvious insofar as Serena is concerned, it is less so in the case of the narrator. Nevertheless, it clearly serves the narrator's purposes to shape Lagrange as someone different to him in every respect, someone who has no real purpose, in effect, apart from that alterity. That alterity demands to be interrogated, however. A moment ago, I mentioned that the relationship of the narrator and Lagrange, taken on its own, would seem to be reducible to a set of commonplace gender binaries. Yet the introduction of the *fiévreuses* inhibits such an easy reduction, making it clear that it is not *merely* a question of gender, nor *merely* a question of binaries. "Avec une fiévreuse, c'était une autre paire de manches," states the narrator (82). First and most obviously, the narrator presents the *fiévreuse* as someone who is as absolutely different from Lagrange as it is possible to be. "Rien de comparable," he reflects, "entre l'utilité reconnue d'une épouse et la flagrante inutilité d'une fiévreuse"—indeed, to his way of thinking, these two kinds of women are so dissimilar that it is difficult to imagine them as belonging to the same sex (48-49). Once again, the terms the narrator uses are loaded ones. The "practical" quality of a wife is broadly recognized, he claims, appealing to the same kind of consensus that he denounces so vigorously in other instances. And one may wonder for *whom* the "useless" quality of a fiévreuse is so "flagrant," in view of the fact that the narrator seems to be alone in recognizing that kind of woman, just as if the *fiévreuses* were figments of his imaginations.

Since in any case it is principally a question of imagination in *L'Acrobate*, from first page to last, we can perhaps concede that a figment may exert just as much psychic force as an individual of real flesh and blood. Yet it is the tenuous distinction between the two that constitutes the tightrope upon which the narrator must perform his acrobatics. "Pire qu'un acrobate," remarks Jean-Baptiste Harang, "c'est un homme coupé en deux, écartelé par l'idée qu'il se fait des femmes, les fiévreuses qu'on ne saurait épouser et les épouses dont aucune fièvre n'est à espérer." The division from which the narrator suffers is clearly bound up in the way he regards women, in the way he imagines himself with regard to women, and (quite simply) in the way he conceives himself as an individual. But it is difficult to determine which of those three optics activates the other two. Moreover, it is possible that the narrator experiences that division not only as an affliction, but also as a stimulant. In other words, perhaps the idea of a dramatically divided self is something that enables the narrator to imagine himself in a satisfying manner. In such a perspective, the *fiévreuses* would be affiliated with the side of himself that he sees as fundamentally wild and untamable, bohemian and creative—in short, with his "artistic" side.

In *Les Fiévreuses*, Serena describes his encounter with a young woman who immediately facinates him: "Cherchant où aller pisser, revenant pour la énième fois longer un couloir mal éclairé, je vois Lodz, la divine Lodz, la légendaire muse des premiers films de Carrare, couchée sur un sofa" (57). The word "muse" does not appear in *L'Acrobate* (neither does the word "acrobate," for that matter), but the notion of the muse is deeply bound up in the way that the narrator conceives the *fiévreuses*, for the "fever" with which they burn is patently inspirational for him. He mentions that in the past he had tried over and over again to catch that fever,[7] but that he never succeeded in doing so. Perhaps it is because he is beset by another illness. He mentions that he is subject to "crises," attacks of anxiety or panic that he suffers exclusively at night. The origin of those crises is unclear, and the narrator is not precise in describing their effects. Nevertheless, he clearly feels that they constitute an important part of his character. That feeling is echoed in *Les Fiévreuses*, where Serena remarks, in the very first sentence of the text: "Mon atout personnel semblait alors dû au fait d'avoir passé des nuits et des nuits en crise, à étouffer, en attendant d'encore une fois mourir, et puis de, peut-être, une fois encore ressusciter" (7). Claiming these crises as an *atout*—an asset, a trump card, an advantage—is a curious gesture. Yet in *L'Acrobate* as well, one gets the sense of the narrator's psychic attachment to them. For one thing, they are for him indelibly associated with the *fiévreuses*, "Parce que c'est bien au fond des crises que m'était arrivé de voir la première fille de ce genre" (21). His account of that meeting is imprecise, as if he himself were not certain of what had actually taken place. He describes the young woman as an orphan, a fragile silhouette with long dark hair; he calls her his "Vénus des crises" (23), for he does not know her name—and before he can ask her, she vanishes.

That moment plays out as phantasm, as a pure product of the narrator's imagination. Nevertheless, it proves to be both powerful and durable for the narrator, because it is the desire to find the young woman again—or someone just like her—that prompts him to go out at night in search of *fiévreuses*: "Et tout ça, on me dira, ces quêtes soir après soir, jusqu'à ce risque de ne jamais m'en relever, tout ça seulement parce que, au fond de vieilles crises, j'avais entrevu une fille dans ce genre, cette Vénus des crises, comme je disais" (38). Indisputably, she is a muse for him, firing his curiosity and imagination in the way she does. And the same claim might be staked for the narrator's crises, because it is during those difficult moments that his creative faculties seem to be whetted to their keenest edge. Indeed, he remarks that if he goes too long without crises, he begins to miss them (25).

It is during those moments of crisis when the division of the narrator's self yawns most broadly. He is abundantly aware of his divided self; and in some sense he appears to cultivate it, as well. From time to time, he *reads* that division, as if it were a text. One such moment occurs when he finds himself in front of a mirror:

> Moment fort, quand je me voyais dans le miroir au-dessus de l'évier, mon Dieu. Difficile à dire, l'impression. La preuve que la figure d'un homme tenait d'habitude par un effort de volonté. Visant à masquer l'inanité de sa figure. S'étant oublié, il se découvrait tel quel. Sans espoir, sans désir, sans charme. Odieux, soumis, humble. Humblement odieux sans sa soumission. Salut, tu vis ici? Tu es qui, déjà? Et mon nom murmuré à voix basse s'émiettait en sons étranges, ne m'évoquant rien de particulier. (24)

Mirror scenes are often sites of rare narrative privilege in literature, and this one is no exception.[8] They put on stage the *gnothi seauton*, the imperative of self-knowledge upon which much of Western culture is founded. Typically, gazing into the mirror, the subject sees himself or herself as an *other*, and it is thanks to the mediation of this notional, heuristic other (as Pierre Bayard suggests) that the subject comes to a better understanding of himself or herself. In the passage quoted above, the narrator's interrogation of himself does in fact wager upon a willingness to look at himself as someone else. Yet the truths about himself that the gaze puts in evidence are not particularly flattering ones. Moreover, the fact that his name is enunciated in a fractured, unrecognizable whisper suggests that this moment of introspection does not provide any satisfactory resolution to the narrator's quest to understand himself.

One thing that it does provide, however, is fuel for the narrator's writing, just like his crises, just like the *fiévreuses*. For he gazes at the page he is writing much as he gazes into the mirror: "Trois cheveux à moi sur ma page. Écrire et écrire, d'accord mais, à force. Cheveux qui tombent, joues qui pendent. Le tribut à payer pour revisiter les pauvres errances du passé. Tenter de voir à en comprendre le sens. Avec l'espèce d'envie d'autre chose qui évidemment pointe son nez" (106). In that activity a kind of feedback loop is established wherein the will to understand himself gives forth into writing, which in turn stokes his desire to understand himself, and so forth.

He does come to understand that a reflection too closely focused on the past is more perilous for him than it might be for most people, more threatening to the precarious psychic balance that he has sought to achieve:

> Ce qu'il faudrait pouvoir éviter, alors, c'est de regarder en arrière. Parce qu'en arrière, il y a les faits et que, pour les faits, rien moyen de changer. Et difficile d'éviter, surtout si on écrit. Parce que l'écriture, pas moyen de l'empêcher d'aller où elle veut. Si elle veut revenir tourner autour d'un soir en particulier, nous y revoilà. Pas à tortiller, il faut suivre. Plus qu'essayer, tant qu'on peut, quelques omissions, là ou là. Mais on peut mal, avec les faits de certaines nuits, omettre. Espérer oublier, à force, et encore. Pas trop espérer. Et est-ce qu'on espère vraiment, c'est ça aussi. (52)

It is not particularly astonishing that his writing efforts should lead him back to those moments in his past that are, by his own admission, the most psychically charged ones. What ought to be noted however is his own conflicted position with regard to that very process. For if his past is the thing that bedevils him the most, his manner of *being* in the past is something that he seeks to preserve—or to revivify—through writing. Thus, when Lagrange attempts to persuade him to write more conventionally and more tastefully, it is on precisely those grounds that he indicts her: "Son but est clair: annihiler en moi jusqu'à l'ombre de la dernière bribe de mon ancienne vie" (6).

The role that Lagrange plays with regard to the narrator's writing is an intriguing one, despite the way that he dismisses her; and it is perhaps not too much of an exaggeration to suggest that she functions as a kind of muse, much like the *fiévreuses*, if in a rather different mode. He claims that she prevents him from writing, but that claim does not stand up to scrutiny. To the contrary, he writes under her gaze, imagining her as his first reader, and trying to anticipate her reaction: "Sera donné de connaître la profondeur de ce monde à qui aura été toute une nuit face à une fille maquillée pour rien. Voilà ce que je viens d'écrire. Quand Lagrange va lire ça" (68). On those occasions when she does in fact read him, Lagrange is not shy about letting him know what she thinks of his writing: "Elle lisait une de mes pages et m'a demandé, un peu soucieuse: Pourquoi fais-tu dire à cette fille: chlic, chlic, c'est ridicule" (89). The real problem, for the narrator, seems to be that Lagrange doesn't find his writing interesting enough. She fails to see, in his evocation of his obsession with the *fiévreuses*, the kind of absolutely crucial, transcendent dilemma that he wishes to convey. "Ne l'intriguent pas le moins du monde, Lagrange, mes éternelles héroïnes maigres," he complains. "Mes inspiratrices moins de cinq pour cent de matière grasse. Au point que j'en arrive à me demander si elle lit vraiment mes pages" (75).

In other terms, it is not that Lagrange prevents him from writing that irks him so, nor is it that she refuses to read him: the real problem in his view is that Lagrange is a bad reader. The manner in which the narrator arrives at that conclusion is, once again, more than passingly conflicted. For he faults Lagrange both for being too literalist and for not being literalist enough. Too literalist because she finds certain features of his writing "ridiculous" by virtue of the fact that they stray too far from a realist view of things. Not literalist enough insofar as she stoutly refuses to take what he writes as the literal truth, preferring to read it as fiction. And there is the rub, precisely. Whatever may be their actual ontological status in the world that he inhabits, for the narrator the *fiévreuses* are *real*, such is the psychic power they exert upon him. He clings to that notion with a great deal of energy, yet he is not certain of his purposes when he puts it forward in his writing. Once again, as he ponders that problem, he reflects on the way that Lagrange will read him: "M'arrive encore de craindre que Lagrange se mette un jour à soupçonner, en lisant ce que j'écris, que je n'invente pas. De le craindre et, bien sûr, au fond, d'un peu l'espérer" (43). His hesitation recalls Georges Perec's characterization of writing as a game of hide-and-seek: "Une fois de plus, les pièges de l'écriture se mirent en place. Une fois de plus, je fus comme un enfant qui joue à cache-cache et qui ne sait pas ce qu'il craint ou désire le plus: rester caché, être découvert" (14). For the narrator of *L'Acrobate*, the alternatives are both attractive and repugnant, depending upon the angle from which he considers them—just like the *fiévreuses* themselves.

The game of hide-and-seek that the narrator plays with Lagrange hinges squarely on the notion of fiction. "Qui dit fiction dit feintise réciproque," as Gérard Genette reminds us (15), and it is largely in the reciprocal relation, the *articulation* of the narrator and Lagrange that problems posed by the idea of fiction become apparent. "Lagrange est de ces doux niais pour qui un auteur écrit à partir de son vécu et invente," says the narrator. "Alors que c'est évidemment dans l'autre sens que ça marche. On vit ce qu'on écrit et n'invente donc rien, jamais" (14). His remark is intriguing, taken in the broad context of his writing project and the claims that he stakes for it. For in this case at least, there is no pretense of a referential reality to which he seeks to remain faithful. To the contrary, in this instance imagination *manufactures* reality. That puts a very different cast upon the question of the ontological status of the *fiévreuses*, of course. And it would seem to lay the question to rest conveniently enough, were it not for the fact that the narrator wavers so dramatically in his thinking. At times, he appears to be just as literalist as he accuses Lagrange of being, such as the moment when he visits a gallery and by mistake drops a photograph of a *fiévreuse* on the floor (32). He is immediately afraid for his reputation, imagining what his colleagues in the world of plastic art would say about him if they were to become aware of his obsession. If those colleagues were able to dismiss it as fiction, there would be no problem whatever; but the narrator needs it to be *real*, and that need is all-consuming. It leaves him painfully suspended in a kind of limbo, for the principle of the real taking shape in fiction and that of fiction shaping the real are equally important to him.

An interesting case study in that dynamic is provided by the narrator's account of a young woman he calls "Sophie Roche." He met her in a bar, he remarks, and she wrote her name on his arm. She gave him a photo of herself, and when he asked if he might take his own photo of her, she agreed, merely stipulating that he should come back the next day, when sober. More than anything else, the narrator was impressed by the fact that when speaking with her, this young woman took him *seriously*. Yet the next morning, he cannot recall in which bar they met. He looks for her desperately, because he senses that she holds the key to the kind of life he wishes to live: "J'étais sûr que ma vie aurait pris un sens, si je m'en étais souvenu" (43). He returns to her again and again in his narrative: she disappears and reappears, but she is always on his mind in one way or another. Nevertheless, his account of her is transparently thin from beginning to end, as if Sophie Roche were a principle rather than an individual. And indeed that may be part of what is going on here. In conversation with Jean-Baptiste Harang, Serena remarks, "Mes fiévreuses, au début je ne savais pas qu'il y en avait plusieurs, c'est le texte qui me l'a offert: dès la deuxième description, j'ai bien vu que ce n'était pas la même, j'ai laissé, voilà tout, elles s'appellent Sophie Roche." In one sense, then, Sophie Roche stands in for all of the other *fiévreuses*. In another perspective, however, it is her very multiplicity that puts one of the most basic properties of fiction on display, the way it enables us (by "us" I mean people who read, *and* people who write, as well) to imagine ourselves as multiple, capable of inhabiting several worlds simultaneously. Pierre Bayard, for example, sees that multiplicity as an essential feature of our way of being, and argues for a very literal, fundamentalist view of it.[9] Other critics, such as Lionel Ruffel, contend that the principles of multiplicity, heterogeneity, and amalgamation are deeply imbricated in the manner in which we imagine our contemporary world.[10]

We find our way through that world in multiple ways, of course—and indeed that is one of the lessons that *L'Acrobate* puts on offer. In terms of the narrator's efforts to find his way, Sophie Roche comes to his assistance in very substantial ways. For just when he thinks he has lost her forever, she appears at the door of his house, seeking to sell him a vacuum cleaner (53). She seems not to recognize him, but despite that, they use the *tu*, the informal mode of address, with each other right from the start. The narrator's account of the scene is thin with regard to the broader narrative weft of the novel, as if the events he describes were hypothetical. Moreover (and most importantly) the scene is peppered with allusions to the gestures of writing. Those allusions take different shapes. Speaking about his conversation with Sophie Roche, for example, the narrator mentions that it is "Confus, comme un texte écrit par-dessus un autre" (66): the evocation of a palimpsestic discourse should not be lost in a text as heavily overwritten as this one appears to be. The narrator further remarks that Sophie Roche "avait les yeux cernés de rimmel, trop de rimmel" (67), and such a remark cannot be taken as innocent when one remembers that Jacques Serena is the author of a text entitled *Rimmel*. When the narrator, some twenty pages later in the text, hears Lagrange walking about under the mezzanine where he is writing and asks her if one can spell "rimmel" without a capital letter (88), the story that Serena is telling becomes more complex still, with its different levels of appearance and reality calling each other dramatically into question.

What seems beyond question, however, is Serena's desire to put on display a fable of literary creation. The multiple worlds that he limns in *L'Acrobate*—the phenomenal world, the fictional world, Lagrange's world, the narrator's world, the world that Sophie Roche inhabits, to name only the most obvious ones—are mutually permeable in certain intermediary points. That is, they tend to bleed into each other a bit, especially when they are subjected to the kind of close scrutiny that the narrator exerts upon them. Those intermediary sites, Serena suggests, are ones of exceptional privilege, both for writers and for readers, for they enable us to be both *here* and *there*, simultaneously.[11] That manner of being is surely the one that the narrator adopts, for better or for worse. The way that he continues to imagine Sophie Roche from his writer's perch in the mezzanine is emblematic. He wonders if she has been hospitalized; he speculates that she has gone to a home for young women in La Rode; he pictures her speaking to a sailor. He even imagines that she has come to live in his home, hired by Lagrange as a housemaid. The improbable nature of such an eventuality is eclipsed by the necessity that drives it, because the young woman's *fever* is something the narrator cannot do without: "Avec Sophie Roche, rien que de tenir sa main m'irradiait" (93). Yet the image of Sophie Roche is difficult to sustain. Without constant and vigilant cultivation, it tends to fade, to the narrator's chagrin: "Tard dans la soirée," he remarks, "je me taillais les cheveux quand elle s'est redressée. Sans son sweat. Nue, assise sur le matelas. Sa présence, comment dire. Elle existait de moins en moins" (100).

Fictions are undoubtedly more ontologically slender than most of the objects we encounter, but the power they exert over certain subjects can be very considerable indeed. Ensuring their viability comes at a cost, entailed by the abstraction into which the narrator deliberately immerses himself. It is an intermediate state, one in which the boundaries of different kinds of worlds are largely blurred, to his creative advantage. One finds him in just that state at the end of *L'Acrobate*, writing away:

> Plongé dans ma page, me semble parfois entendre en bas Lagrange crier. Et Sophie Roche émettre quelque chose entre le grognement et le rire. Nouveau cri, durci, de Lagrange. Nouveau rire, renforcé, de Sophie Roche, ou grognement. Et on dirait bien que monte jusqu'ici un brouhaha depuis la cage d'escalier. Comme un choeur, en sourdine, un terrible rire mais encore engourdi. J'ai encore soif mais je préfère continuer d'écrire. (125)

Serena proposes his narrator to us as an exemplary figure, trusting that we will recognize in his grapplings with the real and the imagined something that corresponds, however distantly, to our own experience. That correspondence devolves upon the abstraction into which we plunge when we read fiction, certainly; but it also points toward how we allow ourselves to be *divided* in order precisely to inhabit more than one world. Perhaps we live much of our lives in a divided state, more than we commonly acknowledge—though the extent, degree, and tenor of that phenomenon vary greatly in function of circumstance, cultural norms, and personal inclination. Whatever else it may offer, literature provides a space where we assume that division as a matter of free choice, confiding that its fictions will afford us mobility, intrigue, consternation, fascination, and satisfactions of still other stripes. Unlike Serena's benighted narrator, however, we are free to leave that space whenever it suits us to do so, blithely abandoning the fictions that animate it, even as we set off in search of others.

Julia Deck's Geometries

SECOND NOVELS are often where literary careers are made, or on the contrary where they founder. Julia Deck's *Le Triangle d'hiver* (2014) amply fulfills the rich promise of her first novel, *Viviane Élisabeth Fauville* (2012), putting on display a pleasing lightness of touch and an impressive degree of narrative confidence.[1] That latter quality serves Deck particularly well, for the story she tells contains more than a few twists. Its protagonist is a young woman identified only as "Mademoiselle." Having no real achievements to her credit, and still less ambition, she finds herself in straightened circumstances, having lost her job in a household appliance store after attacking her boss with a blender-mixer. Reasoning that she must make a change, she will henceforth present herself to the world as the novelist "Bérénice Beaurivage." It is an identity that demands more and more upkeep the longer she maintains it, for sooner or later, one expects a novelist to write something, whether good, bad, or indifferent, and Bérénice Beaurivage will grapple unequally with that problem.[2] Things are constantly in flux in this novel, and appearances are in some ways more reliable than realities. The action moves from Le Havre to Saint-Nazaire, to Marseille, to Paris, and back again to Le Havre. When Mademoiselle meets and seduces the "Inspecteur," one might imagine that her circumstances will improve. And indeed they do for a moment, until the journalist "Blandine Lenoir" imposes her troubling—and triangulating—presence. One follows the characters in their peripatetics with assurance, until it becomes clear that they are not the people one understood them to be. The correspondences and personal reciprocities that prevail among them are highly contingent, and the terms upon which they rest can be recast in the blink of an eye. Even the most attentive of readers is likely to nonplussed at some point in this novel. But that sort of narrative sleight of hand is part of the fun, of course; and like any successful feat of prestidigitation, it relies on our willingness to be fooled.

Among all of this book's virtues, I am chiefly intrigued by the quirky geometries that animate it, and that inflect every dimension of the text: the relations of the characters, the objects in their world, the landscape upon which the events play out, the plot structure, and more still. The most obvious geometrical shape in the novel is the triangle that the title announces. It is a figure that Julia Deck uses (and sometimes abuses) throughout the text. On occasion the figure appears visually, and as if anecdotally. Such is the case when Mademoiselle finds herself "face au grand A de la tour Eiffel" (142). At other times, the reference is more literal. Her panties are described, for instance, as a "triangle de dentelle" (72), and the prewrapped sandwich that she consumes takes the shape of "triangles superposés à la rosette de Lyon ou l'emmental" (169). I mentioned a moment ago that Blandine Lenoir serves to triangulate the relationship of Mademoiselle and the Inspecteur, and Julia Deck takes care to ensure that we should understand that function, most notably when Mademoiselle comes upon the two others in the Inspecteur's apartment: "J'ai frappé à la porte. Elle s'est ouverte comme s'ils m'attendaient, et tout à coup nous avons formé un triangle parfaitement équilatéral" (149). At other moments in the text, it seems as if the figure is written in the stars. An ocean liner plays a significant role in the plot. Its name is *Sirius*, which is, as one of the boat's stewards complaisantly informs Mademoiselle, "une des trois étoiles du Triangle d'hiver, qui de notre point de vue semble presque équilatéral" (33). The Inspecteur is a man of more learning than the steward, and his comment upon the name of the ocean liner is consequently a bit more involved: "Oui, ils ont fini par l'appeler comme ça. J'aurais préféré *Alpha Canis Majoris*, qui est son nom scientifique, la première étoile de la constellation du Grand Chien, mais ça compliquait tout car Sirius fait également partie du Triangle d'hiver" (89). If we readers were asked to choose between the Great Dog and the Winter Triangle however, our choice would be clear enough, guided as we are by the book's title. When yet another ocean liner appears on the horizon, and we learn that its name is *Procyon* and that it is the sister ship of

Sirius, we are amply confirmed in that choice, presented with a triangulation wherein only Betelgeuse is lacking.

That lack is one of the abuses of the triangle that Julia Deck commits, and I believe that it is strategic in nature. For if geometries can be perfect in the mind, they cannot be so in the world—or in a novel like this one that puts on offer a deeply flawed world. In her novel, the protagonist's itinerary, from Le Havre to Saint-Nazaire, to Marseille, to Paris, and back to Le Havre, does not describe a perfect triangle.[3] Yet it is close enough for real-world purposes, one might concede; and the return to the point of departure after all of the acutely angular plot turns is surely a calculated effect. In that perspective, the use that Deck makes of the triangle far outweighs its abuse, and I hope to have shown that its occurrence in her novel is far more programmatic than anecdotal. Moreover, many other analogous figures appear in the narrative weft of the text, serving to complement the triangle and to suggest that Deck's novel is deeply conditioned by geometries of different sorts. One notes, for example, objects and structures described as quadrangles, orthogonals, parabolic hyperbolics, trapezoids, circles, cubes, and parallelepipeds.[4]

More broadly still, the fictional world that Deck puts on offer is strikingly architectonic. Once again, that effect is sometimes cast in a figural manner, sometimes far more literally. During Mademoiselle's stay in Paris, she walks a great deal in order to pass the time. Deck mentions that she circles the Arc de Triomphe twice, contemplating the avenues that lead out from it, each of which appeals to her (142). The moment is an exemplary one, I think. On the one hand, the Place de l'Étoile clearly participates in the astral theme of the novel. On the other hand, and more importantly, Mademoiselle is patently fascinated by the symmetries that it displays. Like many people, she finds symmetry consoling, reassuring, and she seeks it pretty much everywhere. She finds it, for instance, in her lover's face: "Les lèvres de l'Inspecteur pourraient aussi bien ne produire aucun son, occupées seulement à découvrir les dents qu'il a fort bien alignées, maxillaire inférieur emboîté au millimètre derrière le supérieur, incisives au cordeau et canines à peine plus effilées préparant en souplesse la transition vers les prémolaires" (65). The small apartment that she occupies in Le Havre displays the same effect: "Les aménagements intérieurs du studio, tout en angles droits, équipements fonctionnels et baies verticales, témoignent du style qui prédominait à la Reconstruction" (18). And in fact the city itself seems to be laid out according to the same principles:

> Sur le quai de Southampton, il n'y a pas un chat ni même un arbre, l'architecte de la Reconstruction ayant estimé que la verdure eût inutilement distrait le regard de ses édifices en béton armé. De fait, les volumes quadrangulaires dégagent une belle impression d'équilibre grâce aux variations de hauteur, au jeu des éléments horizontaux—placettes, portiques, balcons, terrasses—, qui modulent en douceur la composition des façades. (25)

It should be remembered that Le Havre was leveled during the latter part of the Second World War, and rebuilt largely from scratch in the postwar period—the "Reconstruction" that the narrator mentions in the two passages I have just quoted. The lead architect on that rebuilding project was Auguste Perret, and the success of his undertaking (which lasted for twenty years, from the mid-1940s to the mid-1960s) was such that in 2005 UNESCO declared Le Havre a World Heritage Site. It is not for nothing that Julia Deck chooses a passage from Perret's *Contribution à une théorie de l'architecture* as the epigraph for her novel. That gesture announces the architectonic principle very explicitly, and prompts us to be attentive to further manifestations of that principle, in a process that Umberto Eco has called "constructing the reader."[5] Those manifestations are not hard to find in *Le Triangle d'hiver*, and they constitute an important dimension of Deck's geometrical play. Several of them bear the stamp of Perret himself, notably the moment when Mademoiselle visits the Église Saint-Joseph, one of Perret's key designs in the rebuilding project: "Tour fusiforme de cent cinquante mètres de hauteur, l'église révèle une dentelle de béton armé, élégante peau minérale constellée de vitraux géométriques" (164).

August Perret was especially known for his innovative use of reinforced concrete, and for the orthogonal lines that such a technique facilitates. Mademoiselle perceives such orthogonality in all of the cities she visits. In Saint-Nazaire, for instance, she comes upon "une esplanade clôturée par un bloc de béton brut" (50); in Marseille she is impressed by "la ville orthogonale de l'après-guerre" (108); and we have noted her fascination with the Place de l'Étoile in Paris. In the company of her lover, she spends a long moment in the bomb burst chamber of the submarine base in Saint-Nazaire. The lines, the right angles, and the seemingly infinite iteration of the site speak to her powerfully—and most compellingly the fearful symmetry of the way its space is organized. If that organization testifies to delirium or obsession, it is nonetheless appealing to Mademoiselle's mind. For it is the case that, wherever she may go, her gaze is seized by architectonics, by orthogonality, by symmetry, by constructed and shapely order.

Yet hers is surely not the only gaze to be thus captivated, for Julia Deck's gaze is quite obviously focused on those principles, too. And granted that Deck is constantly putting images structured according to those principles before us, we readers find ourselves by force of repetition more than usually attentive to *shapes* in this novel—and indeed to the very idea of shape. Encountered again and again in this way, the notion of shape itself tells a story. For when recognizable shapes recur with regularity, according to patterns that can be apprehended, they certify that someone *has been there*, and has acted intentionally to arrange things in a pleasing manner. While it is undoubtedly true that symmetry can occur in nature (in a snowflake, for instance, or in the features of a human face), it is symmetry as a cultural phenomenon that interests me more. By that I mean the way we construct things in such a way that *this* reflects and complements *that*; but I also mean the way we think about such constructions, through the very principles of their elaboration. If those principles are sharply foregrounded in a given artifact—as they seem to be in Julia Deck's novel—they oblige us to think about process issues. *Le Triangle d'hiver* constantly asks the question of how we organize space, whether it be the space of the city or the space of the book. It is a fundamental question in an ontological perspective most certainly,[6] but I find it still more intriguing in terms of aesthetics, and most particularly in terms of fiction. For if it is true that people can do whatever they wish in fiction, it is nonetheless true that fiction is always organized. It is constructed, composed, hammered out—in a word, it is *shaped*. And when the notion of shape itself is thematized as insistently and as geometrically as it is in *Le Triangle d'hiver*, it invites us to reflect upon what that idea means and what purpose it may serve for the characters in the fictional world, and for the writer who deploys it so relentlessly, and indeed for ourselves, whether in our readerly lives or in our many other modes of being.

In Mademoiselle's case, the gaze that she casts upon the world is both measured and measuring. It quantifies, it selects, it postulates hierarchy and coherence, it judges. And it performs those operations with astonishing alacrity: "Son œil dérive vers la fenêtre, cadre opaque où se reflètent les clients—des groupes d'étudiants mais surtout des couples, très classiquement composés d'un homme et d'une femme. Trois costumes-cravate attendent d'être servis au bar, dont l'un, bleu sombre à la limite de l'obsolescence, dénote le voyageur de commerce en transit" (30). She is equally quick to size up Blandine Lenoir, and equally cool when it comes to assessing how Blandine might inflect the geometries of her relation with the Inspecteur. Mademoiselle gazes consciously, attentive to whatever she may see, but also constantly aware that she is looking, even in those moments when she is not looking for anything in particular: "Le verre occupe un peu. Elle l'entoure de ses mains, étudie le reflet des néons dans le liquide, le porte à ses lèvres puis observe à nouveau le verre, la salle, la salle dans la vitre puis le verre dans la vitre, la vitre dans le verre, la salle dans la vitre du verre, la salle la vitre le verre la vitre la salle le verre, ce doit être l'effet des cocktails, le regard s'énerve tout seul" (30). If Julia Deck takes such pains to describe Mademoiselle as an observer, it is perhaps because she wishes to sharpen our own powers of observation. Just as Mademoiselle sees shapes in the fictional world that she inhabits, so too may we perceive shapes of different ilks in the novel; and in both cases those shapes make navigation possible.

Speaking of navigation, the ocean liner *Sirius* sails through this tale as an example of pure form, pure shape, pure construction. It serves moreover to put the very idea of construction on display, for when Mademoiselle first sees it in Saint-Nazaire, *Sirius* has just been launched from its shipyard, fresh as a new penny. Its life is nearly coextensive with that of Mademoiselle's tale, for it catches fire and burns, just off of Marseille, toward the end of the novel. Its lines are sleek and symmetrical; its dimensions are impressive; it is coolly and unquestionably majestic. It embodies the very principle of luxury, and in this it cannot fail to impress Mademoiselle. Interestingly enough, when she first claps eyes upon it, she reads it in largely mathematical terms:

> Insérée dans l'embouchure du fleuve comme la dent d'une fourchette, la pointe de Floride accueille les navires de passagers en escale. Un paquebot est venu pendant que la jeune femme honorait son rendez-vous à l'agence pour l'emploi. C'est un navire de croisière moderne, trois cents mètres de long et dix étages érigés sur l'eau calme. Quatre mille personnes circulent peut-être à l'intérieur de ses superstructures, mais la paroi étincelante ne laisse rien deviner de cette agitation, parfaitement étrangère à la ville qui s'étend au-delà du quai. (17)

That sort of reading allows Mademoiselle to make sense of the ship's shape, and thus enables her to understand it in a way that is, for her at least, immediate. Furthermore, that takes its place in a sustained pattern of simple mathematical calculation in *Le Triangle d'hiver*, wherein things come to *be* by virtue of being surveyed, scanned, or measured.

The manner in which Julia Deck wagers upon mathematics may seem surprising at first. But in a country with a legacy of mathematical inquiry as strong and venerable as that of France, it is undoubtedly inevitable that mathematics should have inflected other cultural traditions, here and there, and that certain figures in the history of French culture should have mixed their math and their aesthetics very liberally indeed. One thinks of Descartes for instance, and Pascal, and d'Alembert, and of Lautréamont, who included an "Éloge des mathématiques" in his *Chants de Maldoror*. More recently, Paul Valéry comes to mind, as do the surrealists,[7] and the Ouvroir de Littérature Potentielle (Oulipo), cofounded by Raymond Queneau and François Le Lionnais with the explicit intent of encouraging the articulation of mathematics and literature.[8]

For Mademoiselle herself however—and perhaps for Julia Deck as well—something else is at stake, in addition to quantification and measurement. The gestures that mathematics involves are deeply soothing to Mademoiselle, a notion that Deck is careful to underscore. In order that her reader should appreciate the importance of that notion, Deck stakes it out early in her novel, couching it in an unmistakably Proustian moment when Mademoiselle is having tea and *madeleines*, while gazing once again at the ocean liner *Sirius*: "Elle avale une dernière madeleine et se dirige vers la fenêtre pour compter le nombre de ponts sur le paquebot (11), le nombre de hublots par pont (55), puis les multiplier pour obtenir 605—il y a au moins 605 cabines sur ce clapier à touristes flottant. L'arithmétique apaise. Repose à tel point qu'elle y a développé ses dons" (22). Mademoiselle seeks that calming effect in a broad variety of situations: not only when she surveys the *Sirius*, but also when she thinks about the trip from Le Havre to Saint-Nazaire, or from Saint-Nazaire to Marseille; or when she savors the symmetries of the Place de l'Étoile and those of the bomb burst chamber of the submarine base; or when she contemplates the postwar architecture of Le Havre; or when she scrutinizes the shape of her lover's face. Or indeed when she thinks about herself, trying to decide who she is and where she might go from here: "Vous avez, mettons, une trentaine d'années. Cela fait environ trois cent mille heures que vous apprenez à vous connaître, en comptant le temps de sommeil qui n'a guère moins de raisons de fournir des informations sur la personne du dormeur que les instants de veille" (74).

Most fundamentally thus, it is a matter of counting, of simple enumeration that serves to put Mademoiselle's mind at ease. She engages in that activity in a largely automatic fashion, as if it were a natural part of the gaze that she casts upon the world. Typically, she registers her enumerations in lists, cataloguing the phenomena she encounters one after the other, as if the mere act of accretion were sufficient to make things understandable. The novel teems with those catalogues, to a very telling degree. Mademoiselle makes lists obsessively, and without a great deal of conscious thought. She catalogues for instance the items lying on the floor of her apartment, which is in significant disarray (18); she notes all of the things she has packed in her valise, during an otherwise empty moment of her trip from Le Havre to Saint-Nazaire (42); she lists the things she sees as her gaze traverses the port of Saint-Nazaire (51); she inventories the effects with which the architects of the Second Empire embellished the facades of their buildings (61-62); during a visit to the National Naval Museum in Paris, she passes in review all of the French ports that Claude-Joseph Vernet painted (144). In short, whatever she may be doing, and quite regardless of the relative importance of the phenomena she considers, Mademoiselle counts and catalogues. That is just the way she is. Counting, listing, and classifying: clearly enough, that behavior testifies to a desire for harmony.

I wonder if that same impulse animates the manner in which Julia Deck constructs her fictional world. That world is a broadly specular one (like that of many novels in our time) wherein Mademoiselle's tale is intricated with a reflection upon writing and its uses. The vectors of that intrication are sometimes linear and reasonably frank, at other times interrupted and ironic. Yet in the backing and forthing that they describe, significant geometries become apparent, as if fiction itself were subject to the logic of shape. Deck lays the foundation of her fictional world in the novel's incipit, and it consists in a name: "Bérénice Beaurivage. Je le tourne, le retourne et n'y discerne pas un pli. Oui, ce nom m'irait à la perfection, réfléchit-elle en pivotant vers la fenêtre qui encadre une rue morne" (9). It is not for nothing that Roland Barthes viewed the name as the prince of signifiers,[9] and Deck has commented upon the importance of the name in her own practice of writing.[10] Quite clearly and explicitly, she suggests that when Mademoiselle adopts her new name, that very action suffices to set the stage for this fictional world, and to put the intrigue in motion: "Bérénice Beaurivage. Il suffit de prononcer ce nom et tout de suite la perspective se déploie, l'horizon s'élargit" (9).[11] Mademoiselle resolves to become the woman that this euphonious name limns, and she is only momentarily discomfited by the fact that she has borrowed the name from a film: "Se profile un léger embarras. Car ce nom, je ne l'ai pas inventé, il appartient à une autre, quoique pour ainsi dire à moitié. Mon nom est occupé par une actrice dans un film d'Éric Rohmer, la comédienne Arielle Dombasle y interprète le rôle de la romancière Bérénice Beaurivage" (10). Christine Marcandier underscores the irony of Mademoiselle's act, choosing a name from cinema in order to launch the fiction of herself as a writer (120), yet the role comes readymade to Mademoiselle, because Bérénice Beaurivage is a novelist in Rohmer's film, *L'Arbre, le maire et la médiathèque* (1993). Moreover, it is not a very broad leap from a novel to a film, insofar as both serve as privileged vehicles of fiction.

We are frequently confronted with leaps of just that sort in *Le Triangle d'hiver*, where Rohmer's movie plays constantly in the background, as it were. As Mademoiselle builds up and inhabits the fiction of her new life, she finds that it pays a very good return, especially with regard to the men she encounters. The Inspecteur in particular is fascinated by the fact that she is a novelist, making her living with her imagination, while he is an engineer, closely focused on hard fact.

He remarks that she bears a superficial resemblance to the actress Arielle Dombasle, whom he had seen on television fifteen or twenty years previously; a bit later he recalls having seen Arielle Dombasle in a film by Éric Rohmer entitled *Pauline à la plage* (1983). Deck exploits that moment lustily, for if Arielle Dombasle did indeed play a role in *Pauline à la plage*, it was not that of Bérénice Beaurivage. Yet even in his mistake, the Inspecteur comes closer to the truth than he might have suspected. Furthermore, that passage plays out a dynamic that is a crucial one in Julia Deck's novel: the manner in which fictions communicate with each other, contaminate each other, give rise to other fictions, and compete in the world with verifiable fact.

In Mademoiselle's case, that latter competition gradually turns in favor of fact, because the fiction that she has elaborated is not sustainable. She pretends to be a writer, yet quite clearly she cannot write, and the veneer of Bérénice Beaurivage wears thinner by the day in the Inspecteur's eyes, from the moment she moves in with him. It is the devious Blandine Lenoir who precipitates the crisis of the affair, sending an article to the Inspecteur that explodes the myth of Bérénice Beaurivage. Like any good engineer, he checks his facts twice, and then confronts his lover with the truth: "Je t'ai cherchée sur Internet, Bérénice, et tu n'existes pas" (117). Faced with Mademoiselle's reluctance to abandon her pretense, he continues, "il suffisait d'entrer ton nom dans un moteur de recherche pour comprendre qu'il n'y a pas de Bérénice Beaurivage. Sinon au cinéma, dans un film de 1993. Tu es le personnage d'une comédie dramatique tournée il y a plus de vingt ans, et tu n'as pas du tout vieilli, je dirais même que tu parais plus jeune, car c'est vrai que tu lui ressembles, à cette actrice" (118-119). Such a verdict would seem to be beyond appeal, were it not for the way that Mademoiselle clings to the fiction that she has elaborated, and the forbearance of the Inspecteur. As a final piece of evidence, he gives her a copy of Rohmer's film, and she watches it:

> Ensuite j'ai pris le DVD. Il s'agissait d'un long métrage d'Éric Rohmer intitulé *L'Arbre, le maire et la médiathèque*, formule étrange qui ne m'a pas encouragée à l'insérer tout de suite dans le lecteur. Pour ce faire, j'ai attendu que l'Inspecteur parte travailler le lendemain matin, et je me suis installée à mon aise dans le canapé.

> L'intrigue, au demeurant fort mince, reposait sur le triangle composé par un homme et deux femmes, le rôle principal échéant au comédien Pascal Greggory, qui d'abord vivait avec Arielle Dombasle puis, au fil d'interminables arguties, se retrouvait avec Clémentine Amouroux. J'ai pensé que je ressemblais assez à la première, on me l'avait déjà fait remarquer, mais en dehors de ce détail, rien dans le film ne pouvait éclairer ma situation présente. (140)

Several things should be noted here, beginning with the fact that this is the first and only time that the title of Rohmer's film appears in *Le Triangle d'hiver*, despite the fact that the movie has been virtually present since the first page of the novel. Second, Mademoiselle sits down to watch the film as if for the first time, whereas we know that her familiarity with it is longstanding. Third, she recognizes the way that the events of the movie reflect the recent events of her life, yet she seems to dismiss that effect as anecdotal. We readers may react a bit differently however, perceiving the mise-en-abyme quality of this passage, which is of course underscored by the evocation of the *triangle*. Briefly stated, this is a deeply specular moment in the novel, one where Julia Deck invites us to consider the reflections that she constructs. Those latter are many, and they may be dizzying. Most obviously there is the analogy of the two triangulated relations, Mademoiselle/Inspecteur/Blandine on the one hand, and Arielle Dombasle/Pascal Greggory/Clémentine Arnoux on the other. The simplicity of that analogy is significantly complicated if one adds a third triangle, composed of the fictional characters that the actors in Rohmer's movie play: Bérénice Beaurivage/Julien Dechaumes/Blandine Lenoir. In other words, "Blandine Lenoir," just like "Bérénice Beaurivage," is a name borrowed from a film, and the person who bears that name in Julia Deck's novel is undoubtedly playing out a fiction just as fanciful as that of the woman she denounces.

In one perspective, Deck is exploiting the hoary trope of life imitating art. But that relation holds only insofar as we suspend our disbelief, for surely enough what is actually going on is art imitating art. Deck suggests that the two fictional worlds on display here, that of Rohmer's movie and that of her novel, are mutually reflective, symmetrical in a sense, and complementary. Yet that is not quite the way it seems to Mademoiselle and to the "Blandine Lenoir" who exposes her, both of whom inhabit the fictions that Rohmer's film proposes. They migrate back and forth between the real and the fictional with very impressive aplomb. One of the keys to that migration is the word *médiathèque*, which is in its own way as overdetermined in this novel as the word *triangle*. It figures in the title of Rohmer's film of course, but Julia Deck is also careful to point out that both Mademoiselle and Blandine frequent their local media libraries,[12] where they undoubtedly contracted galloping cases of bovarysme. Whatever the other consequences of that disease may be, it enables them to shuttle back and forth between fictions very readily indeed, so readily that it is hardly worthwhile to invoke the notion of metalepsis. Moreover, I believe that Julia Deck is subtly suggesting that we readers are likewise capable of the same sort of migration, the same creative duplicity, at least where our readerly selves are concerned.[13] How else to account for the adroitness with which she juggles the fictional worlds of the film and the novel, the insistency with which she argues their mutual complementarity?

That performance becomes more vertiginous still when Deck factors in Racine's *Bérénice*, which effectively functions to triangulate things. It is worth noting that Mademoiselle appropriates that text just as illegitimately as she does in the case of her name, stealing it from a newsstand in the Gare Montparnasse. It is the play's title that catches her eye in the first instance, and quickly thereafter the brief description of the triangular relationship that the cover blurb sketches: "Vraiment joli prénom, Bérénice. Elle extrait le livre, découvre sur le quatrième plat de couverture l'argument de la pièce de Jean Racine. Une femme entre deux hommes dont celui qu'elle préfère lui préfère le pouvoir, voyez-vous cela, ce n'est pas à moi qu'arriverait ce genre de problème" (45). Julia Deck presents that comment to us ironically, for if one steps back from things a bit, as we readers have the leisure to do, it becomes apparent that Bérénice's situation reflects Mademoiselle's all too well. Deck also takes the opportunity to reflect a bit on the distinctions we commonly draw between "high" culture and "popular" culture, because Mademoiselle had passed over detective novels and romance novels "par principe" (45) before settling upon *Bérénice*. Yet she will not get very far with it, finding herself quickly bored: "Près du lit traîne Jean Racine, elle l'ouvre au hasard, tombe sur Bérénice reprochant à son amant de lui offrir un diadème au lieu de sa présence, ça l'énerve, elle ferme le livre" (55).[14] Later, very much at loose ends in the Inspecteur's Parisian apartment, she turns toward *Bérénice* once again, with little more success:

> De dépit, comme j'avais lu tous les romans de la bibliothèque, je me suis tournée vers la pièce de Jean Racine, qui n'avait pas regagné le dernier tiroir, intitulée *Bérénice* et que j'ai parcourue d'un œil distrait, n'étant guère portée vers la tragédie. J'ai tout de même enregistré la coïncidence entre les deux Bérénice, le personnage interprété par Arielle Dombasle dans le film d'Éric Rohmer s'appelant ainsi. (141)

Whatever other purpose it may serve, that moment confirms in Mademoiselle's mind the triangle effect that structures her circumstances so uncannily. And indeed how could she not recognize that shape, defined as it is by three individuals named "Bérénice"?

It will be clear by now that this novel teems with triangles of different sorts. Those figures are in broad conversation with each other, moreover, for each of them comments upon, complements, and calls into question each of the others. The Bérénice/Bérénice/Bérénice triangle is the most obvious one, undoubtedly, but it is closely followed by the Mademoiselle/Inspecteur/Blandine and the Arielle Dombasle/Pascal Greggory/Clémentine Arnoux triangles. Insofar as Mademoiselle becomes more and more consumed by the fiction she has invented for herself, it is legitimate to imagine her as occupying one of the angles of a Rohmer/Mademoiselle/Racine triangle. Moreover, in view of the complex and wry game the Julia Deck is playing, one might suspect that yet another triangle is in operation here, one wherein Mademoiselle serves as a stalking-horse for Deck herself—but in an unbalanced and extremely mordant way. Indeed, one can hardly avoid that suspicion, in view of the fact that Mademoiselle presents herself as a novelist in the role she scripts for herself.

The figure that then emerges, which one might imagine as Rohmer/Deck/Racine, enables Julia Deck to play on several fronts, and once again the vectors of that play are both frank and ironic, in turn. Frank, because she has very serious things to say about literature and its uses. Ironic, because a chasm yawns between Deck and her protagonist on the one hand, and between Deck and Rohmer and Racine on the other. When it is a question of that latter relation, Deck encourages us to think about how stories are told in different cultural traditions—classical drama, film, the contemporary novel—and how those traditions come into come into conversation with each other, either diachronically or synchronically. Deck also asks us to reflect upon influence and appropriation, for in point of fact her own appropriation of the name "Bérénice" is no less brazen than Mademoiselle's. I argued a moment ago that the triangulation is unbalanced, and that is certainly the case, if one imagines Deck as suspended between a pillar of the French neoclassical canon like Racine and a broadly acknowledged contemporary master like Rohmer. Yet it is also unbalanced by virtue of the fact that when Deck takes Mademoiselle's place in the triangle the disparity between them is dazzling. It hinges precisely upon writing, an effect that Deck exploits with a great deal of brio. Mademoiselle's attempts to pass herself off as a novelist are comical, especially when she is asked to explain how she goes about the practice of her craft: "Oh. C'est assez simple. Et en même temps. Très compliqué. Il faut. On doit. Utiliser les mots. Utiliser sa voix. Oui, c'est la voix qui fait tout. Avec les mots, bien entendu. Vous comprenez?" (64-65). In those moments when she does try to write, she grapples unequally with the demands that writing imposes upon her, with the notionally simple gesture of putting words down on paper, one after the other:

> Elle farfouille dans son fourbi, exhume un carnet décoré d'étoiles en strass. De fines lignes bleutées attendent de guider l'écriture à travers les pages, et par prudence elle l'ouvre à la troisième, ayant observé qu'il est souvent préférable de ne pas commencer par le début.
>
> Après quoi il n'y a plus qu'à. Mâchouiller le bout de son stylo, lever les yeux au plafond, ébaucher un bout d'idée, le transcrire avant de s'apercevoir qu'il est trop bête. Rayer trois mots, recommencer. Refaire du thé, repasser devant le paquebot qui obstrue toujours son champ visuel, libérer son esprit des pensées parasites, récrire trois mots en se disant Après tout, il s'agit d'avancer, je corrigerai plus tard. Relire ces trois mots, les barrer avec force, la page se déchire. (21)

That passage is a poignant one for anyone who writes, and Deck is attentive to that poignancy. Yet, stepping back from the fictional world once again, it is beyond dispute that this description of a novelist who cannot write has been written by a novelist who *can*, that Julia Deck has in this very case put 126 words on paper, one after the other, in such a way that they make excellent sense to a reader. It is trivially true to say that such a process lies at the heart of this novel. More consequentially however, in *Le Triangle d'hiver* Deck is speaking about writing as *building*, as construction, and about the architectonics and the suave geometries that subtend that process. In that perspective, the novel itself plays out the key features of the figure it adopts as its totem. One of the most pleasing things about a triangle is that if one follows the line that it traces, one eventually finds one's way back to the point where one began. But it is not quite the same point after all, for it has been subtly reconfigured by everything that has preceded. And if one were to take another trip around the perimeter of the figure, one might expect that trip to be rather different from the first.

Christine Montalbetti's Mission

UNDER NORMAL circumstances, one wouldn't look for a fish in a tree. Yet when Christine Montalbetti looks through her family tree in order to find the oldest ancestor whom she can identify, she comes upon one Jules Poisson (1833-1919), her great-great-grandfather. Her efforts to understand what sort of a person he was involve both a quest and an inquest. She chronicles those efforts in *Mon ancêtre Poisson* (2019), a book quite unlike any other that she has written to this point. The text bears the traces of a variety of techniques. A great deal of documentary, archival research certainly went into it, but so did a lot of speculation. Hard fact and objective, even scientific data rub elbows with very personal considerations. Flatly declarative narration gives way to an impassioned intergenerational conversation, and vice versa, turn and turn about. This hybridity of conception and execution is so pronounced that one hardly knows what to call the book. Thankfully enough, the Éditions P.O.L provide an answer of sorts on both the cover of the book and the title page, with the indication "Roman." Upon reflection—and granted the capacious dimensions of that genre—that suggestion makes a good deal of sense.

By any standard, Jules Poisson's career was exceptional. He began his working life when he was just two months shy of his tenth birthday, as an apprentice gardener at the Jardin des Plantes, in Paris. Drawing upon a sharp intelligence as well as a vast curiosity about the natural world, and by dint of extraordinary effort, he would become a distinguished, broadly published botanist. Among his other legacies, he is the object of a Wikipedia entry, a solid claim to achievement in our ephemeral digital age. There, the "partial" list of his publications runs to forty-odd entries, on subjects as diverse as the flora of the Quai d'Orsay Palace, the echinocactus genus in Baja California, rhododendrons, kudzu, palm trees, yuccas, fig trees, agaves, giant sequoias, orchids, and new techniques in potato preservation. Clearly, he was a man whose mind ranged widely, a polymath equally intrigued by the big and the small, the near and the far, the familiar and the exotic. According to family legend, he met his wife, Sophie, in Corsica. They would have three children, one of whom would be Christine Montalbetti's great-grandmother.

As her title indicates, Montalbetti wagers heavily upon the proper name in her book, especially in its liminal moments, as she sets the stage for what follows and coaxes her reader into a posture of narrative complicity.[1] It is not for nothing that Roland Barthes designated the proper name as the prince of signifiers,[2] and the onomastic strategy that Montalbetti deploys is very efficient indeed. She plays upon the cratylic value of her forebear's name, considering it in different lights, and inviting her reader to play along with her. In the first instance—that is to say, in the first sentence of the novel—that invitation takes the form of a thought experiment. "On pourrait appeler ça l'expérience de l'aquarium," muses Montalbetti, urging us to imagine ourselves in front of an aquarium, nose to nose with a fish. "Que se passe-t-il dans ce moment où vous fichez vos yeux chacun dans ceux de l'autre?" she asks (7-8). Well, one thing that might happen is an absolutely unanticipated moment of recognition:

> Est-ce qu'il n'y a pas quelque chose qui s'agite en vous sans forcément que vous parveniez à en identifier la cause? Une mémoire obscure qui vous revient, une intuition bizarre, quelle rumeur, quel savoir? Vous, sollicité par la bestiole, intrigué par la nature de cette rencontre, et est-ce que ce n'est pas parce que, malgré vous, dans cet instant, vous regardez une ancienne forme de vous-même? (8)

In a similar manner, when Montalbetti casts her glance on another sort of fish—not across the vastness of evolutionary time, but across four generations—she recognizes something of herself therein. She plays upon that analogy with a good deal of glee, insisting upon the term that serves as its linchpin, the name, "Ton nom précieux pour moi, emblématique [. . .], ton nom qui naturellement te désigne comme une origine" (18). Jules Poisson's name is thus doubly *original*. Montalbetti wonders if he himself remained throughout his life attentive to its homonymic resonance. Certainly he must have recognized it as a child, but perhaps thereafter it became transparent for him. If not, Montalbetti reasons, if her forefather continued to think about his name in other contexts, he must have had ample occasion to muse wryly upon it, as does Montalbetti herself. Fish swim throughout this book in a variety of guises. For example, among all of her other archival activities, Montalbetti collects a dossier of articles devoted to fish appearing in the journal *La Nature* during her ancestor's lifetime. As a subscriber and frequent contributor to that publication, he must have seen those pieces and been amused by them, Montalbetti reflects; and she reads them over his shoulder, as it were, in an effort to understand him and thus to bridge the daunting gap between herself and this forebear whom she never met.

The manner in which she addresses him is very much a part of that strategy. Karin Schwerdtner has studied the modalities of address in Montalbetti's work, arguing that since her very first book, the attention she has paid to address has been an important facet of her style (Schwerdtner 171). Noting that there are two principal axes of address in the novel *Trouville Casino* (2018), one directed toward the protagonist using the second person singular, and one toward the reader using the second person plural, Schwerdtner frames that dynamic as a wager. When she invites Montalbetti to comment upon that effect in an interview, Montalbetti confirms that doubling of address: "Il y a effectivement un double dialogue dans *Trouville Casino*: d'une part, avec le lecteur et, d'autre part, avec mon protagoniste" (171), while affirming that the notion of address is fundamental to her own conception of literature.[3] She mentions that the *tutoiement* that she uses with her character helps her to recognize a kind of commonality that they share, while the *vouvoiement* with which she addresses her reader is a form of "délicatesse" rather than a means of keeping the reader at a distance (173). Yet Montalbetti is careful to note another reason for that technique: "D'autre part, la deuxième raison pour laquelle j'ai eu envie de conserver ce 'tu,' c'était parce que cela me plaisait beaucoup de me trouver dans la situation de la double-adresse. C'était un plaisir d'écriture que de m'adresser tour à tour à un 'vous' et à un 'tu,' voire d'interpeller parfois les deux destinataires dans la même phrase. Cela introduit dans ma phrase une énergie nouvelle" (173).

Now, this discussion of the technique of double address concerns *Trouville Casino*, which was Montalbetti's most recently published book when Schwerdtner interviewed her. Montalbetti calls upon that technique once again in *Mon ancêtre Poisson*, which appeared the following year; but this time the stakes are a bit higher. For her protagonist is no longer an individual whom she picked out of the back pages of the newspaper and with whom she claims no real connection, but rather her great-great-grandfather. The *tu* through which she addresses him is thus far more charged with affect. And the double address that she practices in *Mon ancêtre Poisson* puts her readers into a rather different situation, insofar as we witness Montalbetti's search for a "commonality" with her protagonist that is far more urgent than in *Trouville Casino*. That very urgency, that strong desire for connection, lies at the very center of the thematics of *Mon ancêtre Poisson*. It is something that Montalbetti calls upon us to recognize, and to ratify, early on in her book: "Ta présence flotte ici, un fantôme bénéfique, et qui m'apaise. Cette affection inconsidérée qu'on peut ressentir pour des ancêtres qu'on n'a pas connus, vous devez bien savoir aussi de quoi je parle" (27). Such solicitation is part of a broader strategy intended to engage the reader, certainly; but the terms of that engagement are likewise more urgent here than in Montalbetti's previous books. It is reasonable to believe that her intent is that some small part of her affective engagement with her protagonist will color the way we respond to him, as well—and will inflect the way we understand the mission that she has undertaken in this curious book.

The stories that Montalbetti tells here are various and multicolored. Parts of these stories are also imbricated in what is more properly called history, for in his eighty-six years of life Jules Poisson was witness to a great many events that we now designate as important ones. "Comment est-ce que tu la vis, toi, la Commune," asks Montalbetti, "et avant ça la guerre de 1870, comment est-ce que ça se passe, pour toi, le siège de Paris?" (50). She remarks that he was there for the birth of cinema; she wonders if he saw the First World War coming; she knows that he lived long enough to see the end of that war and the Treaty of Versailles (108, 181, 221-22). Inscribing her ancestor in history in that manner is a way of guaranteeing his existence, of making that existence more objective, concrete, and phenomenal. It also provides Montalbetti with a set of handholds as she reaches back into a past that is well beyond her own, in search of a person with whom she was not acquainted. In that dimension of her project, then, she wagers upon the *real*.⁴

Far more often, however, Montalbetti is obliged to call upon her imagination in order to animate her great-great-grandfather for herself, and for us. This is especially true when she tries to conjure up the fabric of Jules Poisson's daily life: "Tu sors de l'immeuble, tu remontes cette rue timide, tu marches dans Paris, passent les voitures à cheval, c'est un bruit constant de sabots, de cliquetis de harnais, de frottement de roues en bois, on ne pense pas toujours à imaginer la nature des sons qui entourent tes promenades, et parfois dans l'air le sifflement d'un fouet. Placez un hennissement, c'est possible, un brouhaha de naseaux qui s'ébrouent" (108). Thankfully, Montalbetti's imagination is fertile; and as the latter passage demonstrates, she is not shy about putting it on display. Such a gesture serves to call us to attention, and to enlist us as active participants in the process of envisioning Jules Poisson. It is not the *real* that she offers us here, of course, but something that seeks to approximate the real. Imagining this man walking in the streets of Paris in a soundscape of clopping hooves, the clacking of wooden wheels on cobblestones, and the whinnying of horses is certainly credible enough, suggesting as it does some of the thickness of the real. Moreover, it corresponds closely to what Pierre Bayard has termed a *vérité subjective*, which he views as more powerful and stable than mere fact, by virtue of the impressive consistency it enjoys in the mind of the subject who proposes it (*Comment parler des faits qui ne se sont pas produits?* 26).⁵

Montalbetti nevertheless recognizes the limits of that process of imagination, and she calls our attention to them from time to time. The profiles of those limits become particularly clear in cases where imagination stumbles upon the world of phenomena. When Montalbetti imagines her ancestor fretting about people who die from ingesting poisonous mushrooms, for instance, she regrets that she cannot comfort him by her touch: "Cet enjeu qui te pèse, ton sérieux, ta volonté de bien faire, tout est contenu dans ce petit pli sur lequel je ne pourrai pas passer mes doigts, tout doux, tout doux, pour tenter de t'apaiser" (126). Neither is it possible, she laments, for her to hear his voice: "Ta voix, Jules, je n'aurai pas eu la chance de ça, ta voix hors d'atteinte, ta voix disparue pour toujours" (87). Fundamentally, the problem is one of *contact*, and that is a notion with which Montalbetti grapples throughout this book, in a variety of different ways and in many different contexts.

On occasion, Montalbetti asks herself what her forefather would think of the story she is telling about him. Once, as she describes a scene of Jules Poisson and his son Eugène writing a scientific text together, and the son chafing under the authority of the father, Montalbetti wonders if that same father, that great-great-grandfather, would not be tempted to call her to account in order to rein in her writerly imagination. "Parce que tu vas me dire que je brode" (131), she worries. The word *broder* is an interesting one, insofar as in its most literal sense it suggests work typically associated with women, work undertaken in an aesthetic spirit rather than a strictly utilitarian one, something supplemental rather than essential. Yet if one cares to parse those cultural clichés in a more serious manner, taking into account considerations of gender and the way we think about science on the one hand and literature on the other, one of the central piquancies of this book soon becomes apparent. For it is a matter of verifiable fact that this supremely pragmatic man of science engendered, through a few intermediary generations, a novelist.

As Montalbetti surveys the task that she has set for herself, in the early pages of her book, she recognizes that Jules Poisson's life has something fundamentally *romanesque* to it. She suspects that in some sense, the novel she wishes to write is already present in latent form—or perhaps in fragments waiting only to be reassembled:

> Ta vie, Jules, c'est avant tout une série de petits romans, et d'abord les romans que les uns et les autres, dans la famille, on s'est faits à ton sujet.
>
> Chacun le sien, chacun privilégiant un aspect, tirant sur un fil plutôt que sur un autre, chacun selon sa sensibilité, mais tous aussi oeuvrant au même roman commun, l'entérinant, le répétant, nous le refilant, de génération en génération, et puis le faisant circuler à qui veut bien l'entendre.
>
> Un roman troué, bien sûr, un roman lacunaire.
>
> Un roman XIXe, puisque tu nais en 1833, et qui déborde sur le siècle suivant au point que tu connaîtras toute la guerre de 14, une vie longue, oui, puisque tu sauras comment va le monde jusqu'en 1919. (9)

One might suppose thus that Montalbetti's project resembles that of someone assembling a jigsaw puzzle, to borrow an image from Georges Perec. More a matter of reception than of production, more readerly and less writerly, Montalbetti's responsibility would be to collect those disparate narrative fragments and to construct a coherent whole out of them. Yet, having adumbrated that idea, she is quick to disabuse us of it, stressing the fact that she herself has stories to tell,[6] and that she is eager to begin telling them:

> Et puis il y a aussi tous les romans qu'à partir de maintenant je vais me faire de toi. Parce que voulant gratter le vernis du roman familial pour tenter de faire apparaître une vérité (oh, j'y parviendrai peut-être parfois, quelques fulgurances de vérité, le frisson de ça), je m'en invente aussi d'autres. La moindre information ouvre une perspective dans laquelle mon imagination forcément s'engouffre, un nouveau roman hypothétique se dessine alors, qui complète ou d'autres fois corrige le précédent, qui parfois infirme non seulement le roman familial (et l'enquête est bien là pour ça), mais celui que je m'étais fait à mon tour. Et de sorte qu'ici ce sont aussi toutes sortes de petits romans successifs de ta vie, comme une addition de petits romans, tu vois, prends-les comme ça. (10-11)

Moreover, it is useful to recall that Montalbetti's project is not merely biographical in character. It is a novel, after all, and if its main protagonist often occupies the center of the narrative stage, the book is not solely and uniquely about him. That is, just as Montalbetti is not exclusively occupied here in collecting and assembling the stories that others told about Jules Poisson, neither is she merely interested in collecting and assembling incidents of his life. For a life—any life—is not a mere series of incidents, it is far more dynamic and complex than that.[7] That is true of Jules Poisson's life, and it is also true of Christine Montalbetti's life. And if she is demonstrably concerned with understanding who her great-great-grandfather was in his life, she is also concerned with what that very understanding might mean in her own life. In other terms, this is a book about him, but it is also a book about her—and about the vexed notion of *contact* between one person and the other.

In Montalbetti's view, the most reliable way of facilitating the sort of contact she seeks is through reading. I have mentioned that she reads articles in contemporary journals that Jules Poisson must have read, telling herself that she is in a sense reading along with him.[8] She also attempts to read as much of his own writing as she possibly can. She reads some of his letters, the ones that are on file in the Muséum National d'Histoire Naturelle. But she concentrates most closely upon his scholarly, scientific writings, which he published in journals such as *La Revue horticole, Le Bulletin du Muséum, Le Bulletin de la Société botanique de France*, and especially *La Nature*. She reasons that it is there that her ancestor as he really was is to be found. Moreover, the archives of those publications can now be accessed online, and thus Montalbetti can consult them without leaving home, at her ease.

When she comes upon Jules Poisson's first published sentence, she finds it very striking: "'Le genre *Casuarina* forme à lui seul la petite famille des Casuarinées.' La voilà, ta première phrase publiée, celle par laquelle tout commence, et cette expression, 'petite famille,' qu'est-ce que tu veux, aussitôt, ça me fait fondre. 'Petite famille,' je me dis, c'est tout nous, ça" (60). Yet reading that sentence, Montalbetti over-reads it, for surely her forebear did not have her in mind—or indeed any branch of his own family—when he wrote it. But that sort of readerly projection, fueled by desire, is very much a part of Montalbetti's project. It is a way of abolishing the distance that looms between her and Jules Poisson. More cannily, and in a less obvious manner, it is also a way of soliciting our complaisance and, eventually, our active collaboration. For in this instance, as we ourselves read, we are watching Montalbetti read, and she wagers that the analogies circulating in that dynamic will prove to be strongly affiliative.[9]

As she reads her ancestor's writings, Montalbetti is principally interested in the way that the writer attempts to be as non-intrusive, as "objective," as transparent as possible. Yet it is also true that any writing bears traces of the writer to some degree, however minimal. Christine Montalbetti is an extremely attentive, resourceful reader, and she is willing to go to very considerable lengths in order to identify traces of the *je* in her forefather's writings. She seizes upon the smallest indication that might reveal a detail of his daily life, using those moments to paint a picture of Jules Poisson in his own element. Among all of those instances, she is most deeply fascinated by the passages that suggest an affinity between her ancestor and herself. She thinks of those cases as moments of "proximity," a powerful notion deeply imbricated in the longing for contact that lies at the heart of her project:

> Je continue à me frayer un chemin dans tes articles. Ce qui me frappe aussi, nos proximités. Oh, parfois ce sont des détails. Tu orthographies mal Mississippi, par exemple (moi pareil—on doit être quelques-uns dans ce cas). [. . .] Ou une proximité stylistique, comme ça. Tu écris qu'une plante pousse 'sans broncher,' et je trouve à ta phrase quelque chose de familier. 'Sans broncher,' va savoir, j'aurais pu écrire ça d'une plante. (81-82)

Clearly enough, these "proximities" devolve upon writing itself, and upon the small, barely noticeable tics of personal style. Sometimes, however, considerations a bit broader in scope are at stake. Montalbetti registers and applauds the attentiveness with which Jules Poisson addresses his readers, seeing therein a significant feature of her own writerly practice. She thinks about the way he imagines the "communauté floue" (82) of his readership, recognizing two things: one the one hand, that she now belongs to that very community; on the other, that she and her ancestor are both extraordinarily heedful of their readers. Reading through his published works, Montalbetti notes that he wrote quite a bit about Japan and about America, just as she herself has done,[10] and she takes that as yet another sure sign of their connection, as uncanny as it may be. Identifying those points of connection is one thing, but nourishing that connection is another. To Montalbetti's way of thinking, that latter process can take place only in the active, sustained communication between a writer and a reader. She remarks that, whatever else may be going on in Jules Poisson's life, he continues to write: "C'est ce que tu fais. Comme je continue à te lire. Un compagnonnage, c'est comme ça que je le vis" (86). More than anywhere else, it is in that uninterrupted, purposeful dynamic of production and reception that Montalbetti finds connection: "Je me sens comme en duplex avec toi, un duplex temporel, toi, enfoui dans ton XIXe, et moi depuis ce XXIe" (87). Yet the truth of the matter is that in her case at least, it is not a simple question of production and reception, because it is her reading of her forefather's writing that fuels her own production:

> Ce que je fais, longtemps, je te lis et à tes phrases je noue les miennes. Chaque matin à m'asseoir à ma table, à parcourir lentement un de tes articles. Je prélève certains de tes mots, je les enrobe de guillemets et je les dépose délicatement sur ma page (ils passent ainsi de ta main à mes doigts), et tes phrases font naître les miennes, elles en appellent d'autres, qui me viennent en réponse. C'est comme une folle conversation avec toi, une tresse joyeuse de nos phrases, qui s'entremêlent. (63)

Moreover, patently enough, we readers are invested with the reception of that production. Again and again, however, Montalbetti suggests that reading—whether it be hers or ours—is not a merely passive activity, but that it must involve an active, critical engagement, and in fact some form of production. Thus, in the way that Montalbetti reads her great-great-grandfather, I am obliged to recognize the way that I read Montalbetti, even though the situation and the stakes of those gestures are very different. In that very perspective, the logic of Montalbetti's attentiveness to her reader becomes clearer. In encouraging us to believe that we have something to *do* here,[11] she is promoting a highly interactive vision of writing and reading, one in which communication flows in both directions, rather than just from writer to reader. In the first instance, and most obviously, that stance is calculated to heighten the sense of connection that we feel with her. In another light, and more particularly, it suggests that the kind of connection that she is seeking with her grandfather is far more plausible than it might have appeared to be at first glance.

Since the beginning of her career, a strong current of metacommentary has characterized each of Christine Montalbetti's novels. In *Mon ancêtre Poisson*, however, the wager that subtends that technique is much more urgent, and its dimensions are considerably more vast. One manifestation of that current is the narrative "intrusion" that Montalbetti typically practices, an effect that she has honed over the course of her career, and that she uses broadly in this book. At its simplest level, that effect serves to remind us that a story is being told by a narrator who is making certain choices with regard to the telling. For example, when Montalbetti uses the interjection "mazette," she intervenes to add, parenthetically: "j'adore dire mazette quand je parle à quelqu'un du XIXe siècle" (73). Obviously enough, the *je* alerts us to the fact that the focus of the telling has shifted from Jules Poisson to the narrator herself (though we may eventually be tempted to ask ourselves if that shift is quite as dramatic as it seems in the early portion of the novel). Calling attention explicitly to the way she uses language, the narrator encourages us to be mindful of that dimension of her storytelling. Questions of authority and control are also in play here, for the narrator is also gently reminding us that she will tell this story in the way she deems best.

Other instances of that technique are a bit more involved, and serve to underscore other considerations. Addressing her ancestor in the second person singular, Montalbetti says: "Au printemps (je te la fais bucolique), il paraît que ce sont d'abord le lilas, l'anémone et la primevère qui fleurissent" (60). The evocation of flowers puts this remark squarely in Jules Poisson's wheelhouse, yet the question of address is not as simple as it seems. For Montalbetti is clearly calling our readerly attention to the way in which she sets this scene: among all of the possibilities available to her, she has chosen to present that particular spring as "bucolic." That it should be bucolic or otherwise is a matter of little importance; what counts is the way in which she places the issue of narrative choice on center stage and causes it to perform.

From time to time, Montalbetti invokes the *here* and the *now* of the narration itself: "Je me sens un peu agitée. La porte-fenêtre est ouverte, même si la nuit est proche. Ça a été une belle journée d'octobre. Une moto passe au loin. Des bruits parviennent des jardinets alentour, mal identifiables, on commence peut-être à préparer le repas" (137). This too is a kind of mise en scène, the construction of a decor and a context for the narrator and the task she has set for herself, the problems she faces, her disposition of spirit as she grapples with those problems, and so forth. Whereas in this passage, it is simply a question of the telling, without further specification of the nature of that activity, in certain other passages Montalbetti makes it clear that her own telling, in this instance, takes the form of *writing*. "Je remplis des pages et des pages," she remarks, "sur un fichier préparatoire (à la fin, plus de 800, tu parles, qui font comme une tour de Pise, toute de guingois, pile énorme et bancale, qui manifeste mon enthousiasme, mais voilà où j'en serai, mon pauvre Jules, à crouler sous les brouillons—si tu savais dans quel état parfois ça me met)" (64). Other moments in the text are more explicitly metanarrative in character, moments when Montalbetti not only reminds us that she is telling a story, but also defends her particular way of telling it: "Des revirements, ici, il va y en avoir, des reconfigurations de la légende familiale, des changements de perspective, des renversements" (39). But what is the sense of that defense? It is not as if we readers were in possession of the *true* story of Jules Poisson's life, nor of the way that life is remembered in Montalbetti's family. We have no grounds to criticize the fidelity of her storytelling, granted that her story of Jules Poisson is the only one we have. Something else is at issue here, I believe.

It is reasonable to infer that that "something else" may be involved with storytelling itself, with its possibilities and its limits, its vexations, its relation to its subject and its object. On several occasions, Montalbetti reflects upon narrative insufficiency, upon the way that any story, when parsed with a critical eye, seems incomplete. Such is the case of the stories that she seeks in the archives of the Museum or in her family mythology, and such is also the case of the story that she herself tells. "Le plaisir qu'il y a à se les faire, ces petits romans, la nécessité aussi, comme s'il fallait ne pas laisser trop de zones vides, pas trop de blancs dans les histoires d'où l'on vient et qui sont déjà si trouées, si faites de manques, alors on se lance dans le mouvement des hypothèses et, toutes fragiles qu'elles sont, elles viennent combler quelque chose qui s'inquiétait en nous" (73). The hard truth is that any story has interruptions and lacunae. Those phenomena can be more or less pronounced—and to the extent that they seem pronounced, a storyteller (or indeed a reader) may wish to repair them somehow. But how is that latter gesture to be achieved? Is it a matter of bridging those narrative gaps, or of filling them up with palliative material, or of configuring things such that they loom less large? Or might one choose to call attention to them and to highlight the manner in which they affect both the storyteller and the reader?

That is of course Montalbetti's strategy. It is an efficient way to encourage us to think about narration, and more broadly about representation. Fiction and the real are both at issue here, each interrogating the other. The hybridity of Montalbetti's storytelling serves to persuade us that those two worlds are less dissimilar than we might have thought, at least when it is a question of representation. Montalbetti frets that she cannot describe all of the people who played a role in Jules Poisson's life, all of these "personnages secondaires" (76), as they necessarily become in the *story* of his life. What fuels that remark is the desire for totalization, and what Montalbetti is chafing against is the impossibility of ever saying everything about anything. Both in her work as a novelist and as a literary theorist, she has without a doubt been long aware of that impossibility, and yet she discovers it again and anew in this text, "cette évidence que personne ne peut raconter votre vie exactement comme elle a été" (144). The only way to live with that impossibility is to recalibrate one's expectations, such that they become a shade more modest, and indeed that is precisely what Montalbetti does. In a passage devoted to Edison's experiments with voice recordings, she might just as well be speaking about her own project: "Retenir des traces, en tout cas, voilà à quoi on s'occupe" (87).

All of that reflection upon the work of narration and the novel's horizon of possibility leads Montalbetti to new ways of thinking about both reading and writing:

> Tout ce que la phrase de roman draine et ne cesse de réinventer pour le transformer en une fête bizarre. Car est-ce que ce n'est pas ça, la lecture, une fête bizarre, la célébration étonnée des sentiments divers qui nous traversent, et qui ne sont pourtant pas tous heureux, loin de là? Et le moment de l'écriture aussi, fête bizarre, car à sa façon la phrase, au moment où elle prend vie, en même temps la donne, elle a ce pouvoir de produire des mondes, elle procure cette joie puissante. Une fête, oui, indéniable; et pourtant, pourquoi est-ce que tu me fais penser à ça, ce geste a quelque chose aussi du celui de Frankenstein, le savant qui dans le roman de Mary Shelley travaille à inventer une créature, car il le fait, quelle horreur, avec des bouts de cadavres qu'il accole, comme nous avec nos morts, nos morts dont on ne sait pas bien faire le deuil, ceux qu'on connaît et ceux qu'on ignore (et dont parfois on finit par apprendre l'existence). (168)

The bizarrerie of reading and writing pales, however, in comparison to that of the competing analogies that Montalbetti implicitly invokes in this passage. For if she can be imagined as a Mary Shelley inventing her Frankenstein, she can also be imagined as a Frankenstein inventing his monster. Those analogies take on additional piquancy when one recalls that Montalbetti has chosen men of science as her protagonists upon a couple of other occasions. In her second novel, *L'Origine de l'homme*, for example, she focuses on Jacques Boucher de Crèvecoeur de Perthes, a nineteenth-century French archaeologist interested in the Stone Age. In 2010, Montalbetti conceived a one-man-show for the actor Denis Podalydès, entitled *Le Cas Jekyll*. Just like Victor Frankenstein, Henry Jekyll's experiments would go badly awry. And for largely the same reasons, because both of them abuse the creative powers that science affords them. When Montalbetti draws our attention to the fact that, "il y aura eu quelques savants dans mes livres" (34), it is more than a simple instance of autoallusion, I think. It is also a tactful and mildly oblique manner of mooting the issue of scientific investigation and creativity, a question that echoes throughout *Mon ancêtre Poisson*, in different guises. For she herself is of course engaged both in investigation and creation here, in ways that are more than merely anecdotal.

That is not to belittle the anecdote, however, because as a theorist of narrative and also as a novelist, Montalbetti is well placed to measure its potential. Just like the question of narrative choice, she theatricalizes the anecdote in her novel and enlists it in the drama she proposes to us. In the liminal moments of the text, she announces, "C'est un roman qui s'organise autour de deux anecdotes, toujours les mêmes" (9), adding that these anecdotes were fundamental to her family mythology, told over and over again at gatherings of one sort or another. She mentions that when she was a little girl, she would be called upon to recite those anecdotes for the benefit of guests. "Je vous les raconterai" (10), she promises us—for in this instance, we are of course her guests. Thus does she launch one dimension of the hermeneutic code in this novel, an effect that she will cultivate throughout the text, with very considerable care. She alludes to those two anecdotes from time to time, even suggesting on one occasion, provocatively, that there may be a third. She muses upon their role in the family dynamic, suggesting that they served as pawns in a conversational game, and musing that her great-great-grandfather seemed to have been the only member of her family to have been enshrined in anecdote. When Montalbetti decides that the moment has come to reveal those two anecdotes to us, she gives us only the first, describing it as "un peu potache" (149), a bit puerile. And indeed it is innocent enough, involving someone who gave fish eggs to Jules Poisson, asking him to identify what plant they came from, and thinking thus to trick him. Poisson immediately sees through the fishiness of that proposition, but he delays his answer in order to heighten the suspense of the moment—just as his great-great-granddaughter delays the telling of those anecdotes in her novel.

Montalbetti underscores that delay for our benefit in an effort to pique our readerly curiosity still further:

> Oui, je le sais, qu'il y a la deuxième anecdote.
> Peut-être que tu trembles un peu, que tu préférerais que je la taise. Ou bien est-ce que c'est moi qui n'en mène pas large?
> On la racontait si facilement, quand j'y pense. Les temps ont changé, il faut croire. Je me laissais faire par l'entrain des adultes; aujourd'hui, elle me bouleverse.
> Ça ne vous plaît pas trop, en général, qu'on fasse de la rétention, mais voilà, il y a quelque chose là qui me paraît impossible à dire. (152)

What could have been so easily sayable in the family gatherings of her youth, but is now impossible to say? Quaint then, but terrible now? She informs us again that she is not ready to disclose that second anecdote to us, adding that she is resisting the temptation to do so. "Pour le moment je résiste, pour le moment je tiens bon," she remarks (197). She wonders if it is legitimate to confine that anecdote to the shadows of her novel, to what Gerald Prince terms the "unnarratable,"[12] or if to the contrary she owes it to us to reveal it. When finally Montalbetti does put that anecdote on the table, what we have been conditioned to anticipate as an explosion of truth proves to be not much more than a muted snap of the fingers. The anecdote involves a dinner that Jules Poisson hosted, or at which he was a guest, in which the attendees were led to believe that they had been served human flesh. The impact of that revelation is underwhelming; one can certainly understand that the anecdote circulated freely in the family mythology; and one is left to wonder if there is not something else of far greater importance that has not yet been said.

As to that mythology, what is its function, if not to certify the absolute, uninterrupted continuity of the family? That notion is an important one for Montalbetti, because it serves to make the difficult prospect of *contact* a bit more plausible. Speaking about her grandmother, she remarks: "Elle avait tant de plaisir à me parler de toi, ma grand-mère-ta-petite-fille" (27). More than anyone else, her grandmother is the person who links her to her great-great-grandfather. Montalbetti knew her, and she knew him: is it thus unreasonable to believe that Montalbetti can come to some knowledge of him? And yet it is undoubtedly not merely a question of knowledge, for that lineage is cemented and guaranteed, in Montalbetti's view, by love: "Elle t'aimait (toi, délicieux, facétieux, comme elle te décrivait), je l'aimais, je vous dis les choses simplement" (28). Montalbetti reflects that both she and Jules Poisson had gazed upon her grandmother, and that idea prompts her to think about what it is to see and what it is to understand. Another event that Montalbetti recounts serves to materialize and reinforce that same theme. When her mother learns that she is writing about Jules Poisson, she makes a gift of his eyeglasses to her. For Montalbetti, the significance of that is a matter of *touch*—"tenir entre mes doigts ce que tu avais tenu," she remarks (46)—, but it is also a matter of *sight*, and of the kind of *insight* that she is trying to achieve in her project. All of those considerations serve to buttress the curious sense of connection in the present moment, "ce sentiment d'accompagnement" (28) that she feels with regard to her ancestor.

That sense of connection is colored by sadness and by a kind of mourning. I qualify that latter term because Montalbetti herself expresses some skepticism about it. On one occasion, she confesses: "j'ai toujours eu du mal avec les affaires des morts" (47). And one will recall that in her remarks about the way Frankenstein creates his monster out of several different cadavers, Montalbetti suggests that we do largely the same with the dead whom we mourn, both those whom we knew well and those whom we knew far less well, "nos morts dont on ne sait pas bien faire le deuil" (168). In other words, for her, the act of mourning is never given and simple; it is always something questionable. Her project puts that dubious character of mourning massively on display, most especially in those moments where Montalbetti reflects upon some of the tensions that subtend it:

> C'est le moment du songe, une histoire de famille aussi, ce songe d'Athalie, de deuil, et rêver des morts, est-ce que ce n'est pas de ça ici qu'il s'agit? Et à ma façon, de réparer

> l'irréparable, incomplètement, naïvement, éperdument, dans le deuil où je suis non seulement de toi mais aussi de notre rencontre impossible, parce que oui, c'est ce à quoi ce récit tend, sa mission déraisonnable, combler à la fois certaines des lacunes de ton histoire et ce fossé qui nous sépare, qui fait que nos corps ne se seront jamais croisés dans ce Jardin où nous ne marchons pas au même moment, et de sorte que les pages de ce livre sont le seul lieu où nous pouvons nous tenir ensemble, fragilement. (48-49)

Montalbetti is fully aware of the fundamentally quixotic nature of her project, and of the desire for an "impossible encounter" that fuels it. She furthermore realizes that the "mission" she has set for herself is "unreasonable": it is not *reasonable* to think that she will be able to fill in all of the gaps in her forefather's life story, nor is it reasonable to believe that by virtue of her efforts she can bridge the distance between him and her. Most obviously, it is not reasonable to mourn a great-great-grandfather whose existence came to an end fully two generations before one's own existence began. Freud describes mourning as a reaction to loss,[13] but in what sense can Montalbetti claim to have "lost" Jules Poisson? Once again, it seems legitimate to ask if there is not something else going on here, something undisclosed that amplifies the way that Montalbetti mourns her ancestor.

Sadness is not lacking in the way she thinks about him, to be sure. She sees a sadness in him that she had not expected, granted the way he was enshrined in family legend as a calmly confident, quietly joyful figure. She discerns that sadness immediately in the photo of Jules Poisson that she contemplates, and she wonders about its source. She sees pain in her forefather's face, too, and she speculates that he himself may have been in a state of mourning at the time the photo was taken, remembering his son Eugène, who had died, alone, in Africa. As Montalbetti thinks about Jules Poisson and his son, and about the incomplete nature of their story and thus hers, she too is afflicted by sadness, as if through inheritance: "Parfois, je regrette le flou, l'indécision, les questions encore en suspens au sujet de ton fils. Des tristesses me viennent que je n'aurais pas eues sinon" (165).

Yet is it really a matter of inheritance, or rather of something else? Just as Montalbetti wonders about the origin of Jules Poisson's sadness, it is plausible that we should wonder about the cause for her sadness, if the sources that she has adduced thus far seem insufficient. And if mourning is so insistently at issue in this book, it is useful to ask who is the object of that mourning, if indeed it seems *unreasonable* that it should be one's great-great-grandfather. Bringing her novel to its end, Montalbetti speaks again of her desire for connection with her ancestor, remarking that she would like to link arms with him and stroll along the paths in the Jardin des Plantes. She imagines that she might confide in him "quelque chose [. . .] qui aujourd'hui distille en moi un genre de tristesse, à cause d'un événement survenu depuis et de sorte que j'ai l'impression que désormais je la porterai toujours en moi, cette tristesse" (229). She realizes that that "something" is parked, mutely, in a dark place within her, but she knows that it will emerge one day, perhaps when she is very old. She imagines herself in a nursing home, grappling with her memories, confusing past and present, trying to explain herself to the staff responsible for her care:

> Et ce dont je leur parlerai, il y a cent à parier contre un, de ma fille, Suzanne, comme si je l'avais vue la veille (Suzanne, je le laisserai passer dans ma bouche, ce prénom, frôler mes lèvres chaque fois qu'il sortira—mes lèvres un peu baveuses, tenez, essuyez-vous, elles me tendront le mouchoir que je porterai d'une main tremblante à ma bouche), la chose qui ne passera pas, ce sera elle, de l'avoir portée un temps (un peu plus de cinq mois) et de ne pas l'avoir connue; la chose qui remontera de là où je l'ai enfermée et qui déjà la nuit revient parfois dans l'obscurité de la chambre. À toi, mon savant fantôme, mon vieux jardinier, à toi je voudrais le dire, commencer à le dire, comme je peux, et puisque c'est ça aussi qui vous relie, toi et elle, le fait que je ne vous connaîtrai jamais, toi, qui es trop ancien, et elle, qui aurait dû s'appeler Suzanne. (230-31)

It makes a good deal of sense to understand this as that "something else" to which the anticlimactic family anecdotes seemed to point, and as that "something else" that explains the depth of sadness Montalbetti displays in this book. At first glance, this disclosure may seem like a trick, a narrative sleight of hand intended to take us by surprise, and obliging us to rethink the way we understand the diegetic economy of this novel and its teleology. Yet I believe that something more serious is at work here, and that it is more useful to understand this moment as involving addition rather than substitution. That is, it is not so much the case that "Suzanne" has been substituted for "Jules Poisson" as the object of mourning, as that she has been positioned alongside him.

The full power of this book becomes apparent only in that juxtaposition. One story is extremely rich in detail; one is very impoverished in that respect. One reaches far into the past; the other is far more recent. One demands a good deal of archeology on Montalbetti's part as she delves into dusty archives; the other demands quite a different sort of archeology. One story is far easier to tell than the other. Yet the meaning of the one amplifies and sharpens the meaning of the other; each brings the other into focus. Reflecting on her own situation, Montalbetti regrets that she cannot tell the story of her great-great-grandfather to her daughter. Yet that does not mean that the story cannot be told, as she clearly recognizes: "moi qui ne pourrai pas raconter ton histoire à ma fille, ni à ces petits-enfants que je n'aurai pas, mais qui, est-ce pour cette raison, la raconte ici à tout le monde, pour que le souvenir de toi ne se perde pas" (231-32). In that very perspective, her mission in this book is perhaps less unreasonable that it might have seemed. For as much as she insists upon lineage and descendance here, something else is at issue as well. Genealogy is a matter of biology undoubtedly, but the way we understand it is bound up in narrative. The notion of ancestry makes very little sense if it is stripped of the stories in which we wrap it, and similarly the idea of family. Like families, stories tend to ramify, if not always directly and immediately, in a linear fashion. Some stories come to an end more obviously and literally than others—yet even those stories continue to signify if they are passed on to others. In *Mon ancêtre Poisson* that dynamic of transmission is everywhere apparent; and it is at least double, for just as Christine Montalbetti is telling us a story, she is telling one to herself, as well. It is in that doubling, I think, that her mission can be appreciated in its broadest sense, and where it may be understood as far more reasonable than we might have suspected.

Notes

Raymond Queneau's Constraint

1. The other signataries were Jacques Baron, Georges Bataille, J.-A. Boiffard, Robert Desnos, Michel Leiris, Georges Limbour, Max Morise, Jacques Prévert, Georges Ribemont-Dessaignes, and Roger Vitrac.
2. See Le Lionnais, "Raymond Queneau"; and Roubaud, "Mathématique."
3. In fact, Queneau was off by an order of ten: at the rate he suggests, it would take more than ten centuries to finish the text.
4. See also *Bâtons* 322, where Queneau again invokes the figure of the artisan.
5. See also *Voyage* 125: "Ce qui compte est ce qui est le plus difficile, non le moins."
6. See Le Lionnais, "Premier Manifeste" 22: "Un mot, enfin, à l'intention des personnes particulièrement graves qui condamnent sans examen et sans appel toute oeuvre où se manifeste quelque propension à la plaisanterie. / Lorsqu'ils sont le fait de poètes, divertissements, farces et supercheries appartiennent encore à la poésie. La littérature potentielle reste donc la chose la plus sérieuse du monde. C.Q.F.D."
7. See for example *La Littérature potentielle*; *Atlas de littérature potentielle*; *La Bibliothèque Oulipienne*.
8. In fact, poems 16 and 28 have more than five syllables in the interlude verses. Poem 16 seems in fact to proclaim this aberrance, dealing as it does with Achilles's heel. See Oulipo, *Atlas* 249-50; and Jouet, *Raymond Queneau* 79.
9. See particularly Calame, Debon, Eruli, Métail, Mouchard, Naudin, and Panaitescu.

10. See for instance Fournel; Lescure, "Moraliste"; Oulipo, *Atlas* 249-53; Perec, *Clôture* 71-72; and Queval.

Edmond Jabès's Margins

1. In what follows, for the sake of efficiency, I shall refer to Jabès's works by abbreviations: A *Aely*; CS *Ça suit son cours*; DD *Dans la double dépendance du dit*; DL *Du désert au livre*; E *Elya*; EA *Un étranger avec, sous le bras, un livre de petit format*; EL • *(El, ou le dernier livre)*; LD *Le Livre du dialogue*; LP *Le Livre du partage*; LQ *Le Livre des questions*; LR *Le Livre des ressemblances*; LY *Le Livre de Yukel*; P *Le Parcours*; PL *Le Petit Livre de la subversion hors de soupçon*; RL *Le Retour au livre*; SD *Le Soupçon le désert*; Y *Yaël*.
2. See Derrida 409: "Ce centre avait pour fonction non seulement d'orienter et d'équilibrer, d'organiser la structure—on ne peut en effet penser une structure inorganisée—mais de faire surtout que le principe d'organisation de la structure limite ce que nous pourrions appeler le *jeu* de la structure."
3. See for example Auster 9: "I have always refused to join any kind of group"; and DL 31: "mon incapacité profonde à m'intégrer à un groupe, à moins d'y être poussé par l'urgence et la nécessité d'une action directe."
4. See for instance the remarkable text Jabès wrote for a UNESCO anti-apartheid publication, reprinted in DD 45-47.
5. See for example Derrida 100: "Et par une sorte de déplacement silencieux vers l'essence, qui fait de ce livre une longue métonymie, la situation judaïque devient exemplaire de la situation du poète, de l'homme de parole et d'écriture"; and Blanchot 876: "Et l'on comprend alors que la méditation du poète Jabès sur l'acte et l'exigence poétiques puisse aller de pair avec la méditation sur son appartenance, invétérée et réfléchie, récente et sans date, à la condition juive."
6. For a more ample discussion of this notion, see Motte, *Questioning Edmond Jabès*, especially chapter 5.
7. See PL 17: "Ce petit livre, par son titre, à travers l'ouvrage qui le contenait déjà, se rattache aux dix volumes du 'Livre des Questions.'"

8. For a review of the clinamen as a critical construct, see Motte, "Clinamen Redux."

Georges Perec's Work

1. See Freud 244-45. See also Otto Fenichel's discussion of the work of mourning in *The Psychoanalytic Theory of Neurosis* 21, 162, 393-94, 572.
2. See for instance Fenichel, who speaks of "a gradual 'working through' of an affect" (162), and John Bowlby: "Again and again emphasis will be laid on the long duration of grief, on the difficulties of recovering from its effects, and on the adverse consequences for personality functioning that loss so often brings" (8).
3. See Philippe Lejeune on the emotive function of understatement in Perec (21).
4. See for example Marcel Bénabou 24-29 on the notion of lack, and the portion of Lejeune's *La Mémoire et l'oblique* entitled "Dire l'indicible" (13-57).
5. Perec's scar also plays an important role in a broader pattern of signs and structures in his work that are marked, usually by emptiness or incompletion, in their lower left-hand corners, a consideration that several of his readers have pointed out. See for instance Magné 84-86, Motte, "Embellir les lettres" 110-11, and Pawlikowska 80-82.
6. The edition of *Un homme qui dort* that I use offers a particularly egregious example of that phenomenon, giving the author's name on the cover as "Pérec."
7. Bénabou sees in the account of Cinoc's name a "heavy-handed caricature" of Perec's experience with his own name (30).

Marcel Bénabou's Rhetoric

1. See the "Préambule" of *La Vie mode d'emploi*: "On en déduira quelque chose qui est sans doute l'ultime vérité du puzzle: en dépit des apparences, ce n'est pas un jeu solitaire: chaque geste que fait le poseur de puzzle, le faiseur de puzzles l'a fait avant lui; chaque pièce qu'il prend et reprend, qu'il examine, qu'il caresse, chaque

combinaison qu'il essaye et essaye encore, chaque tâtonnement, chaque intuition, chaque espoir, chaque découragement, ont été décidés, calculés, étudiés par l'autre" (18).

2. For the sake of economy, I shall refer to them in what follows as *Pourquoi*, *Jette*, and *Jacob*, respectively.

3. See Gilles Deleuze's remarks about the cry in Francis Bacon's paintings: "Si l'on crie, c'est toujours en proie à des forces invisibles et insensibles qui brouillent tout le spectacle, et qui débordent même la douleur et la sensation" (41).

4. See Alan Astro 253: "Bénabou, for his part, dreams not of committing the perfect crime, but of writing the perfect book, which would rid him of the obscene desire to write."

5. *Pourquoi* was published when Bénabou was forty-seven years old.

6. See Astro's remarks about the "sacrilege of literary writing" (254).

7. See his comments on the importance of reevaluating the idea of citizenship in a critical perspective, "Surtout quand cette citoyenneté est de part en part *précaire*, *récente*, *menacée*, plus artificielle que jamais" (33; emphasis in original).

8. For a broader discussion of Bénabou's vision of the book, see Motte, "Playing it by the Book," especially 27-31.

9. Except that, according to Bénabou himself, three of those subchapters are "missing," in a sort of false clinamen, or intentionally programmed error in the system.

10. See Astro's comments about the puns on "Bénabou" in *Pourquoi* (Astro 256). See also the various inflections of the totemic verb *aboutir* in the French edition of *Jacob* (for instance, 49, 170, 238, 243, 244, and 247).

11. See Jean-Claude Raillon's remarks about *Pourquoi*: "l'ouvrage compte manifestement parmi les productions trop rares qui s'écrivent sur le mode de leur propre lecture" (58).

12. In the body of my text, that is, rather than in a footnote, because those references, as Bénabou conceives them, are central rather than marginal, authoritative rather than exegetic, text rather than pretext.

13. See Derrida's comments on the language of Metropolitan France, as seen from the perspective of French Algeria: "En tant que modèle du bien-parler et du bien-écrire, il représentait la langue du maître (je crois n'avoir d'ailleurs jamais reconnu d'autre souverain dans ma vie)" (73).

14. See also Bénabou's discussion of Perec in "Perec et la judéité," and Astro's remarks about Perec and Bénabou (257-58).
15. See Deleuze on painting: "l'acte de peindre est toujours décalé, ne cesse d'osciller entre un avant-coup et un après-coup: hystérie de peindre" (63).
16. Claude Burgelin remarks: "Marcel Bénabou vient rappeler, avec le sérieux et l'humour indispensables, qu'écrire est une affaire trop grave pour qu'on l'entreprenne" (4).
17. See Beaujour's discussion of that game as it is played by the Dadaists and the surrealists ("The Game of Poetics," especially 62-63).

Jacques Jouet's Exhaustion

1. See for example Calvino, "Myth in the Narrative" 76: "literature itself is merely the permutation of a finite set of elements and functions."
2. For instance, Noël Arnaud, Jacques Bens, André Blavier, Paul Fournel, François Le Lionnais, Jean Queval, and Jacques Roubaud.
3. *Trois fois trois voeux* (*Scène* 155-90), *Les Z'hurleurs 2* (*Scène* 285-305), *La Femme aux cendres* (*Scène* 315-46), *Danse, distance, photographie* (*Morceaux* 143-226), and *Ils n'ont plus de vin* (*Morceaux* 289-312).
4. The Oulipian *Épaisseurs* were Marcel Bénabou, Jacques Bens, François Caradec, Paul Fournel, Michelle Grangaud, Jouet himself, Hervé Le Tellier, and Jacques Roubaud.
5. I am pleased to report, however, that the "Guère Épais" have risen again, phoenix-like, from their ashes. Even as I write this (in early summer 1999) the Éditions Plurielle have launched a new collection entitled "Les Guère Épais Civilisations," with a first volume already in print and three more announced as forthcoming. Interested amateurs may inquire about them at the Éditions Plurielle, 15 rue du Petit Musc, 75004 Paris.
6. See Raymond Queneau's remarks about the potential that the sestina form offers to contemporary literature, in an essay from 1964 entitled "Littérature potentielle" (*Bâtons* 317-45, especially 329-32). See also Jacques Roubaud's "Hortense" novels which, like *Fins*, borrow their structure from that of the sestina.
7. He is referring to Lautréamont's celebrated dictum, "La poésie doite être faite par tous. Non par un."

Notes

Marie NDiaye's Narrative

1. Dominique Rabaté, *Marie NDiaye* 9.
2. K. Ambroise Teko-Agbo, "*En famille* or the Problem of Alterity" 163.
3. Nora Cottille-Foley, "Les Mots pour ne pas le dire ou encore l'indicibilité d'une visibilité frottée de fantastique dans les oeuvres de Marie NDiaye" 13.
4. Shirley Jordan, "Marie NDiaye: Énigmes photographiques, albums éclatés" 75.
5. Walter Isle stresses the "outrageous" character of play, arguing that play must have an ostentatious character to it. See "Acts of Willful Play" 63. Johan Huizinga takes a similar position when he suggests that poetry must be playfully exorbitant. See *Homo Ludens: A Study of the Play-Element in Culture* 142.
6. See *Narrative as Theme: Studies in French Fiction* 28-30.
7. Marie-Claire Barnet speaks of "le sens du désarroi dans lequel NDiaye nous plonge." "Déroute d'un *Autoportrait en vert* (mère): Vers l'errance de Marie NDiaye" 159. Dominique Rabaté remarks, "Le donné initial des intrigues pose ainsi un univers insolite où quelque chose d'anormal mine insidieusement les règles de notre compréhension ordinaire" (14).
8. On the idea of the "baffled protagonist," see Lydie Moudileno, "Marie NDiaye's Discombobulated Subject" 86.
9. See "Délits, détours et affabulation: L'écriture de l'anathème dans *En famille* de Marie NDiaye" 442-53.
10. See "*Mon coeur à l'étroit*: Espace et éthique" 171-72: "Les personnages de NDiaye n'abordent qu'avec répugnance la question des possibles différences raciales (soit lorsque, comme Nadia, ils se sentent eux-mêmes impliqués, et honteux; soit, comme chez les personnages d'*En famille* ou de *Mon coeur à l'étroit* qui jugent ou conseillent Fanny et Nadia, parce que l'euphémisme est une des armes les plus virulentes du préjugé). De même, les romans de NDiaye évitent souvent d'être explicites à ce sujet, s'en tenant au point de vue du personnage et déplaçant ainsi la différence et l'exclusion vers des signes extérieurs physiques qui peuvent suggérer diverses formes de marginalisation."
11. See Jordan 68-69: "Plus radicalement, nous pouvons déceler chez NDiaye le thème récurrent d'une défaillance de la vision (on

n'y voit plus clair; on n'y croit plus à ses yeux) qui déroute le protagoniste en train de perdre ses repères, et le lecteur en train de chercher les siens."

12. See Barthes, "Analyse textuelle d'un conte d'Edgar Poe" 34.
13. See Dominique Rabaté 38: "L'énergie romanesque qui habite chacun des textes mène à une sorte d'impasse. La logique narrative, qui a suivi sa course en obéissant au développement de la situation initiale, bute sur l'aporie originaire dont elle était issue."

Marie Cosnay's Characters

1. Roland Barthes, "Analyse textuelle d'un conte d'Edgar Poe" 34. For the Poe text, see *The Complete Tales and Poems of Edgar Allan Poe* 96-103.
2. "Il va de soi qu'une conception du personnage ne peut pas être indépendante d'une conception générale de la personne, du sujet, de l'individu," argues Philippe Hamon in "Pour un statut sémiologique du personnage" 116.
3. See Hamon 118-19: "[C]ette notion de personnage [. . .] est autant une reconstruction du lecteur qu'une construction du texte (l'effet-personnage n'est peut-être qu'un cas particulier de l'activité de la lecture)."
4. In *Le Personnage*, Christine Montalbetti suggests that our readings of character oscillate between two poles, textualist and pragmatic (28). She defines the textualist (or immanentist) position thus: "Le personnage, dans sa définition textualiste, est donc un personnage épuisé, épuisé par la somme même des énoncés qui en rendent compte. Il est sans autre passé que celui qui nous est conté, sans autre généalogie que celle qui nous est présentée, sans autre avenir que celui qui nous est narré, dans quelques clausules sunthétiques ou prospectives" (16). Regarding the pragmatist position, she remarks: "Ces définitions immanentistes du personnage ne tiennent pas compte—ou bien elles l'évacuent comme un objet d'étude non pertinent, ou inaccessible—de la définition pragmatique par où le personnage se trouve saisi dans le mouvement d'une lecture qui participe à sa construction" (21).
5. See Hamon 144: "On pourrait donc définir le personnage comme *un système d'équivalences réglées destiné à assurer la lisibilité du texte*" (emphasis in original).

6. See Montalbetti's discussion of the "crise du personnage" 27-28.
7. Régis Jauffret, *Microfictions*.
8. See Patrick Deville, *Pura Vida: Vie & mort de William Walker*, *Equatoria*, and *Kampuchéa*.
9. See Antoine Volodine, *Dondog* and *Songes de Mevlido*.
10. Marie Cosnay, *Villa Chagrin*. Her other writings include *Que s'est-il passé?*, *Adèle, la scène perdue*, *Le Chemin des amoureux*, *Déplacements*, *André des Ombres*, *Les Temps filiaux*, *Trois Meurtres*, *Entre chagrin et néant*, *Noces de Mantoue*, *La Langue maternelle*, *Où vont les vaisseaux maudits?*, *À notre humanité*, *Des métamorphoses*, *La Bataille d'Anghiari*, *Le Fils de Judith*, *Cordelia la Guerre*, *Sanza lettere*, *Vie de HB*, *Jours de répit à Baigorri*, *Aquerò*, *Épopée*, *If*, and *Comètes et perdrix*.
11. See Ross Chambers, *Loiterature*.
12. See Cosnay's accounts of deportation proceedings in Bayonne from May to September 2008, in *Entre chagrin et néant*.
13. See *Villa Chagrin* 12, 14, 15, 20, 27, 28, 32.
14. Bram van Velde, *Lettres*.
15. See 50: "Un jour je regardais le corps très transparent de l'ami mort, allongé sur le dernier lit, je voyais les paupières et les fils des veines à la circulation précisément arrêtée."
16. See "La Peinture des van Velde ou le Monde et le Pantalon," "Peintres de l'empêchement," "Three Dialogues," and "Bram van Velde," in Samuel Beckett, *Disjecta: Miscellaneous Writings and a Dramatic Fragment*, 118-32, 133-37, 138-45, and 151, respectively.

Bernard Noël's Trips

1. See "La Vie l'écriture" 163: "Tous mes livres sont les fragments d'un journal, mais tous n'en ont pas l'air."
2. Readers interested in Bernard Noël's other "travel writing" may wish to consult *URSS aller retour* and *Le Reste du voyage et autres poèmes*.
3. See *In the Metro* 8: "Subway riders basically handle nothing more than time and space, and are skilled in using the one to measure the other."
4. Working against the grain of habitual ways of thinking, Maurice Blanchot contends that interruption is in fact crucial to the way

we understand phenomena, even when those phenomena appear to be continuous. "L'interruption est nécessaire à toute suite de paroles," he argues, "l'intermittence rend possible le devenir; la discontinuité assure la continuité de l'entente" (*L'Entretien infini* 107).

5. See Georges Perec, *L'Infra-ordinaire*; Jean-Philippe Toussaint, *La Salle de bain* and *La Télévision*; Christian Oster, *Loin d'Odile*.

6. Adelaide Russo remarks much the same effect when she analyzes the way that Noël looks at André Masson's work: "Ce regard 'dans le silence et par le silence' est en fait une écoute" ("Collage Incipit Atelier" 203). Michael Brophy notes the precision of Noël's gaze ("Bernard Noël: Entre chute et élan" 127).

7. See Chambers, *Loiterature* 8-9: "A reason I'm interested in loiterly literature, then, is that it has this characteristic of the trivial: It blurs categories, and in particular it blurs those of innocent pleasure taking and harmless relaxation and not-so-innocent 'intent'—a certain recalcitrance to the laws that maintain 'good order.' In so doing, it carries an implied social criticism. It casts serious doubt on the values good citizens hold dear—values like discipline, method, organization, rationality, productivity, and, above all, work—but it does so in the guise of innocent and, more particularly, insignificant or frivolous entertainment: a mere passing of the time in idle observations or witty remarks, now this, now that, like the philosopher pursuing his ideas as he sits daydreaming on his bench. Or like the poet mooching along, his idleness a contrast to the busy street, going to the bank and the bookstore, doing this, then that."

Jean Rolin's Mourning

1. See for example Mélanie Lamarre, "Ivresse et militantisme: Olivier Rolin, Jean Rolin, Jean-Pierre Le Dantec" and Sarah Sindaco, "*La Clôture* de Jean Rolin: Le territoire parisien: Entre ironie et mélancolie."

2. See "Mourning and Melancholia" 243-44: "The correlation of mourning and melancholia seems justified by the general picture of the two conditions. Moreover, the exciting causes due to environmental influences are, so far as we can discern them at all,

the same for both conditions. Mourning is regularly the reaction to the loss of a loved person, or to the loss of some abstraction which has taken the place of one, such as one's country, liberty, an ideal, and so on. In some people the same influences produce melancholia instead of mourning and we consequently suspect them of a pathological disposition. It is also well worth notice that, although mourning involves grave departures from the normal attitude to life, it never occurs to us to regard it as a pathological condition and to refer it to medical treatment. We rely on its being overcome after a certain lapse of time, and we look upon any interference with it as useless or even harmful."

3. See for instance Joshua Armstrong, "Writer, Window, World: Jean Rolin's Perishing Panoramas and François Bon's Fleeting Frame"; Aline Bergé, "L'Homme oiseau de la zone frontière"; Warren Motte, "Jean Rolin's Explosion"; Catherine Poisson, "Terrain vague: *Zones* de Jean Rolin"; and Bruno Thibault, "Rives et dérives chez Jean Rolin, J. M. G. Le Clézio et Pascal Quignard."

4. See for example 65, 102, 131.

5. See *Le Dénouement*, especially 88-89.

6. See *Mémoires de l'oubli* 13: "J'ai voulu, dans ce livre, interroger l'irréparable, tel qu'il surgit dans certaines oeuvres hantées par les morts des catastrophes modernes. Les récits de William Faulkner, Joseph Roth, Georges Perec et W. G. Sebald naissent dans le sillage de désastres historiques dont presque tous leurs récits portent l'empreinte. De la défaite de l'armée confédérée à l'éclatement de l'Empire austro-hongrois, de Waterloo à la destruction des villes allemandes, des massacres coloniaux au génocide des Juifs d'Europe, l'histoire contemporaine apparaît comme une longue série de calamités, laissant les survivants en proie à une mélancolie sans remède."

7. See *Black Sun* 9: "loss, bereavement, and absence trigger the work of the imagination and nourish it permanently as much as they threaten it and spoil it."

8. See Barthes, *La Chambre claire* 135: "Toute photographie est un certificat de présence."

9. See for example 8, 18-19, 21, 51-52, 58, 61-62, 69, 72, 73, 103, 118, 123-24.

10. See especially 133 and 176-79.

11. See "The Game of Poetics," especially 61-63. In particular, Beaujour remarks, "Thus playing a very serious game in order to lose is a very sophisticated behaviour, and perhaps the ultimate sophistication within a given culture" (62).
12. Raphaëlle Guidée speaks of "les limites de la représentation du passé, et la nécessité d'inscrire, à défaut d'une présence restaurée, les signes du manque" (221).

Jacques Serena's Fever

1. I am of course thinking of the incipit of *Anna Karenina*: "Happy families are all alike; every unhappy family is unhappy in its own way" (3).
2. See Barthes, *S/Z* 26: "L'inventaire du code herméneutique consistera à distinguer les différents termes (formels), au gré desquels une énigme se centre, se pose, se formule, puis se retarde et enfin se dévoile (ces termes parfois manqueront, souvent se répéteront; ils n'apparaîtront pas dans un ordre constant)."
3. See Frédéric Martin-Achard 184-185: "Dans *L'Acrobate*, le narrateur évoque avec un humour très noir et une fausse désinvolture son absence se 'souci de soi.'"
4. Jean-Baptiste Harang quotes Serena himself on this feature of *L'Acrobate*: "Lagrange, pur produit de la télé, pur produit Bilalian, non, je ne lui ai pas donné de prénom, sans raison, il me semble qu'avec un nom et un prénom on est quelqu'un, Lagrange n'est personne, c'est un nom que j'ai lu sur un poteau indicateur."
5. The feature of Georges Perec's writing that Philippe Lejeune finds most attractive involves the active role that Perec reserves for his reader: "il y a dans tous ses textes une place pour moi, pour que je fasse quelque chose" (*La Mémoire et l'oblique* 41).
6. See *Postscript to* The Name of the Rose, where Eco devotes a chapter (47-53) to that notion.
7. See 30: "Voilà donc ce que j'aurais cherché, soir après soir: attraper la fièvre."
8. See Martin-Achard, speaking about Serena's *Isabelle de dos*: "La relation spéculaire est fréquente chez Serena: au cours d'un instant de rapprochement avec sa compagne Isabelle, le narrateur contemple, dans un miroir, la scène qui se déréalise sous ses yeux.

Notes

La médiatisation par la glace réfléchissante la transforme en image, comme si le personnage se changeait métaphoriquement en photographies: la présence est perdue au moment même où la scène est vécue par le narrateur. Elle est immédiatement convertie en souvenir, entraînant un défaut irrémédiable de présence. Le présent se transforme en passé, tandis que l'individu se métamorphose en pierre tombale" (190).

9. See the way Bayard presents what he calls a "realist" theory of parallel worlds: "Elle consiste à prendre au sérieux les affirmations de certains physiciens et à considérer que nous existons réellement à une multitude d'exemplaires dans une pluralité de mondes différents, et que la croyance en notre personnalité unique est une illusion, dommageable à notre compréhension du réel" (*Il existe d'autres mondes* 44-45). The claims that he stakes for that theory in *Le Titanic fera naufrage* are likewise interesting: "En cela, la théorie des univers parallèles offre une proposition alternative cohérente à la psychanalyse. Alors que celle-ci construit des modèles fondés sur l'idée d'un clivage interne du sujet—nous serions divisés entre des parties contradictoires de nous-mêmes—, la théorie quantique défend l'idée d'un clivage externe, la division s'exerçant bien entre nous-mêmes et nous, mais un *nous* situé à l'extérieur d'un monde que nous croyons à tort unique" (105).

10. See Ruffel 29: "Il s'agit de comprendre le contemporain comme la levée, la suspension, de la représentation du temps comme flèche. Il renoue avec ce qu'est le temps: hétérogène, mélangé, que ce soit sur le plan des subjectivités ou des collectivités."

11. In *Qui a tué Roger Ackroyd?* Bayard emphasizes the dimensions of such sites, pointing toward "l'immense monde intermédiaire entre le monde de l'oeuvre et le nôtre" (129).

Julia Deck's Geometries

1. Born in Paris in 1974, Julia Deck has to date published five novels at Minuit.

2. In a recent interview, Deck remarks, "Mes deux premiers livres tournent autour de femmes un peu déréglées" ("La Normalité").

3. Christine Marcandier argues that it is more like a Penrose triangle, and points out that *Le Triangle de Penrose* was the novel's working title (121, 125).

4. See 25, 26, 27, 28, 145, 157, and 165, respectively.
5. Eco devotes a chapter of his *Postscript to* The Name of the Rose to that notion (47-53).
6. See James Carse's remark about how we conceive our location: "To be somewhere is to absolutize time, space, and number" (46).
7. Robert Tubbs notes: "the work of the Parisian surrealists illustrates that some of the mathematical ideas influencing artists and writers were not simple geometric or numerical notions; instead, they were sometimes fairly sophisticated and even highly abstract modern mathematical concepts" (1).
8. See Queneau's remarks about the use of mathematics in the novel, in *Bâtons, chiffres et lettres* 33.
9. See "Analyse textuelle d'un conte d'Edgar Poe" 34: "Un nom propre doit être toujours interrogé soigneusement, car le nom propre est, si l'on peut dire, le prince des signifiants; ses connotations sont riches, sociales et symboliques."
10. In her conversation with Johan Faerber, she remarks: "D'abord, je ne peux pas développer un personnage, je ne peux même pas lui faire boire un café si je ne sais pas comment il s'appelle."
11. See Marcandier's observation about "la fiction mystificatrice de Bérénice Beaurivage" (118).
12. See for example the description of Mademoiselle's apartment, with "ouvrages de la médiathèque écrasés pages contre terre" (18); and the moment when Deck notes of her, "Elle a commencé de fréquenter la médiathèque" (25). As to Blandine, the novel ends in this fashion: "Elle pourrait aussi faire un tour à la médiathèque, rapporter le film qu'elle a emprunté en début de semaine, un long-métrage d'Éric Rohmer dont le titre l'intriguait. Une des actrices lui ressemblait de façon troublante, et le nom de son personnage, singulière alliance de tonalités contraires, l'avait frappée au point qu'elle s'était demandé ce que pouvait être la vie de celle qui le portait. Si ça vaudrait la peine de l'emprunter. Oui, elle aimerait bien, pour essayer, devenir en tout point le personnage interprété par la comédienne Clémentine Amouroux dans le film d'Éric Rohmer. Blandine Lenoir. Un nom qui m'irait à la perfection" (175).
13. Pierre Bayard is one of the principal champions of that plurality. See especially *Il existe d'autres mondes*.

14. See Marcandier 119-120: "Pour Bérénice Beaurivage dans *Le triangle d'hiver* le grand écart se fera entre *Bérénice* (forcément) et *Madame Figaro*, alors que la romancière s'amuse, elle, à parodier la madeleine de Proust."

Christine Montalbetti's Mission

1. Umberto Eco characterizes that latter process as "constructing the reader," and devotes a chapter to it in his *Postscript to The Name of the Rose*. See particularly 50: "What model reader did I want as I was writing? An accomplice, to be sure, one who would play my game."
2. See Barthes, "Analyse" 34: "Un nom propre doit être toujours interrogé soigneusement, car le nom propre est, si l'on peut dire, le prince des signifiants; ses connotations sont riches, sociales et symboliques."
3. See Schwerdtner 173: "Car, de mon point de vue, l'écriture est toujours un geste adressé, qui n'a de sens que dans l'idée que le texte en cours sera lu."
4. See Jonathan Cohen, *Apart from Freud: Notes for a Rational Psychoanalysis* 222: "The hallmark of a rational pursuit of knowledge is not pessimism but skepticism about dogmas and an insistence on theories that move closer and closer to reality."
5. See *Comment parler des faits qui ne se sont pas produits?*, 26: "La notion de vérité subjective est inacceptable au regard de celle de vérité factuelle et ne saurait lui être substituée. Elle est pourtant déterminante dans nos comportements. Refuser d'y prêter attention, c'est prendre le risque de ne rien comprendre à la manière dont nous mêlons sans cesse dans nos vies imaginaire et réalité, et aux raisons pour lesquelles nous aimons disserter inlassablement de faits qui ne se sont pas produits."
6. See Bayard, who speaks of "le droit imprescriptible de l'être humain à raconter des histoires" (154).
7. See Marc Le Bot, *Les Yeux de mon père*, 12-13: "Nos oeuvres, et nos écritures, n'accompagnent pas la vie afin d'en conserver pieusement des fragments. Elles accompagnent la vie parce qu'elle part, qu'elle ne cesse de partir et que, nécessairement, on l'accompagne. À sa suite on erre."

8. See for example 215: "Je lis par-dessus ton épaule, tiens, quelque chose sur l'usage militaire des pigeons voyageurs, et je me plonge avec toi dans ces histoires de volatiles auxquels on confie des missions d'État."

9. On strategies of engagement in Montalbetti's writing, see Motte, "Christine Montalbetti's Engaging Narrations."

10. Montalbetti's "Japanese cycle" includes works like *L'Évaporation de l'oncle*, *Love Hotel*, and the short story "Hôtel Komaba Éminence." Her "American cycle" includes *Western*, *Journée américaine*, *En écrivant* Journée américaine, and *Plus rien que les vagues et le vent*.

11. See Philippe Lejeune's remark about Georges Perec's writing: "Il y a dans tous ses textes une place pour moi, pour que je fasse quelque chose. Un appel à moi comme à un partenaire, un complice, je dois prendre le relais" (41).

12. See *Narrative as Theme* 28-29: "More specifically, we are all familiar with the category of the unnarratable or nonnarratable, which evokes the topos of the inexpressible without being limited to it and which comprises everything that *according to a given narrative* cannot be narrated or is not worth narrating—either because it transgresses a law (social, authorial, generic, formal), or because it defies the power of a particular narrator (or of any narrator), or because it falls below the so-called threshold of narratability (it is not sufficiently unusual or problematic: that is, interesting)."

13. See "Mourning and Melancholia" 243: "Mourning is regularly the reaction to the loss of a loved person, or to the loss of some abstraction which has taken the place of one, such as one's country, liberty, an ideal, and so on."

Bibliography

Armstrong, Joshua. "Writer, Window, World: Jean Rolin's Perishing Panoramas and François Bon's Fleeting Frame." *Contemporary French and Francophone Studies* 17.4 (2013): 462-71.

Arnaud, Marthe. *Manière de Blanc*. Paris: Éditions Sociales Internationales, 1938.

Astro, Alan. "Bénabou bien abouti." *Pardès* 14 (1991): 252-59.

Augé, Marc. *In the Metro*. Trans. Tom Conley. Minneapolis: University of Minnesota Press, 2002.

Auster, Paul. "Book of the Dead: An Interview with Edmond Jabès." In *The Sin of the Book: Edmond Jabès*. Ed. Eric Gould. Lincoln and London: University of Nebraska Press, 1985. 3-25.

Barnet, Marie-Claire. "Déroute d'un *Autoportrait en vert* (mère): Vers l'errance de Marie NDiaye." In Andrew Asibong and Shirley Jordan, eds. *Marie NDiaye: L'étrangeté à l'oeuvre*. Spec. issue of *Revue des Sciences Humaines* 293 (2009): 153-70.

Barth, John. *The Friday Book, or, Book-Titles Should Be Straightforward and Subtitles Avoided*. New York: Putnam, 1984.

Barthes, Roland. "Analyse textuelle d'un conte d'Edgar Poe." In Claude Chabrol, ed. *Sémiotique narrative et textuelle* (Paris: Larousse, 1973). 29-54.

—. *La Chambre claire: Note sur la photographie*. Paris: Gallimard / Le Seuil, 1980.

—. *S/Z*. Paris: Seuil, 1970.

Bayard, Pierre. *Aurais-je été résistant ou bourreau?* Paris: Minuit, 2013.

—. *Comment parler des faits qui ne se sont pas produits?* Paris: Minuit, 2020.

—. *Il existe d'autres mondes.* Paris: Minuit, 2014.

—. "Pour une nouvelle littérature comparée." In Pierre Bayard, ed. *Pour Eric Chevillard.* Paris: Minuit, 2014. 93-118.

—. *Qui a tué Roger Ackroyd?* Paris: Minuit, 1998.

—. *Le Titanic fera naufrage.* Paris: Minuit, 2016.

Beaujour, Michel. "The Game of Poetics." In Jacques Ehrmann, ed., *Game, Play, Literature.* Boston: Beacon, 1971. 58-67.

Beckett, Samuel. *Disjecta: Miscellaneous Writings and a Dramatic Fragment.* Ed. Ruby Cohn. New York: Grove, 1984.

Bénabou, Marcel. *Jacob, Ménahem et Mimoun: Une épopée familiale.* Paris: Seuil, 1995.

—. *Jette ce livre avant qu'il soit trop tard.* Paris: Seghers, 1992.

—. "Perec et la judéité." *Cahiers Georges Perec* 1 (1985): 15-30.

—. *Pourquoi je n'ai écrit aucun de mes livres.* Paris: Hachette, 1986.

—. "La Règle et la contrainte." *Pratiques* 39 (1983): 101-06.

—. *La Résistance africaine à la romanisation.* Paris: Maspero, 1976.

Bens, Jacques. "Queneau oulipien." In Oulipo, *Atlas de littérature potentielle.* Paris: Gallimard, 1981. 22-33.

Bergé, Aline. "L'Homme oiseau de la zone frontière." *Contemporary French and Francophone Studies* 16.5 (2012): 635-43.

Blanchot, Maurice. *L'Entretien infini.* Paris: Gallimard, 1969.

—. "L'Interruption." *Nouvelle Revue Française* 137 (1964): 869-81.

Boucheron, Patrick, and Mathieu Riboulet. *Prendre dates: Paris, 6 janvier-14 janvier 2015.* Lagrasse: Verdier, 2015.

Bounoure, Gabriel. *Edmond Jabès: La demeure et le livre.* Montpellier: Fata Morgana, 1984.

Bowlby, John. *Attachment and Loss.* Vol. 3. New York: Basic Books, 1980.

Brophy, Michael. "Bernard Noël: Entre chute et élan." *Dalhousie French Studies* 38 (1997): 127-33.

Burgelin, Claude. "*Pourquoi je n'ai écrit aucun de mes livres* ou le livre sur tout." Unpublished typescript.

Calame, Alain. "La Place des mathématiques dans Morale élémentaire I." *Lectures de Raymond Queneau* 1 (1987): 93-104.

—. "La Place des mathématiques dans Morale élémentaire II et III." *Lectures de Raymond Queneau* 1 (1987): 105-17.

Calvino, Italo. *The Castle of Crossed Destinies*. Trans. William Weaver. New York: Harcourt Brace, 1979.

—. *Comment j'ai écrit un de mes livres*. Paris: Bibliothèque Oulipienne, 1983.

—. *If on a winter's night a traveler*. Trans. William Weaver. New York: Harcourt Brace, 1981.

—. "Myth in the Narrative." Trans. Erica Freiberg. In Raymond Federman, ed. *Surfiction: Fiction Now and Tomorrow*. Chicago: Swallow Press, 1975. 75-81.

Carse, James P. *Finite and Infinite Games: A Vision of Life as Play and Possibility*. New York: Free Press, 1986.

Chambers, Ross. *Loiterature*. Lincoln and London: University of Nebraska Press, 1999.

Cohen, Jonathan. *Apart from Freud: Notes for a Rational Psychoanalysis*. San Francisco: City Lights, 2001.

Cosnay, Marie. *Adèle, la scène perdue*. Le Chambon-sur-Lignon: Cheyne, 2005.

—. *André des Ombres*. Paris: Laurence Teper, 2008.

—. *À notre humanité*. Meudon: Quidam, 2012.

—. *Aquerò*. Paris: Éditions de l'Ogre, 2017.

—. *La Bataille d'Anghiari*. Las Couti: L'Or des Fous, 2013.

—. *Le Chemin des amoureux*. Limoges: Le Bruit des Autres, 2007.

—. *Comètes et perdrix*. Paris: Éditions de l'Ogre, 2021.

—. *Cordelia la Guerre*. Paris: Éditions de l'Ogre, 2015.

—. *Déplacements*. Paris: Laurence Teper, 2007.

—. *Des métamorphoses*. Le Chambon-sur-Lignon: Cheyne, 2012.

—. *Entre chagrin et néant*. Paris: Laurence Teper, 2009.

—. *Épopée*. Paris: Éditions de l'Ogre, 2018.

—. *Le Fils de Judith*. Le Chambon-sur-Lignon: Cheyne, 2014.

—. *If*. Paris: Éditions de l'Ogre, 2020.

—. *Jours de répit à Baigorri*. Paris: Créaphis, 2016.

—. *La Langue maternelle*. Le Chambon-sur-Lignon: Cheyne, 2010.

—. *Noces de Mantoue*. Paris: Laurence Teper 2009.

—. *Où vont les vaisseaux maudits?* Serres-Morlaàs: Atelier in 8, 2011.

—. *Que s'est-il passé?* Le Chambon-sur-Lignon: Cheyne, 2003.

—. *Sanza lettere*. Bordeaux: Éditions de l'Attente, 2015.

—. *Les Temps filiaux*. Serres-Morlaàs: Atelier in 8, 2008.

—. *Trois Meurtres*. Le Chambon-sur-Lignon: Cheyne, 2008.

—. *Vie de HB*. Caen: Nous, 2016.

—. *Villa Chagrin*. Lagrasse: Verdier, 2006.

—. Trans. Ovide. *Les Métamorphoses*. Paris: Éditions de l'Ogre, 2017.

Cottille-Foley, Nora. "Les Mots pour ne pas le dire ou encore l'indicibilité d'une visibilité frottée de fantastique dans les oeuvres de Marie NDiaye." In Andrew Asibong and Shirley Jordan, eds. *Marie NDiaye: L'étrangeté à l'oeuvre*. Spec. issue of *Revue des Sciences Humaines* 293 (2009): 13-23.

Debon, Claude. "Sinon comment entrer?" *Lectures de Raymond Queneau* 1 (1987): 85-91.

Deck, Julia. *Monument national*. Paris: Minuit, 2022.

—. *Propriété privée*. Paris: Minuit, 2019.

—. *Sigma*. Paris: Minuit, 2017.

—. *Le Triangle d'hiver*. Paris: Minuit, 2014.

—. *Viviane Élisabeth Fauville*. Paris: Minuit, 2012.

—, and Johan Faerber. "'La Normalité est une fiction sociale' (Le grand entretien)." *Diacritik*. diacritik.com/2017/09/13/julia-deck-la-normalite-est-une-fiction-sociale-le-grand-entretien/#.

Deleuze, Gilles. *Francis Bacon: Logique de la sensation*. Paris: Éditions de la Différence, 1996.

Derrida, Jacques. *L'Écriture et la différence.* Paris: Seuil, 1967.

—. *Le Monolinguisme de l'autre.* Paris: Galilée, 1996.

Deville, Patrick. *Équatoria.* Paris: Le Seuil, 2009.

—. *Kampuchéa.* Paris: Le Seuil, 2011.

—. *Pura Vida: Vie & mort de William Walker.* Paris: Le Seuil, 2004.

Eco, Umberto. *Postscript to* The Name of the Rose. Trans. William Weaver. New York: Harcourt Brace, 1984.

Eruli, Brunella. "Pour une morale élémentaire: Queneau et le Yi-King." *Lectures de Raymond Queneau* 1 (1987): 35-66.

Fenichel, Otto. *The Psychoanalytic Theory of Neurosis.* New York: Norton, 1945.

Fernandez Zoïla, Adolfo. *Le Livre, recherche autre d'Edmond Jabès.* Paris: Jean-Michel Place, 1978.

Fournel, Paul. "Elémentaire morale." In Oulipo. *La Bibliothèque Oulipienne.* Vol. 1. Paris: Ramsay, 1987. 2 vols. 139-63.

Freud, Sigmund. "Mourning and Melancholia." In *The Standard Edition of the Complete Psychological Works of Sigmund Freud.* Ed. and trans. James Strachey. Vol. 14. London: Hogarth Press and The Institute of Psycho-Analysis, 1957. 237-58.

Genette, Gérard. *Postscript.* Paris: Seuil, 2016.

Guglielmi, Joseph. *La Ressemblance impossible: Edmond Jabès.* Paris: Les Éditeurs Français Réunis, 1978.

Guidée, Raphaëlle. *Mémoires de l'oubli: William Faulkner, Joseph Roth, Georges Perec et W. G. Sebald.* Paris: Garnier, 2017.

Hamon, Philippe. "Pour un statut sémiologique du personnage." In R. Barthes, W. Kayser, W. Booth, and P. Hamon. *Poétique du récit.* Paris: Le Seuil, 1977. 115-80.

Handelman, Susan. "'Torments of an Ancient Word': Edmond Jabès and the Rabbinic Tradition." In *The Sin of the Book: Edmond Jabès.* Ed. Eric Gould. Lincoln and London: University of Nebraska Press, 1985. 55-91.

Harang, Jean-Baptiste. "Serena sur un fil." *Libération*, October 21, 2004. http://next.liberation.fr/livres/2004/10/21/serena-sur-un-l_496660

Huizinga, Johan. *Homo Ludens: A Study of the Play-Element in Culture.* Boston: Beacon, 1950.

Isle, Walter. "Acts of Willful Play." In Gerald Guinness and Andrew Hurley, eds. *Auctor Ludens: Essays on Play in Literature.* Philadelphia and Amsterdam: Benjamins, 1986. 63-74.

Jabès, Edmond. *Aely.* Paris: Gallimard, 1972.

—. *Ça suit son cours.* Montpellier: Fata Morgana, 1975.

—. *Dans la double dépendance du dit.* Montpellier: Fata Morgana, 1984.

—. *Du désert au livre: Entretiens avec Marcel Cohen.* Paris: Belfond, 1980.

—. • *(El, ou le dernier livre).* Paris: Gallimard, 1973.

—. *Elya.* Paris: Gallimard, 1969.

—. *Un étranger avec, sous le bras, un livre de petit format.* Paris: Gallimard, 1989.

—. *Le Livre des questions.* Paris: Gallimard, 1963.

—. *Le Livre des ressemblances.* Paris: Gallimard, 1976.

—. *Le Livre de Yukel.* Paris: Gallimard, 1964.

—. *Le Livre du dialogue.* Paris: Gallimard, 1984.

—. *Le Livre du partage.* Paris: Gallimard, 1987.

—. *Le Parcours.* Paris: Gallimard, 1985.

—. *Le Petit Livre de la subversion hors de soupçon.* Paris: Gallimard, 1982.

—. *Le Retour au livre.* Paris: Gallimard, 1965.

—. *Le Soupçon le désert.* Paris: Gallimard, 1978.

—. *Yaël.* Paris: Gallimard, 1967.

Jauffret, Régis. *Microfictions.* Paris: Gallimard, 2007.

Jordan, Shirley. "Marie NDiaye: Énigmes photographiques, albums éclatés." In Andrew Asibong and Shirley Jordan, eds. *Marie NDiaye: L'étrangeté à l'oeuvre.* Spec. issue of *Revue des Sciences Humaines* 293 (2009): 65-82.

Jouet, Jacques. *Actes de la machine ronde.* Paris: Julliard, 1994.

—. *Actes du jésus.* Paris: Éditions du Paon-Saint-André, 2001.

BIBLIOGRAPHY 221

—. *Agathe de Mek-Ouyes*. Paris: P.O.L, 2011.
—. *L'Amour comme on l'apprend à l'École hôtelière*. Paris: P.O.L, 2006.
—. *Annette et l'Etna*. Paris: Stock, 2001.
—. *Les Annexes de l'oeil*. Antibes: Editions Anna Tanaquilli, 1997.
—. *L'Anse*. Paris: Editions du Limon, 1988.
—. *Un art simple et tout d'exécution*. Belfort: Circé, 2001. With Marcel Bénabou, Harry Mathews, and Jacques Roubaud.
—. *À supposer. . . .* Caen: Nous, 2007.
—. *Autre couture*. Paris: Bibliothèque Oulipienne 134, 2004. With Ian Monk, Paul Fournel, Frédéric Forte et Olivier Salon.
—. *Le Bestiaire inconstant*. Paris: Ramsay, 1983.
—. *La Bibliothèque de Poitiers*. Poitiers: La Licorne, 1999. With Michelle Grangaud and Jacques Roubaud.
—. *La Bibliothèque oulipienne*. Vol. 2. Paris: Ramsay, 1987. With Oulipo.
—. *La Bibliothèque oulipienne*. Vol. 3. Paris: Seghers, 1990. With Oulipo.
—. *La Bibliothèque oulipienne*. Vol. 4. Bordeaux: Le Castor Astral, 1997. With Oulipo.
—. *Bodo*. Paris: P.O.L, 2009.
—. *Le Bourgeois versifié*. Paris: P.O.L, 2017.
—. *Cantates de proximité*. Paris: P.O.L, 2005.
—. *Castel del Monte ou l'octagone*. Bari: Mario Adda, 1999. With Nicola Amato.
—. *107 Âmes*. Paris: Ramsay, 1991.
—. *Ce que rapporte l'Envoyé*. Illkirch: Le Verger, 1999.
—. *Le Cocommuniste*. Paris: P.O.L, 2014.
—. *Une chambre close*. Paris: Bibliothèque Oulipienne 78, 1996.
—. *Le Chant d'amour grand-singe*. Paris: Bibliothèque Oulipienne 62, 1993.
—. *Le Chantier*. Paris: Éditions du Limon, 1993.
—. *Danaé (trentine)*. Paris: Bibliothèque Oulipienne 143, 2006.

—. *La Dernière France*. Paris: P.O.L, 2018.

—. *De la justice et du travail: Scènes et portraits de groupes*. Biache Saint-Vaast: TEC, 2003.

—. *Des ans et des ânes*. Paris: Ramsay, 1988.

—. *Le Dictionnaire des Papous dans la tête*. Paris: Gallimard, 2007. Éd. Françoise Treussard.

—. *Le Directeur du Musée des Cadeaux des Chefs d'État de l'Étranger*. Paris: Seuil, 1994.

—. *Distiques Jiānpū*. Paris: Bibliothèque Oulipienne 237, 2019. With Frédéric Forte.

—. *Dos, pensée (poème), revenant*. Paris: P.O.L, 2019.

—. *Du jour*. Paris: P.O.L, 2013.

—. *Du monostique*. Paris: Bibliothèque Oulipienne 135, 2004.

—. *Du W, de Cortázar et de Li Po*. Paris: Bibliothèque Oulipienne 161, 2007.

—. *[ə]*. Paris: Bibliothèque Oulipienne 64, 1993. With Jacques Roubaud.

—. *Échelle et papillons: Le pantoum*. Paris: Les Belles Lettres, 1998.

—. *L'Éclipse*. Paris: Bibliothèque Oulipienne 28, 1984.

—. *Un énorme exercice*. Lausanne: Art et Fiction, 2008. With Tito Honegger.

—. *Espions*. Paris: Bibliothèque Oulipienne 44, 1990.

—. *L'Évasion de Rochefort*. Saint-Quentin: Festival de la Nouvelle, 1997.

—. *Exercices de la mémoire*. Paris: Bibliothèque Oulipienne 82, 1996.

—. *Fins*. Paris: P.O.L, 1999.

—. *Frise du métro parisien*. Paris: Bibliothèque Oulipienne 97, 1998. With Pierre Rosenstiehl.

—. *Glose de la Comtesse de Die et de Didon*. Paris: Bibliothèque Oulipienne 56, 1992.

—. *Guerre froide, mère froide*. Villelongue d'Aude: Atelier du Gué, 1978.

BIBLIOGRAPHY

—. *Hinterreise et autres histoires retournées.* Paris: Bibliothèque Oulipienne 108, 1999.
—. *Histoire de Paul Gauguin et de son divan.* Paris: Éditions Plurielle, 1996.
—. *L'Histoire poèmes.* Paris: P.O.L, 2010.
—. *Je me souvins.* Paris: Bibliothèque Oulipienne 205, 2014.
—. *Jules et autres républiques.* Paris: P.O.L, 2004.
—. *Kayserberg.* Paris: Éditions Plurielle, 1997. With Claudine Capdeville, Pierre Laurent, and Georges Kolebka.
—. *Une mauvaise maire.* Paris: P.O.L, 2007.
—. *Makhambet Utemissov. L'armoise rouge de la steppe: Poèmes kazakhs.* Trans. Jacques Jouet. Paris: Caractères, 2003.
—. *Mek-Ouyes amoureux.* Paris: P.O.L, 2006.
—. *Mon Bel Autocar.* Paris: P.O.L, 2003.
—. *Monostication de La Fontaine.* Paris: Bibliothèque Oulipienne 72, 1995.
—. *La Montagne R.* Paris: Seuil, 1996.
—. *Montagneux.* Lausanne: Art et Fiction, 2012. With Tito Honegger.
—. *Morceaux de théâtre.* Paris: Éditions du Limon, 1997.
—. *Les Mots du corps dans les expressions de la langue française.* Paris: Larousse, 1990.
—. *MRM.* Paris: P.O.L, 2008.
—. *Muséification de Notre Dame.* Paris: Éditions Plurielle, 1997.
—. *Navet, linge, oeil-de-vieux.* 3 vols. Paris: P.O.L, 1998.
—. *Nos Vaches.* Bordeaux: L'Attente, 2001.
—. *Obernai.* Paris: Chez l'Auteur, 1999.
—. *L'Oulipien démasqué.* Paris: Bibliothèque Oulipienne 38, 1990.
—. *Les Papous dans la tête.* Paris: Gallimard, 2007. Éd. Bertrand Jérôme et Françoise Treussard.
—. *Paresse.* Lausanne: Art et Fiction, 2010. With Tito Honegger.
—. *Le Paris de Caradec.* Paris: Bibliothèque Oulipienne 186, 2010.

—. *Pas de deux: Comédrame booléen*. Paris: Bibliothèque Oulipienne 120, 2002. With Olivier Salon.

—. *Pauline (polyne)*. Paris: Bibliothèque Oulipienne 93, 1997.

—. *Petites Boîtes, sonnets minces et autres rigueurs*. Paris: Bibliothèque Oulipienne 134, 2004.

—. *Poèmes avec partenaires*. Paris: P.O.L, 2002.

—. *Poèmes de métro*. Paris: P.O.L, 2000.

—. *Le Point de vue de l'escargot*. Strasbourg: L'Alsace et Le Verger, 1994.

—. *Portraits mosnériens*. Paris: Virgile, 2007. With Ricardo Mosner.

—. *14 Réguliers comprenant leur désir*. Paris: Saint-Germain-des-Prés, 1978.

—. *Qui s'endort*. Remoulins-sur-Gardon: Éditions Jacques Brémond, 1988.

—. *Raymond Queneau*. Lyon: La Manufacture, 1988.

—. *Récapituls, grands et petits*. Paris: Bibliothèque Oulipienne 224, 2015.

—. *La Redonde*. Paris: Bibliothèque Oulipienne 107, 1999.

—. *Rendez-vous dans ma rue*. Paris: Passage Piétons, 2001.

—. *La République de Mek-Ouyes*. Paris: P.O.L, 2001.

—. *La République romaine*. Paris: Collection Afat Voyages, 1997.

—. *Une réunion pour le nettoiement*. Paris: P.O.L, 2001.

—. *Romillats*. Paris: Ramsay, 1986.

—. *Rumination de l'essai oulipien*. Paris: Bibliothèque Oulipienne 164, 2007.

—. *Rumination du dialogue*. Paris: Bibliothèque Oulipienne 189, 2010.

—. *Ruminations de l'atelier oulipien, de l'improvisation du potentiel*. Paris: Bibliothèque Oulipienne 203, 2014.

—. *Sauvage*. Paris: Autrement, 2001.

—. *La Scène est sur la scène*. Paris: Éditions du Limon, 1994.

—. *La Scène usurpée*. Monaco: Éditions du Rocher, 1997.

BIBLIOGRAPHY

—. *Les Sept Règles de Perec*. Paris: Bibliothèque Oulipienne 52, 1990.

—. *La Seule Fois de l'amour*. Paris: P.O.L, 2012.

—. *Un train traverse le jour*. Paris: Bibliothèque Oulipienne 178, 2009.

—. *Trois Pontes*. Paris: P.O.L, 2008.

—. *Vanghel*. Paris: P.O.L, 2003.

—. *Vies longues*. Paris: Bibliothèque Oulipienne 124, 2003.

—. *La Voix qui les faisait toutes*. Montreuil, Roubaix, Lille: V. O. Editions, TEC / CRIAC, Sansonnet, 1999.

—. *Le Voyage du Grand Verre*. Paris: Bibliothèque Oulipienne 162, 2007.

Kristeva, Julia. *Black Sun: Depression and Melancholia*. Trans. Leon Roudiez. New York: Columbia University Press, 1989.

Lamarre, Mélanie. "Ivresse et militantisme: Olivier Rolin, Jean Rolin, Jean-Pierre Le Dantec." *Contextes: Revue de Sociologie de la Littérature* 6 (2009). http://journals.openedition.org/contextes/4450

Le Bot, Marc. *Les Yeux de mon père*. Paris: P.O.L, 1992.

Lejeune, Philippe. *La Mémoire et l'oblique: Georges Perec autobiographe*. Paris: P.O.L, 1991.

Le Lionnais, François. "Raymond Queneau et l'amalgame des mathématiques et de la littérature." In Oulipo. *Atlas de littérature potenielle*. Paris: Gallimard, 1981. 34-41.

—. "La LiPo: Le Premier Manifeste." In Oulipo. *La Littérature potentielle: Créations, re-créations, récréations*. Paris: Gallimard, 1973. 19-22.

—. "Le Second Manifeste." In Oulipo. *La Littérature potentielle: Créations, re-créations, récréations*. Paris: Gallimard, 1973. 23-27.

Lescure, Jean. "Moraliste élevé." In Oulipo. *La Bibliothèque Oulipienne*. Vol. 1. Paris: Ramsay, 1987. 2 vols. 68.

—. "Petite Histoire de l'Oulipo." In Oulipo. *La Littérature potentielle: Créations, re-créations, récréations*. Paris: Gallimard, 1973. 28-40.

Magné, Bernard. "Le Puzzle, mode d'emploi." *Texte* 1 (1982): 71-96.

Marcandier, Christine. "Les Lois de l'abstraction: Le blanchiment du noir chez Julia Deck et Tanguy Viel." *Revue critique de fixxion française contemporaine* 10 (2015): 116-25. www.revue-critique-de-fixxion-francaise contemporaine.org/rcffc/article/view/fx10.13/929.

Martin-Achard, Frédéric. "De la difficulté d'être soi: Phénomènes de désubjectivation chez les personnages romanesques de Bon, Mauvignier et Serena." *Relief* 10.1 (2016): 179-193.

Mathews, Harry. "L'Algorithme de Mathews." In Oulipo. *Atlas de littérature potenielle*. Paris: Gallimard, 1981. 91-107.

—. *Cigarettes*. New York: Weidenfield and Nicolson, 1987.

Métail, Michèle. "Une petite musique chinoise." *Lectures de Raymond Queneau* 1 (1987): 69-83.

Missac, Pierre. "Marge pour deux regards." *Les Cahiers Obsidiane* 5 (1982): 44-53.

Montalbetti, Christine. *Le Cas Jekyll*. Paris: P.O.L, 2010.

—. *En écrivant* Journée américaine. Paris: Biro/P.O.L, 2009.

—. *L'Évaporation de l'oncle*. Paris: P.O.L, 2011.

—. "Hôtel Komaba Éminence." In *Petits Déjeuners avec quelques écrivains célèbres*. Paris: P.O.L, 2008. 191-215.

—. *Journée américaine*. Paris: P.O.L, 2009.

—. *Love Hotel*. Paris: P.O.L, 2013.

—. *Mon ancêtre Poisson*. Paris: P.O.L, 2019.

—. *L'Origine de l'homme*. Paris: P.O.L, 2002.

—. *Le Personnage*. Paris: Flammarion, 2003.

—. *Plus rien que les vagues et le vent*. Paris: P.O.L, 2014.

—. *Trouville Casino*. Paris: P.O.L, 2018.

—. *Western*. Paris: P.O.L, 2005.

Motte, Warren. "Christine Montalbetti's Engaging Narrations." *French Forum* 32.1-2 (2007): 189-213.

—. "Clinamen Redux." *Comparative Literature Studies* 23 (1986): 263-81.

—. "Embellir les lettres." *Cahiers Georges Perec* 1 (1985): 110-24.
—. "Jacques Jouet's Magic Mountain." *French Review* 72.3 (1999): 503-14.
—. "Jean Rolin's Explosion." *Review of Contemporary Fiction* 28.3 (2008): 123-41.
—. "Playing it by the Book." *SubStance* 82 (1997): 16-33.
—. *Questioning Edmond Jabès*. Lincoln and London: University of Nebraska Press, 1990.
—. "A Soulful Jouet." *Neophilologus* 78.4 (1994): 549-59.
Mouchard, Claude. "Raymond Queneau: Puissance de l'indéterminable." *Critique* 37 (1977): 101-13.
Moudileno, Lydie. "Délits, détours et affabulation: L'écriture de l'anathème dans *En famille* de Marie NDiaye." *French Review* 71.3 (1998): 442-53.
—. "Marie NDiaye's Discombobulated Subject." *SubStance* 111 (2006): 83-94.
Naudin, François. "Quelques réflexions sur *Morale élémentaire* en général, et sa première partie en particulier." *Lectures de Raymond Queneau* 1 (1987): 17-33.
NDiaye, Marie. *Autoportrait en vert*. Paris: Mercure de France, 2005.
—. *La Sorcière*. Paris: Minuit, 1996.
—. *Un temps de saison*. Paris: Minuit, 1994.
Noël, Bernard. *Le Reste du voyage et autres poèmes*. Paris: Seuil, 2006.
—. *Un trajet en hiver*. Paris: P.O.L, 2004.
—. *URSS aller retour*. Paris: Flammarion, 1980.
—. "La Vie l'écriture: Entretien de Bernard Noël avec Jean-Marie Le Sidaner." *Europe* 606 (1979): 159-75.
Oulipo. *Atlas de littérature potentielle*. Paris: Gallimard, 1981.
—. *La Bibliothèque Oulipienne*. Paris: Ramsay, 1987. 2 vols.
—. *La Littérature potentielle: Créations, re-créations, récréations*. Paris: Gallimard, 1973.

Oster, Christian. *Loin d'Odile*. Paris: Minuit, 1998.

Panaitescu, Val. "Le Quennet." *Les Amis de Valentin Brû* 19 (1982): 33-39.

Pawlikowska, Ewa. "La Colle bleue de Gaspard Winckler." *Littératures* 7 (1983): 79-87.

Perec, Georges. *"53 Jours"*. Paris: P.O.L, 1989.

—. *La Clôture et autres poèmes*. Paris: Hachette, 1980.

—. *La Disparition*. Paris: Denoël, 1969.

—. "Entretien: Perec / Jean-Marie Le Sidaner." *L'Arc* 76 (1979): 3-10.

—. "Histoire du lipogramme." In Oulipo. *La Littérature potentielle: Créations, re-créations, récréations*. Paris: Gallimard, 1973. 77-93.

—. *Un homme qui dort*. 1967. 2nd ed. Paris: Union Générale d'Éditions, 1976.

—. *L'Infra-ordinaire*. Paris: Le Seuil, 1989.

—. *Penser/Classer*. Paris: Hachette, 1985.

—. *Les Revenentes*. Paris: Julliard, 1972.

—. *Tentative d'épuisement d'un lieu parisien*. Paris: Bourgois, 1982.

—. *La Vie mode d'emploi*. Paris: Hachette, 1978.

—. *W ou le souvenir d'enfance*. Paris: Denoël, 1975.

Perret, Auguste. *Contribution à une théorie de l'architecture*. Paris: André Wahl, 1952.

Poe, Edgar Allan. *The Complete Tales and Poems of Edgar Allan Poe*. New York: Modern Library, 1938.

Poisson, Catherine. "Terrain vague: *Zones* de Jean Rolin." *Nottingham French Studies* 39.1 (2000): 17-24.

Pontalis, J.-B. *Avant*. Paris: Gallimard, 2012.

Prince, Gerald. *Narrative as Theme: Studies in French Fiction*. Lincoln: University of Nebraska Press, 1992.

Queneau, Raymond. *Bâtons, chiffres et lettres*. Paris: Gallimard, 1950. Rev. ed. 1965.

—. *Bords*. Paris: Hermann, 1963.

—. *Cent Mille Milliards de poèmes*. Paris: Gallimard, 1961.

—. *Le Chiendent*. Paris: Gallimard, 1933.

—. *Entretiens avec Georges Charbonnier*. Paris: Gallimard, 1962.

—. *Morale élémentaire*. Paris: Gallimard, 1975.

—. "Poèmes." *Nouvelle Revue Française* 253 (1974): 1-20.

—. *Odile*. Paris: Gallimard, 1937.

—. *Le Voyage en Grèce*. Paris: Gallimard, 1973.

Queval, Jean. "Morale élémentaire (avec un clinamen)." In Oulipo. *La Bibliothèque Oulipienne*. Vol. 1. Paris: Ramsay, 1987. 2 vols. 72.

Rabaté, Dominique. *Marie NDiaye*. Paris: Culturesfrance/Textuel, 2008.

Raillon, Jean-Claude. "Le Fil de la plume." *Conséquences* 11 (1988): 58-77.

Rohmer, Éric. *L'Arbre, le maire et la médiathèque*. Paris: La Compagnie Éric Rohmer, 1993.

—. *Pauline à la plage*. Paris: Les Films du Losange, Les Films Ariane, 1983.

Rolin, Jean. *Un chien mort après lui*. Paris: P.O.L, 2009.

—. *La Clôture*. Paris: P.O.L, 2002.

—. *L'Explosion de la durite*. Paris: P.O.L, 2007.

—. *Ormuz*. Paris: P.O.L, 2013.

—. *Peleliu*. Paris: P.O.L, 2016.

—. *Savannah*. Paris: P.O.L, 2015.

—. *Zones*. Paris: Gallimard, 1995.

Roubaud, Jacques. *La Belle Hortense*. Paris: Ramsay, 1985.

—. *L'Enlèvement d'Hortense*. Paris: Ramsay, 1987.

---. *L'Exil d'Hortense*. Paris: Seghers, 1990.

—. "La Mathématique dans la méthode de Raymond Queneau." In Oulipo. *Atlas de littérature potenielle*. Paris: Gallimard, 1981. 42-72.

—. *Quelque chose noir*. Paris: Gallimard, 1986.

Roussel, Raymond. *Comment j'ai écrit certains de mes livres.* Paris: Alphonse Lemerre, 1935.

Ruffel, Lionel. *Brouhaha: Les mondes du contemporain.* Lagrasse: Verdier, 2016.

—. *Le Dénouement.* Lagrasse: Verdier, 2005.

Russo, Adelaide. "Collage Incipit Atelier." In Fabio Scotto, ed. *Bernard Noël: Le Corps du verbe.* Lyon: École Normale Supérieure, 2008. 199-212.

Schwerdtner, Karin. "Le Pari de la 'double adresse': Entretien avec Christine Montalbetti." *French Review* 93.4 (2020): 171-82.

Serena, Jacques. *L'Acrobate.* Paris: Minuit, 2004.

—. *Artisans.* Montpellier: Publie.net, 2009.

—. *Basse Ville.* Paris: Minuit, 1992.

—. *Diotima.* Paris: Area, 2008.

—. *Elles en premier toujours.* Montpellier: Publie.net, 2012.

—. *Les Fiévreuses.* Paris: Argol, 2005.

—. *Fleurs cueillies pour rien.* Charenton: Flohic, 2001.

—. *Gouaches.* Paris: Théâtre Ouvert/Tapuscrits, 2000.

—. *Isabelle de dos.* Paris: Minuit, 1989.

—. *Lendemain de fête.* Paris: Minuit, 1993.

—. *Musaraignes.* Montpellier: Publie.net, 2013.

—. *Plus rien dire sans toi.* Paris: Minuit, 2002.

—. *Quart d'heure suivi de Clients.* Besançon: Les Solitaires Intempestifs, 2000.

—. *Rimmel.* Paris: Minuit, 1998.

—. *Sous le néflier.* Paris: Minuit, 2007.

—. *Velvette suivi de Jetée.* Besançon: Les Solitaires Intempestifs, 2001.

—. *Voleur de guirlandes.* Barr: Le Verger, 2000.

—. *Wagon.* Montpellier: Publie.net, 2011.

Sheringham, Michael. "*Mon coeur à l'étroit*: Espace et éthique." In Andrew Asibong and Shirley Jordan, eds. *Marie NDiaye:*

L'étrangeté à l'oeuvre. Spec. issue of *Revue des Sciences Humaines* 293 (2009): 171-86.

Simonnet, Claude. *Queneau déchiffré: Notes sur* Le Chiendent. Paris: Julliard, 1962.

Sindaco, Sarah. "*La Clôture* de Jean Rolin: Le territoire parisien: Entre ironie et mélancolie." *Études Littéraires* 45.2 (2014): 83-95.

Stamelman, Richard. "Nomadic Writing: The Poetics of Exile." In *The Sin of the Book: Edmond Jabès.* Ed. Eric Gould. Lincoln and London: University of Nebraska Press, 1985. 92-114.

Téboul, Jean-Pierre. "La Coupure de la trace." *Les Cahiers Obsidiane* 5 (1982): 10-15.

Teko-Agbo, K. Ambroise. "*En famille* or the Problem of Alterity." Trans. Ruthmarie H. Mitsch. *Research in African Literatures* 26.2 (1995): 158-68.

Thibault, Bruno. "Rives et dérives chez Jean Rolin, J. M. G. Le Clézio et Pascal Quignard." *L'Esprit Créateur* 51.2 (2011): 69-80.

Tolstoy, Leo. *Anna Karenina.* Trans. Constance Garnett. Rev. Leonard J. Kent and Nina Berberova. New York: Modern Library, 1965.

Toussaint, Jean-Philippe. *La Salle de bain.* Paris: Minuit, 1985.

—. *La Télévision.* Paris: Minuit, 1997.

Tubbs, Robert. *Mathematics in 20th-Century Literature & Art: Content, Form, Meaning.* Baltimore: Johns Hopkins University Press, 2014.

van Velde, Bram. *Lettres.* Lagrasse: Verdier, 2012.

Volodine, Antoine. *Dondog.* Paris: Le Seuil, 2002.

—. *Songes de Mevlido.* Paris: Le Seuil, 2007.

Also by Warren Motte

Pour une littérature critique (2021) — Ce livre prend comme objet la littérature critique, c'est-à-dire, des ouvrages conçus dans un esprit critique, qui invitent leurs lectrices et lecteurs—soit de façon ouverte, soit de façon couverte, subtile et nuancée—à s'engager avec la textualité de manière critique. Cette dynamique, suspendue entre production et réception, est hypothétique et fragile; elle est difficile à théoriser de façon satisfaisante; elle est ardue à tracer en se servant d'une stratégie lectorale conventionnelle. Pourtant, c'est précisément ce phénomène articulé et réciproque qui fournit à cette sorte de textualité une mobilité tout à fait rafraîchissante, mobilité qui rend possible la signification littéraire sur un horizon ouvert et largement reconfiguré.
188 pages.
ISBN 978-1-60962-209-1 paperback
ISBN 978-1-60962-220-6 ebook

Lydie Salvayre, maintenant même (2021) — Warren Motte, «Dans le vif du vivant» / Lydie Salvayre et Warren Motte, «Une conversation avec Lydie Salvayre» / Lydie Salvayre, «Deux artistes» / Lydie Salvayre, «Projet en cours» / Lydie Salvayre, «Quatre photos» / Bernard Wallet, «Lydie Salvayre, écrivain baroque'n'roll» / David Lopez, «Almuerz» / Marie Cosnay, «Diamant brut» / Mahir Guven, «À propos de Lydie Salvayre» / Stéphane Bikialo, «Éloge de la fuite» / «Ouvrages de Lydie Salvayre»
103 pages.
ISBN 978-1-60962-197-1 paperback
ISBN 978-1-60962-198-8 ebook

www.ingramcontent.com/pod-product-compliance
Lightning Source LLC
Chambersburg PA
CBHW032250150426
43195CB00008BA/394